AN INTRODUCTION TO **ACCOUNTING CASE ANALYSIS**

SECOND EDITION

AN INTRODUCTION TO

ACCOUNTING CASE ANALYSIS
SECOND EDITION

L. S. ROSEN
York University

McGRAW-HILL RYERSON LIMITED
Toronto   Montréal   New York   St. Louis
San Francisco   Auckland   Bogotá   Guatemala
Hamburg   Johannesburg   Lisbon   London
Madrid   Mexico   New Delhi   Panama   Paris
San Juan   São Paulo   Singapore   Sydney
Tokyo

AN INTRODUCTION TO ACCOUNTING CASE ANALYSIS: Second
Edition

Printed and bound in Canada

Care has been taken to trace ownership of copyright material contained in
this text. The publishers will gladly take any information that will enable
them to rectify any reference or credit in subsequent editions.

1 2 3 4 5 6 7 8 9 0 D 0 9 8 7 6 5 4 3 2 1

Canadian Cataloguing in Publication Data

Rosen, L. S. date
  An introduction to accounting case analysis

ISBN 0-07-092450-3

1. Accounting—Case studies. 2. Accounting—
Problems, exercises, etc. I. Title.

HF5635.R67 1981   657'.044   C81-094051-5

Table of Contents

Preface

The first edition of this book was written at a time when case analysis was a relatively new examination technique of the Societies of Management Accountants in Canada (or La Corporation Professionnelle Des Comptables En Administration Industrielle Du Québec) and the Institutes/Ordre of Chartered Accountants in Canada. Considerable space was taken in that edition explaining the benefits of case learning and how students might approach case analysis under examination conditions. An underlying assumption of the first edition was that students had not been exposed to much *accounting* case analysis in university courses, and therefore had to acquire the general ideas quickly. For example, we explained how accounting cases differed from policy and administration cases. We also explained what accounting cases were attempting to test, and how this could differ from testing by use of directive questions.

Six years have gone by since the first edition was written. When the time came to research the state of case usage in Canada prior to writing the second edition we found that conditions varied considerably across the country. Some students were still not being exposed to less directive educational methods in university, college and correspondence accounting courses even though the students' goals were to become qualified accountants. Many lecturers for accounting bodies were not upgrading their classroom style to make it more compatible with case learning and testing. But, other accounting instructors were working hard at less directive styles and were seeking more cases to use in their classrooms.

As a result of the wide variation in educational practice we have chosen to expand the coverage in this book. The first four chapters are designed for everybody who will have to write an accounting case. The illustrations are at a level that can be understood by students who are registered in introductory financial accounting courses. The reason for this level is that we discovered that the first edition was being used in introductory accounting courses at some universities. In keeping with the interactive approach needed to teach case analysis, we have retained the conversational style, and have tried to respond to the "new wave" of student concerns. We have also tried to make the first four chapters as self-supporting as possible for those who do not have access to instructors. Chapter Four has been totally rewritten to provide more practice and feedback. The first three chapters have been updated and reorganized to recognize the variation in student needs.

Chapter Five is unchanged from the first edition and is designed as a follow up to Chapters One to Four for students of the Society of Management Accountants. However, Chapter Five should be of considerable help to those registered in management accounting courses. The case in Chapter Five was first used as a national examination of the Society. They kindly provided access to actual student examination papers in order to help us try to improve case analysis techniques in Canada.

Chapter Six is new and is specifically prepared for persons who are writing the Uniform Final Examination of the Institutes/Ordre of Chartered Accountants in Canada. The case in this chapter was used as a national examination of the Institutes/Ordre. Both the case and a solution to it are reprinted with the permission of the Canadian Institute of Chartered Accountants, Toronto. Special permission was also given to reproduce types of actual student responses written as part of the Uniform Final Examinations. These responses have been analyzed in order to pinpoint student errors in approach and detailed technique. This material should be read carefully by accounting majors in universities so that they can prepare themselves for case learning and examinations.

Chapters Seven to Nine are three comprehensive cases that can be used for teaching purposes. The case in Chapter Eight is more geared to management accounting students than are the other two. All three cases are at the level of students who are preparing for final professional examinations. Qualified instructors (university; in-house; and others) who assign this textbook to groups of students may obtain responses and marking guides for the three cases in the Instructor's Manual to accompany this book.

Acknowledgements

This book would not have been commenced without the encouragement of John Ross and William (Bill) Langdon of the Society of Management Accountants of Canada. They pioneered in improving case learning by allowing access to actual student responses so that the "answers" could be analyzed in a textbook available to any student. They also granted permission to reproduce the Society's examinations. I am grateful to both John and Bill.

The second edition has been considerably strengthened through the cooperation of four persons associated with the Institutes/Ordre of Chartered Accountants in Canada. Eric Reynolds, Leonard J. Brooks, Gordon D. Richardson and Robert Thiessen provided me with types of actual student responses. Len and Bob also read Chapter Six and made helpful suggestions. The student responses are very important because they give insight into the type of "answer" that students must prepare themselves for in a four hour examination. Len and Bob are, of course, not responsible for any oversights in Chapter Six.

One major improvement in case learning, teaching and examining in Canada has occurred at the case marking level. Many people could be included in this category as having developed techniques to sort those who provide reasoning and logic from those who merely regurgitate everything they know, hoping that the markers will be sympathetic. Some of those not already mentioned in previous paragraphs are: Joe Bolla; Ross Denham, Morris Kaiser, Bill King, Harley Mintz, Bob Plaxton, Bill Radburn, John Switzer, and Fernand Sylvain.

Several other persons contributed to this book in different ways. Mike Gibbins, in particular, provided special assistance. Finally, I am grateful to the secretaries who ably typed the manuscript: Nancy Johnstone, Gladys Sierra, Denise Timmons.

Suggestions are welcome.

Toronto, Canada.   L. S. ROSEN

CHAPTER ONE

Educational Objectives Of Cases

LEARNING THE ROPES

Act I (Classroom, on first day of classes):

INSTRUCTOR: "You probably know that I'm new to teaching, but I'd like to welcome you here today. I understand that this has traditionally been an exciting and rewarding course. . . ."

STUDENT 040: "Exciting?? Accounting?? Exciting??"

INSTRUCTOR: "Well, you know what I mean. . . . The course was designed by Professor Bramblebush several years ago and the students have always found it challenging, and . . . at least after they settle down. . . ., I'm told that they like the course."

STUDENT 045: "We've heard that the course is tough, with a lot of vague cases; maybe even unorganized. Is this true?"

INSTRUCTOR: "Most of you are business students. Business is complicated; there are very few right or wrong answers. We can't give you a few simple rules to memorize. Business situations are vague; you have to learn to cope with them. . . . The course requires you to think; if you are not used to doing this the course may be a new experience, but not tough."

STUDENT 045 (*quietly to classmate*): "Think we should try to switch to another section? He sounds a little too keen, and boring."

(*Classmate shrugs his shoulders.*)

STUDENT 040: "We've never done vague cases before."

INSTRUCTOR: "Oh! Then you are worried?"

STUDENT 085: "Some of us would like to go on to more advanced courses and studies. We need high grades to get accepted into other programs. . . . With cases, especially on examinations, you never know how you will do."

INSTRUCTOR: "The course consists of more than cases. We are merely using some in conjunction with other learning techniques and aids. Each one has a place."

STUDENT 060:   "What do you mean by that? Could you please explain?"

INSTRUCTOR: "Well, I, uh, let me see how I might explain, uh, um. . . . Did you watch T.V. last night?"

STUDENT 020:   "How could we? You gave us all that advanced reading to do."

INSTRUCTOR: "I didn't ask you to read it last night. You've had all summer to do it."

SEVERAL STUDENTS: "Groan."

STUDENT 020:   "Maybe I peeked a little at T.V., while doing the reading. What program are you referring to."

INSTRUCTOR: "I was thinking of the educational program on '4', but we can think of any news or public affairs program. Maybe even 'Sesame Street', although. . . . Anyway, what sort of business skills do you acquire or learn from watching T.V., or for that matter, when you are in big classes where you cannot ask questions. Student 070."

STUDENT 070:   "Well, you can learn a lot of things, and have it presented in an interesting way on T.V. Maybe you could get your university degree by watching T.V., and doing some assignments. . . . Actually, why is it that universities don't make more use of T.V. instead of following antiquated teaching methods? Students suffer because instructors aren't familiar with modern technology."

SEVERAL STUDENTS: "Yeh. Why is that?"

INSTRUCTOR: "You don't suffer. . . . Surely you've noticed that the public is not sympathetic towards giving more money to universities. We can't afford the elaborate costs of a polished T.V. show, with many rehearsals and hundreds of technicians. . . . Knowledge is changing quickly; we can't show reruns for 20 years or more to pay for the costs. The videotapes would be obsolete. . . . But there are situations where more T.V. would make sense, and that gets us back to my question."

STUDENT 020:   "Could you repeat the question?"

INSTRUCTOR: "(sigh). What business skills can you learn from non-adaptive (i.e., does not adapt to you) T.V.? Student 080."

STUDENT 080:   "The current techniques; world events and the like."

INSTRUCTOR: "Anybody agree or disagree."

STUDENT 050:   "What are you getting at? Why the mystery? Why don't you just tell us?"

(Instructor smiles, does not speak, and waits for a response.)

STUDENT 070:   "Oh, I think I see what you mean. The T.V. cannot afford to wait for a response or give us enough time to think. So it's not good for, or at least not presently set up for, much on-the-spot thinking."

INSTRUCTOR: "Very good 070. What else."

STUDENT 045 *(quietly to classmate):*   "Let's switch sections. I don't need this hassle."

CLASSMATE TO 045 *(quietly):*   "Wait a minute. Let's hear a little more. We can switch next week if we have to."

STUDENT 020:   "Is this what the class is going to be like all term? *We* have to talk?"

INSTRUCTOR: "*(sigh)* Why? Is this something new?"

STUDENT 020:   "Your way is not very efficient. It's faster if you tell us the answers."

INSTRUCTOR: "*(sigh)* The class time is over for today. Let's continue this same topic next class."

Students leave room. (Student 020 asks a classmate "Why does he 'sigh' so much?")

Act II (Instructors' Lounge, shortly after Act I):

SENIOR PROFESSOR: *(sipping hot coffee)* "How'd your first class go?"

INSTRUCTOR: "Rough. How did some of 'them' get this far with so little understanding of educational philosophy and methods? They seem to idolize T.V. learning, and think that it's the only, and painless, way to educate."

SENIOR PROFESSOR *(now smiling knowingly, and puffing contentedly on his pipe):*   "Maybe they are just testing you. You're new. You're an unknown. They want to see how tough you'll be, what your expectations are, whether you are a spoon feeder, and so on. Some classes try to wear you down or soften you up to what they feel most comfortable with. . . . Some students come to class for a rest. . . . How many students are there in the class?"

INSTRUCTOR: "About 60 I think; maybe 65 when they all show up."

JUNIOR PROFESSOR: "That'll be on exam day if at all, . . . Why did you say the class was 'rough'?"

INSTRUCTOR: "They seemed to be fighting my approach."

SENIOR PROFESSOR: "Bramblebush set up that course to get the educational methods issues aired in a hurry. He wanted the 'war' at the beginning of the course so he could get it over with and get down to business, teaching what he called 'the important cognitive skills' of business. . . . Most classes in that course settle down in five or six weeks."

INSTRUCTOR *(now white faced):*   "That long, eh? . . . Why don't we try the same approach in other classes and spread the pain around, especially the pressure on one instructor?"

JUNIOR PROFESSOR: "Lots of reasons; mostly excuses, though. First, in large classes it's easier to have one-way *(instructor to student)* 'learning.' It's too hard to spend the time encouraging quiet and less gifted students to get involved. Second, if you ask more than memorization of the textbook on examinations, it takes longer to mark examinations. . . ."

SPECIAL LECTURER: "The main reason is that many students fight uncertainty or lack of very explicit direction in courses, especially on examinations. Over the years they've learned to find out what the instructor wants and then give it to her or him. Unfortunately, some instructors like to hear back, on examinations, what they've said in class. I suppose they are flattered to hear their ideas repeated. So students learn to regurgitate a professor's ideas, at least until they pass the course. They do whatever earns them the good grades. It's a competitive society; many want to earn high marks. When you give students freedom to think for themselves their anxiety grows. Most like the idea of freedom, but they want to know what degree of freedom is O.K. and towards what target. They don't believe that they have complete freedom. They still want some hand-holding; they still want to know what actions are rewarded with high marks. Some require more signals than others because of their personality, and the type of teaching they've previously been exposed to. . . ."

JUNIOR PROFESSOR: "He's saying that you have to learn how to provide just the right amount of direction to students at different times as the course progresses. That takes experience; you make mistakes. . . ."

INSTRUCTOR: "I guess I'm not entirely clear on what you mean by direction . . . or the significance of various 'cognitive skills' . . . and how cases fit into all this. . . ."

SENIOR PROFESSOR: "I have some material that you can try out in your next class. Then we can talk about it after the class. Let's go to my office. I should have enough spare copies. . . ."

Act III (Classroom; two days later):

INSTRUCTOR: "Let us pick up on our discussion of the business skills that you require. Last day we were trying to figure out the strengths and weaknesses of T.V., or other forms of what are mainly one-way learning."

STUDENT 020: "When are we going to get to accounting?"

INSTRUCTOR: "When you are ready for it. Now just settle down and listen, and think. You come to schools to develop an open mind, not to pre-judge or show prejudices. Maybe one form of learning is not suitable for all situations and needs. At least try to find out what the other alternatives are, before you make up your mind."

STUDENT 045 (*quietly to classmate*): "See, he's in a bad mood; this is going to be a tough course."

INSTRUCTOR: "What do you think 075?"

STUDENT 075:   "I can see that if you are going to be an automotive mechanic or a doctor or an accountant you have to get some 'hands-on' experience, and that this requires more than watching a T.V. set. But, I'm not sure what and how much practical experience is necessary."

INSTRUCTOR: "Good thinking. To summarize, you are saying that *knowledge* or awareness can come from listening to a lecture or watching T.V. But *application* of the knowledge requires what you call "hands-on" experience, perhaps trial and error or being under the watchful eye of a more experienced person. . . . Student 080 can you add to this?"

STUDENT 080:   "A little maybe. In order to be able to apply you have to be able to *diagnose* a problem. An automotive mechanic often has to do some tests before he knows, for sure, what is wrong. Then he has to figure out how best to solve the problem, especially what is a quick, inexpensive and lasting cure. . . . You don't get any or much of this from spoon feeding lectures, especially the diagnosis part, unless all of the possible cases that you'll encounter are set out one by one for you. . . ."

INSTRUCTOR: ". . . and this is more likely to occur in automotive problems than it is for doctors and accountants. . . ."

STUDENT 080:   "I guess so. . . ."

INSTRUCTOR: "That's just excellent 080. Now we're getting somewhere. Let's summarize again. In business and accounting you need *knowledge* but also should have the *diagnosis* or *assessment* skills; you have to be able to *apply* your knowledge. . . . There's more to business education than these skills, as we shall see after the course gets underway.

The interesting question at the moment is how you acquire the needed skills. To start the course we'll use a range of questions, some of which are highly directed and others that are less directed. We'll also use some cases. . . ."

STUDENT 064:   "What's 'less directed' mean?"

INSTRUCTOR: "Good question 064. Let me hand out a short situation for you to read. Then we'll answer that question together." (Instructor hands out Exhibit One—1).

EXHIBIT ONE—1

Mr. Hustle wants to start a "lunch wagon" service to the many new construction sites on the west side of the city. He figures that with the present competition there is still plenty of opportunity for one truck to travel from site to site selling coffee, hot chocolate, tea, soft drinks, donuts, sandwiches, muffins, candy bars, ice cream, and so forth. A suitable truck will cost $9,500. He will also have to pay about $2,200 to refit the truck to hold coffee machines, other hot and cold containers, racks, and so on.

Mr. Hustle feels that he will have to pay out close to $800 in the first week for a basic inventory of coffee, sugar, soft drinks, and similar items. He thinks that it may take one month to build up enough customers to have cash receipts become equal to cash payments for inventory, gas and oil and similar daily cash expenditures. In the first month Mr. Hustle expects cash disbursements for inventory and daily operating expenses to exceed cash receipts by $400. After one month, daily cash receipts should exceed daily cash disbursements by as much as $250 a day.

Annual costs for insurance, licenses and repairs are expected to be $1,500 and most of these will have to be paid in the first month of starting the business. He can postpone paying the $9,500 for the truck by choosing a time payment plan of $1,000 of down payment plus 24 monthly payments of $440.

INSTRUCTOR: "Now that you have read about Mr. Hustle's idea, let us all play the role of instructor for a few moments. What business skills can you teach from that short situation? How about you 064?"

STUDENT 064: "You could show a class how to compute the amount of cash that Mr. Hustle would need to start up his business."

INSTRUCTOR: "Very good. So, how would we word a question to get students to compute cash needs. In short, *what wording or direction* would you provide."

STUDENT 068: "Oh, I get it now. You want us to learn what is wanted by an instructor from looking at clues such as wording or direction in a situation. And different situations could be teaching us different skills."

INSTRUCTOR: "Exactly. What wording would you use for asking people to compute cash needs?"

STUDENT 064: "Are you looking at me?"

INSTRUCTOR: "I'm hoping that someone, any student, will volunteer. You know my commercial by now. If you want to acquire assessment and application skills you have to get involved in a dialogue or two-way exchange with your classmates and the instructor. Why wait for me to ask?"

STUDENT 064: "How about this: 'compute the amount of cash that Mr. Hustle would need in the first month to start his lunch wagon service'."

INSTRUCTOR: "Umm. How many agree?"

STUDENT 080: "Well, you have to clarify whether the truck is being purchased for cash or on the time payment plan. I'd reword the question like this: "Assuming that Mr. Hustle pays cash for the truck, compute the amount of cash that he would need in the first month to start his lunch wagon service."

INSTRUCTOR: "That's good. Notice how 080's question contains a little more direction or guidance than 064's. There could be two answers to 064's. An instructor has to be alert and see that students recognize this, and provide both. In a minor way 064's question is testing student alertness, ability to recognize that options exist, and so forth. . . . High direction in questions tends to lead to one answer and in doing so may cut off the learning of other skills. . . . If there is only one answer, examinations are easy to mark.

As an aside, but a relevant one, I might add that the politicians and the general public have not looked at the consequences of large class sizes very carefully. If you were an instructor, and were required to teach increasingly large classes year after year (especially in accounting where class sizes at some universities have doubled and tripled in the past decade) you may start looking more and more for short cuts, especially in marking examinations. Marking can be pretty boring. One major unfortunate consequence of the larger classes is that you receive a much more directed education than makes sense. The reality is squeezed out of situations to facilitate standard lectures and common, easy-to-mark examinations. Fit everyone into the same box.

This short run approach catches up with you. If students know that examinations are of the multiple choice variety they can restrict their course preparation. If they know that each multiple choice question is worth the *same* number of marks and will require the same amount of time to complete they probably will concentrate on memorizing knowledge. The testing of skills other than knowledge requires time and very careful design when multiple choice questions are used. If the reward in marks does not exist, few students will study or equip themselves in skills that will not be tested.

Suppose now, that you want to test other than a knowledge and minor application of cash receipts and disbursements. How would you word a question that provides less direction than 064's but encourages people to sharpen their business skills?"

STUDENT 085: "You could ask: what problems will Mr. Hustle encounter in starting his business, and what steps can he take to ensure success? This would test a student's ability to *assess* the situation, allow her to display a *knowledge* of cash accounting and profitability, and to *apply* this knowledge, and to make *recommendations* that head off problems."

INSTRUCTOR: "That's excellent 085."

STUDENT 044: "Isn't that asking too much? We just started the course. You want us to run before we can crawl. It's not fair."

INSTRUCTOR: "How do you know how much I'm expecting? Maybe I just want you to get started down the 'assessment' and 'application' pathways, and not to reach the end. If you don't start, how can you finish? Sure, 085's question has less direction than may seem appropriate at this point, but let us try it anyway. Live and learn; make a few mistakes. Isn't it better to make your mistakes at university than when you have a job?"

STUDENT 049: "You need good grades to get a job."

STUDENT 044: "Isn't the problem exactly this. You have your expectations in your head, and we don't know what they are. You aren't communicating them. You're causing anxiety."

INSTRUCTOR: "Maybe now I am, but what about later? When I mark your cases and similar questions you'll get feedback. Why don't you get involved in class discussion? You'll get instant feedback. . . . We're out of time again. . . . How about trying 085's question for next day? We'll discuss it in class, and I'll give you more guidance."

Act IV (Instructor's Lounge; shortly after Act III):

SENIOR PROFESSOR: "Did that material I gave you on the 'lunch wagon' work?"

INSTRUCTOR: "Yes and no. Do you want to see my wounds? (sigh) Some of the students have tuned in to what I'm trying to do. Unfortunately, others think that they have caught on, and want to learn, but they really are off base. They'll slip in a comment that shows that they want handholding, or have missed the point. They are deeply concerned about grades, about my expectations, and, I'd guess, about missing out on a part of an examination question. Some of them hate the slightest bit of uncertainty."

SENIOR PROFESSOR: "Welcome to teaching. You're 'learning the ropes.' Just don't hang yourself with them. . . . I have some more material for you, to try out next day. Hang in there. Some people hate change and will take their anxiety out on you. Turn it around. *It's their problem.* If they don't want to learn assessment, analysis, application and similar skills with us, they'll have a harder time later on when they enter the job market. Keep your cool. Answer all of their questions as best you can. They'll eventually see the light, and start criticizing some of their previous education for not preparing them. Once they are on your side and they start to notice that they are learning some valuable skills it's all downhill for you.

Your assessment of the situation is pretty good. Keep summarizing for them. Give them written material on the educational objectives of cases. Cultivate the class leaders, win them over with the strength of your logic. Talk to the better professors and find out how they handle the difficult situations."

SUMMARY

(The instructor prepared the following summary, "Educational Objectives of Cases," to give to students at the beginning of the next class.)
1. Business and accounting education require that you develop the following types of skills:[1]
   A. Knowledge, or technical understanding.
   B. Comprehension, or an ability to grasp all parts of a situation.
   C. Assessment, which might include a judgment as to the depths of the problem(s) and the quality of your alternative solutions.
   D. Application, or the ability to choose an appropriate technical tool from your store of knowledge, in order to help solve a problem.
   E. Synthesis, or the ability to pull all of the pieces of a problem together, and to recommend solutions that will help the entire situation (and not make some portions better but others worse).
   F. Evaluation, or the skill to assess as noted in C., to focus on main issues and not symptoms, and to weigh the strengths and weaknesses of alternative solutions.
2. Many of these skills are *not* readily acquired by listening to lectures and being hand-held through identical problems to those that you will see in life. There are simply too many combinations of situations to teach them on a situation-by-situation basis. The number of combinations will increase with the knowledge explosion. Better ways must be found to prepare you for the world of the future.
3. As a result, it is necessary to develop analytical or problem solving skills, utilizing the ingredients noted in 1. Cases and less directive questions help us to develop and sharpen our abilities to handle real problems. They simulate real life in circumstances where we can make mistakes but do not incur heavy costs to our employers.

[1] See, for example, Benjamin S. Bloom, ed. *Taxonomy of Educational Objectives, Handbook I: Cognitive Domain* (Longmans, Green & Co., 1956).

4. The use of cases creates uncertainties for students and therefore may require a change of attitude and study patterns on the part of the student. But this does not mean that your grades in the course will automatically be lower. As you receive more and more feedback the uncertainty will diminish. But life is uncertain. An education that assumes or deals only with certainty and simple situations is a poor preparation for life. When classes are large you have to try harder to participate in discussions and learn skills that are needed in business. Your future employers will not accept excuses that you were in large classes and did not learn well.

5. It is counterproductive for an instructor to make less directive situations simpler by giving you too much help or quick answers. The more direction that you are given the less opportunity you have to develop the full range of cognitive "skills."

6. Business skills can be taught by various means, not just by cases. However, it is often economical to use cases because they can simulate real business situations.

7. The higher you want to rise in an organization's hierarchy of rank (president, vice-president, etc.) the better must be your judgment and analytical skills. The choice is yours.

CHAPTER TWO

Case Analysis Techniques

Act V (Classroom):
(Instructor hands out summary "Educational Objectives of Cases," page 9, and lets the class read it.)

INSTRUCTOR: "Are there any questions about the 'summary'?"

STUDENT 090: "Is it reasonable to conclude that accounting and business have grown in complexity over the years and that university preparation for a business or accounting career has not really kept pace? I have the impression that many courses are still focusing extensively on teaching you the 'current state of the art' even though the material may be outdated by the time you graduate. What you seem to be telling us is that a shift must occur, at least in accounting education, so that equal time is devoted to techniques of analysis, systematic assessment of problems, and similar approaches. You want to play down knowledge memorization and play up analytical skills. Yet, this causes problems because you have to have the knowledge before you can apply it. . . ."

INSTRUCTOR: "Good thinking. Accounting teachers have to perform a balancing act. We feed you some knowledge, then we ask you to assess, evaluate and apply it. We have to be careful to not *restrict* the application, assessment, analysis and similar problem situations to only those that you have just covered in the most recent technical-knowledge textbook chapter. If we inadvertently restrict, you become misdirected and do not learn to apply the most sensible technique in that particular situation. When the problem material pertains to only what is in the most recent chapter students tend to learn to regurgitate everything in the chapter, hoping that a marker will pick out what is relevant, and ignore the rest of the regurgitation.

The balancing act for teachers becomes difficult when we have to decide what knowledge to include and *exclude* from a course. Some instructors try to cram all knowledge 'from the beginning of time' into a course. As a result they do not have any space left to practice the other cognitive 'skills.' The developers of this course have made some hard decisions, and have excluded some technical knowledge material. You will be given references where you can acquire the knowledge. Quite frankly you probably will not have time during this course to do all of this reference reading. But, in order to stay current for the rest of your life you will have to do similar 'after course' reading. A trade-off is necessary in professional education. Education programs have to concentrate on what they do best and what you need. You would be a pretty useless doctor if you memorized all of the ailments and hadn't seen a patient, or vice-versa. *Balancing* is the key. . . . There simply isn't time to do everything, and we want you to have a balanced education. . . ."

STUDENT 090:   "We then have to get used to doing more on our own, especially integrating technical knowledge with application, assessments, etc."

INSTRUCTOR: "Precisely. . . . Let us now move on to the techniques of solving a problem situation such as that being experienced by Mr. Hustle. (Exhibit One—1). In the previous class 085 asked us to list potential problems and how to plan to ensure success for Mr. Hustle.

What we need in handling these broader situations and requests is what is called a 'framework for analysis.' Please bear the following point in mind: *one framework that is always universally effective or correct does not exist.* We will provide you with several frameworks. Initially, you can try one until you become familiar with it. But avoid clinging to it forever. Grow with analysis by developing your own frameworks to suit different situations. . . . The frameworks are designed to help you initially to organize your thoughts, cover important issues and proceed logically; they are an aid and should not be allowed by you to become your 'life boat.'

First, let me give you a simple framework, 'Problem Solving Procedure for Accounting Cases,' to help you point your nose a little. (Instructor hands out Exhibit Two—1 and gives the class time to read it.)

* * * * * * *

INSTRUCTOR: "The 'problem solving procedure' is really just a road map telling you how to go from A to E by passing through 'towns' B, C and D. You are probably asking yourself: 'how do I recognize what constitutes a major problem in a less directive situation? What solutions make sense for the particular situation we are examining'? Well, this is where case analysis gets a little harder. We can help you somewhat by providing a few more analytical frameworks. But, expertise comes from practice, and more practice. . . . Let me give you another framework, 'Success and Failure Pressure Points'." (Instructor hands out Exhibit Two—2 and gives the class time to read it.)

EXHIBIT TWO—1

**Problem Solving Procedure
for Accounting Cases**

One of the simplest problem solving techniques requires you to progress from problem identification through to making recommendations and, depending on the situation, implementing those recommendations. The parts of the process are:
1. *Problem recognition.* Identify the potential problems, and place them in their probable order of importance. Try to group those minor problems that are caused by the same major problem.
2. *Gather the necessary evidence* that enables you to analyze the problem situations.
3. *Perform the necessary data analysis,* which includes both qualitative factors and quantitative computations. Sometimes a solution or recommendation becomes obvious once you have completed the analysis. Other times it merely becomes clearer that you have to give different weights or importance to particular factors and ignore others. In short, a judgment becomes necessary.
4. *Make supported recommendations,* after examining all possible solutions, listing the benefits and weaknesses of each and choosing the solution that seems to have the best chance of success.
5. Where required, *implement the recommendations.* Generally in classroom cases implementation is not required.

EXHIBIT TWO—2

Success and Failure Pressure Points

Accounting has to be placed in the broader framework of business policy formulation, strategic planning, and other functional disciplines of business. The linkages between accounting and the purposes, or the reasons for the existence, of an organization are:
1. *Objectives, goals or purposes of the organization:*
    Each organization was formed for a purpose; some time after its

formation the purpose(s) may have changed; for accounting to be relevant we have to link it to the purpose(s) of the organization; this means that we must ascertain the main desires of the group of people who make the business operational. Is the current purpose survival, or making a satisfactory profit, or the best possible health care, or something else? (Sometimes accounting cases are not clear on these aspects of the organization. But, when they are mentioned we should use the information).

2. *Crucial functions, decisions and events:*
   Each business has a few crucial "pressure points" that spell the difference between success and failure. In a consulting firm (or other professional or service organizations) this would tend to be the people. In a manufacturing organization the quality of the products could be of greatest importance. Within these general areas, specific points tend to be vital. For example, maybe one doctor is the key to a successful type of operation. Perhaps that doctor needs a delicate machine to attain success. Or, one small part in one space craft may prevent "lift off," and cost millions of dollars as well as failure to attain the desired goal. If this crucial function or decision fails, the organization may not attain one short term goal or maybe its long term objectives. At worst the organization could go bankrupt.

   Some accounting cases do not provide enough information to enable us to know what are the crucial decisions or functions. But, when the information exists, however hidden, we must use it. This is how we are able to ascertain which problems are of greatest importance and which are less important or unimportant.

3. *Tying accounting procedures and techniques to crucial functions:*
   Not only should we decide upon the importance of problems by looking to crucial functions and decisions, but we must also make our *recommendations* or suggested cures compatible with an organization's purposes and crucial functions. When cases are employed on examinations we must tackle the important problems first; otherwise, we will run out of time. Similarly, when our data analysis is complete, one solution may not "pop out" as the next obvious step to take. We must then look at each of the possible solutions, choosing the one that is most compatible with organizational objectives and crucial functions.

INSTRUCTOR: "Let us now become familiar with the two frameworks by using them to help us solve Mr. Hustle's situation as expressed by 085.

Step 1: Objectives of the business. In all probability Mr. Hustle is trying to make a living. It is not clear from the case situation what he is doing now (unemployed?), but we can probably assume that he will drive the 'lunch wagon' himself. He may therefore want only a 'satisfactory living.' In contrast, if he is expanding and adding another wagon to his fleet and is hiring another driver we might expect that he would want a specified minimum amount of profit, such as more than he would get by leaving his savings in an interest-bearing bank account. Each situation could have different objectives.

Step 2: Crucial functions and decisions. First, let us just list the items that are important if Mr. Hustle is to succeed and make enough to feed, clothe, etc. his family. Later we can try to pick out those that are more important than others.

Important items seem to be: (a) finding enough customers, who (b) will be attracted by the range and quality (freshness, for example) of products offered for sale, at (c) attractive enough prices, that they will provide Mr. Hustle with reasonable cash receipts. In order to make a living cash disbursements must be less than receipts over the long run. Hence, some important factors in keeping cash disbursements low are: (d) being able to buy at low prices, and (e) in those quantities that can be sold with a minimum of wastage, for (f) distribution in a small enough geographical area that transportation time and expense can be minimized.

Although there might be some minor disagreement, it would appear that (a), (d) and (e) are the most important or crucial factors. Success or profit will arise only if there is sufficient volume of business (times the difference between selling prices and daily expenses) to cover Mr. Hustle's costs of buying and refitting the truck, and paying for annual expenses such as insurance and licenses. We have therefore identified the problems (Exhibit Two—1).

Step 3: Prior to Step 1 we would have clarified precisely what our role was, and what we were being asked to do for Mr. Hustle. It is wise to return to the case or question from time to time and be sure that we are following whatever direction has been provided, be it in the body of the question or under some heading labelled "required." Student 085 has asked us: (a) to list the start up problems, and (b) to indicate the steps that can be taken to ensure success. Parts (a) and (b) are related and can be handled as one.

At this point we face a critical decision. Is 085 asking us for *all* ideas and points that occur to us, or only those that bear on the subject of *accountancy?* Sufficient direction is missing. The boundaries of the subject of accounting are not so clear that we will always know for sure what is a legitimate avenue of pursuit in an accounting case. But it certainly helps to know what is required of us.

Let us *assume* that 085 is using the case to test both our grasp of accounting skills and our ability to make our recommendations compatible with other functional aspects of business. Having made this *assumption* we are able to proceed with our analysis.

(Accounting cases can frequently require us to make assumptions when information and direction are missing. Markers are able to learn a considerable amount about a student from the assumptions that he makes or fails to make. For example, the absence of an assumption may tell the marker that the student did not even recognize that a vital piece of information, crucial to the task, had not been obtained.)

Step 4: Fitting accounting into the decision process of 'steps to ensure success.' Even though some of you may have studied very little accounting at this point in time, it is possible to observe a few 'counting' type exercises that Mr. Hustle could use to help him. (We will not even pretend that our advice can 'assure success'). He might, for instance:

A. Try to prepare a week-by-week forecast of his expected cash receipts and cash payments, say, for the next two or three months. This will tell him if he is likely to be short of cash at any point. Perhaps construction shut downs might occur. Can he survive a strike by construction workers? For how long? (A strike is a 'crucial event' that could cause failure for his lunch wagon business. Does Mr. Hustle have a contingency plan that permits him to survive a strike? He could, for example, make sure that he does not sign a contract that forces him to buy so many donuts per day regardless of sales potential. By doing a cash forecast he may spot problems in time and be able to amend contracts, or otherwise head off trouble). If he also keeps track of actual cash receipts and disbursements he can monitor his success against his predictions. He then can attempt to find reasons for important differences. How might he improve?

B. Keep track of what he sells at each location, and what food is left over on which days of the week, time of year, etc. This could improve his purchasing, and lower his investment in food, etc.

C. Compute whether it is best to buy the truck outright, or use a time payment plan.

D. Compute whether it is best to buy some goods that can be

stored (canned soft drinks, for instance) in bulk at reduced prices, or to buy small quantities on a day-to-day basis.

E. Prepare a monthly or quarterly set of financial statements to show a banker (in the event that he needs a loan and the banker asks for a history of the business). He would also have to have records to be able to prepare his annual income tax return.

(If you are not presently familiar with the techniques involved in C, D, and E do not be concerned. They will be covered in due course in an accounting textbook).

Step 5: At this point we would make recommendations. We would be sure to use language that Mr. Hustle would understand, taking care to explain why our suggestions make sense. We would try to *anticipate* his objections and concerns and build our reasoning process into the list of recommendations. We would explain why what may at first appear to be a sound recommendation is not in fact sensible on further investigation. In short, we would try to put ourselves in the shoes of Mr. Hustle and provide him with *convincing* information and recommendations that he would be willing to implement.

The question does not provide us with enough information about Mr. Hustle's background and abilities. He might need help in implementing all but B. in Step 4. If so, can he afford the cost of assistance? We must match costs and benefits and not overload him with accounting niceties.

We could continue our analysis, but I think that you have a general idea of how to commence case analysis. Are there any questions?"

STUDENT 053: "You covered quite a lot today, and some of it zoomed right over my head. Can we look over the hand outs and ask questions next day?"

INSTRUCTOR: "Certainly. I have another hand out item that tends to cover much of what we just completed for Mr. Hustle. There are a few differences. The slightly different approach may help some of you tie the previous two hand outs together." (Instructor hands out Exhibit Two—3 and gives the class time to read it).

EXHIBIT TWO—3

One Possible Analytical Approach

The following approach may be useful in analyzing an accounting case that (1) provides some information about an organization's purposes; (2) lists or otherwise indicates the existence of some possible problems; (3) gives data that appears to be relevant; and (4) requests recommendations. Note that this approach is not necessarily indicative of how the recommendations or report should be written to satisfy the recipient; it is a starting point for you.

1. Identify the *main* problems, in light of:
   A. Organizational purposes, objectives or goals, both in the short and long term; and
   B. Crucial success or failure factors, such as crucial functions (selling, production, etc.), or decisions (expand or not), or events (a strike).

   In brief, a *main* problem is one that has a direct bearing on whether an organization successfully pursues its objectives, or one that can cause failure. Lesser problems can combine into the equivalent of a main problem. Give attention to any isolated, lesser problems only if time permits.

2. List the main problems in approximate order of *importance*, and approach your investigation in this order.

3. Analyze available qualitative and quantitative data that appears to be relevant so as to:
   A. Clarify the order of importance and magnitude of problems; and
   B. Obtain a better understanding of which solutions (i) are *feasible* or "might work," and also (ii) are desirable or *acceptable* to your client (the recipient of the report).

4. Make *recommendations*, supporting each and explaining why you rejected other possible recommendations. (Some cases want you to make only supported recommendations, and do not call for reasons why you rejected other possibilities. For guidance, look for direction in the cases.)

EXHIBIT TWO—4

Types of Cases

Tier	Percentage Time and Effort Allocation		
	Case A	Case B	Case C
1. Problem Identification	30%	70%	5%
2. Data Analysis	50%	0%	85%
3. Recommendations	20%	30%	10%
Total marks allocated to case	100%	100%	100%

INSTRUCTOR: "We have just enough time left today to cover two more items of importance in case analysis: (1) 'sizing up' a case; and (2) for case examinations, learning to budget your time wisely. Here is another hand out." (Instructor hands out Exhibit Two—4 and gives the class time to read it).

*   *   *   *   *   *   *

INSTRUCTOR: "The hand out (Exhibit Two—4) is showing you that there are different types of cases. We have listed only three, but there are many others. When you have received a little more practice we want you to spend some time deciding what type of case you are facing. Is it one that is primarily problem recognition (Case B)? Or, is it one (Case C) where you are directed to the problems but have to perform data analysis that, once performed, leads to easy-to-make recommendations? Clearly, cases are designed to teach and test different cognitive 'skills.'

When you have learned to 'size-up' the case (and this includes locating the direction in the case) you can budget your time better. Those of you who decide to major in accountancy and have to write qualifying examinations must learn time-saving techniques. It does not take long to evaluate a case; it is certainly worth the effort to learn. This experience will help you 'size up' real life situations.

The final hand out for today is for those who have mastered the other ones and want more depth. Do not read this latest one until you feel comfortable with the others that I have provided. Take your time; you may need a few more weeks before you want to tackle this more complex hand out. (Instructor hands out Appendix Two—A, pages 21 and 22.)

I am going to give you a case to do in class next day. Could you look over what I've given you so far, and what I've said and be as ready as you can be. The ideas behind case analysis are fairly logical; the hard part is practicing and improving your skills."

SUMMARY

Many different types of cases exist[1] in order to encourage and test the development of different cognitive and perceptive "skills." One chapter devoted to case analysis techniques cannot possibly tell someone all that is necessary in order to handle accounting cases. We

[1] See, for example, Robert N. Anthony, "The Case Method in Accounting," in J. D. Edwards, ed., *Accounting Education: Problems and Prospects* (American Accounting Association, 1974).

have tried to provide some common frameworks for analysis in order to get you started. You will acquire the skills only through practice.

Ideally we would like to see you integrate your knowledge with the ability to assess, apply, evaluate and so forth on a day-by-day basis. As you learn a new technique (such as accrual accounting) ask yourself where it can be sensibly applied. Where should it *not* be applied? Accounting techniques and procedures are not of universal applicability. Accounting is not a physical science; there are no accounting equivalents to a "law of gravity." Accounting is a tool to help people; this gets us into personality differences among people. Accounting is used by different businesses in different countries for different purposes.

There are too many possible problem situations to be able to teach you what is a sensible cure for each. As educators we therefore have to strike a balance between teaching knowledge and teaching analytical skills. In the end educational success for you is a function of the amount of effort that you devote to knowledge acquisition and application and finding the balance that suits your needs.

APPENDIX TWO—A
A FRAMEWORK FOR ANALYZING BROAD PROBLEMS

A. A Decision Model	B. Relevant Decision Variables			
	1. Ascertain the organization's goal(s) and principal objectives	2. Specify those factors which are particularly crucial for the pursuit and/or attainment of the goal(s) and objectives	3. List the important recurring and non-recurring decisions that must be made about the crucial factors in the success of the organization	4. Specify the role which accounting control and information systems may play in important organizational decisions
1. Initial Information Search	(a) What are the organization's goal(s)? (b) Obtain evidence as to the clarity with which senior officials perceive the organization's goal(s)	What factors are paramount in the success or failure of this organization?	Divide the important decisions into recurring and non-recurring (or infrequent) categories. If possible, list each decision in order of its importance	(a) Where is accounting and related information now being used? (b) In which decisions is the information being used effectively, and ineffectively?
2. Identify and Clarify the Main Problem(s)	What are the relationships among the main problem(s) and the organization's goal(s) and objectives?	Are the main problems related to the crucial variables? If so, what additional sub-problems exist? If not, employ a less elaborate framework than Illustration III-1.	(a) Is the main problem primarily recurring or non-recurring in nature? (b) Clarify the relationships between the crucial variables and the related decisions	(a) Is the main problem accounting or general management in nature? Whose responsibility? is it to find a solution? (b)
3. Search for Solutions to the Main Problem(s)	(a) Seek solutions which are compatible with the organization's goals and prime objectives. (b) Are "adequate" or "ultimate" solutions to be sought?	Allocate search time and cost in accordance with your view of what is crucial	(a) How will your solutions affect the decision-making routine? (b) Which persons must be educated or informed about each proposed solution?	For each possible solution ensure that your information system can give an early warning should the "solution" prove ineffective or undesirable

APPENDIX TWO—A (cont'd)

A FRAMEWORK FOR ANALYZING BROAD PROBLEMS

4. Ascertain the Probability of Success of each Possible Solution	Which of the proposed solutions is closer to the desired goals of both the organization and the senior managers who must implement the solution?	If your proposed solutions affect the crucial factors for success, list all possible undesirable side-effects for each proposed solution	Can each proposed solution be implemented? Who is involved in implementation, and what other decisions must they make? What conflicts exist with other decisions?	If the solution involves the use of accounting and related data, will the user adequately understand the information? Will the data encourage the user to act in an efficient manner?
5. Estimate the Costs and Benefits of each Possible Solution	(a) What are the expected benefits in terms of the organization's goal(s)? (b) What are the estimated costs of implementing each decision? (c) Match costs and benefits	Relatively more attention should be given to problems affecting the crucial factors, and relatively less should be allotted for minor factors	Be confident that benefits and costs are measured in a long-term sense—especially when recurring decisions are involved	(a) Consider the costs of finding solutions as well as the costs of implementing a solution. (b) Prepare cost/benefit analyses for all complex decisions
6. Ascertain the Desirability of each Solution	(a) Do any of the proposed solutions require an amendment to the organization's goal(s)? (b) List all conflicts with previously implemented policies	Which of the proposed solutions effectively and efficiently protects the crucial factors in the success of the organization?	What subsequent decisions may have to be made as a result of each proposed solution? Are any of the subsequent decisions ones which should be avoided?	What effect does each solution have on the information system? Are there undesirable consequences for the information system?
7. Select the Better Solutions (or Best Solution When Only One is Permitted)	Weigh All of the Above Before Selecting the Best Solution(s)			

CHAPTER THREE

Common Errors In Case Analysis

Act VI (Classroom):

INSTRUCTOR: "As promised I am going to give you a short case to help you improve your analytical skills. When you are doing the case remember that it was designed to test your ability in several cognitive areas, *not* just in knowledge recall. If we wanted to see what you have been able to memorize we would ask very explicit questions with no or little room for ambiguity.

When we leave important information out of a question, or are intentionally vague about what we want you to consider, we are allowing students freedom to display their analytical skills. How much freedom do you have? Look to the direction or guidance in the case and make your best judgment. In accounting cases you have to simulate as best you can the approach that would be taken by a well qualified accountant. Markers do not expect as good a response as a qualified accountant would give, but they would like to see some movement towards the target.

When in doubt use the analytical frameworks that I have provided you with. Try to avoid the common errors in case analysis, which we will talk about in more detail at the next class. Especially resist the temptation to provide a quick "answer" unsupported by reasons and logical thought progressions.

Are there any questions? . . . None? . . . I assume then that you are anxious to get underway. We'll discuss the case at the next class."

(Instructor hands out the case, "Entertaining Aunt Minnie.")

ENTERTAINING AUNT MINNIE

Somehow a tradition became established that Aunt Minnie would come for a visit each August. You cannot remember how the "tradition" started, but, because you are an accountant and August is usually not a busy period, you have never bothered to start a counter movement to the "tradition." Uncle Chester, who died 10 years ago, was one of your favourites, and it somehow seemed fair that you would help his widow with her financial problems. You wish, however, that she would buy that hearing aid so many people have recommended to her. You also keep hoping that her memory of the embarrassing things that you did as a child would fade. However, several people have recently remarked to you that "Aunt Minnie's recall of your childhood seems to get stronger every year."

The other evening after dinner, your wife, Aunt Minnie and you were having tea. During a lull (there was more than one) in the conversation, you brought up the usual enquiries about the state of her finances. (You certainly wanted to avoid asking about the state of her health.) This reminded Aunt Minnie that she had recently received a registered letter asking her to sell her share of the company that Uncle Chester and several others had incorporated. After she located the letter in her purse you excused yourself, much to your wife's annoyance, and went to your den to study the letter and accompanying documents.

You locate your files on Aunt Minnie's recent financial history, in order to refresh your memory, and pull together the following information:

1. The letter is from Philip's Investment Corporation (PIC), a large company listed on several Canadian stock exchanges. PIC are willing to pay $120,000 for Aunt Minnie's shares of Bosomworth's Cable TV Ltd. (BCTVL), the company that Uncle Chester had helped incorporate and build. The offer is subject to government approval because cable TV is federally regulated, but, according to the letter, no problem is expected in this regard. If Aunt Minnie did not want cash for her shares she could accept 10,000 common shares of PIC, which are currently trading for $12 to $12.50 per share. From previous analysis for Aunt Minnie you have observed that somewhere around $125,000 is a fair price for her shares.

2. PIC already owns about 18 percent of BCTVL as a result of purchasing another company that had been owned by one of Uncle Chester's "partners" in BCTVL.

3. Aunt Minnie is somewhere between 76 and 80 years old. (She has always been evasive when you have enquired for 'financial planning' purposes. According to her income tax returns she was 68 for three consecutive years.)

4. BCTVL has exclusive rights to provide cable television service in a

specified region in one Canadian province. Uncle Chester and his "partners" started the company when there were few homes in the region. Expansion of a nearby city into BCTVL's region 12 to 15 years ago used up most of the vacant residential land and provided the company with a stable income. Unfortunately, in view of government regulations on competition, and the clearly defined area in which the company can operate, growth is severely restricted. The only way BCTVL can grow, other than in a minor way, is by buying another cable TV company.

Over the past 10 years, net income of BCTVL has been stable, rising only in proportion to inflation. The rates that may be charged to subscribers are, in effect, set by government. Occasionally net income will rise when BCTVL's management cracks down on costs or on people who illegally tap into the company's main line. (A work crew will be sent to cut cable wires leading to homes of non subscribers to BCTVL's service. If the wires are cut half way through the airing of an interesting movie, or sporting event, or beauty contest, or cartoon hour on a rainy day, illegal non subscribers tend to get the message and sign up for cable service).

5. As a consequence of the financial stability of BCTVL, the directors of the company have paid a fairly constant quarterly dividend to shareholders. The dividend is adjusted upwards usually six months after the government allows the company to raise its monthly charge to subscribers. In recent years Aunt Minnie has received a dividend cheque of $2,000 per quarter.

6. Recently, interest in the cable TV business has increased because new, full length, feature movies might be permitted by government to be shown through cable TV. In order to do this, expensive additional equipment would have to be installed by BCTVL. However, a new source of revenue would finally be available to the company.

7. Some uncertainties surround the cable TV business. For example, government regulations might change. Also, some subscribers may try to intercept transmissions from satellites, regardless of whether this is legal.

8. Aunt Minnie could invest the $120,000 cash, if she chose to accept it, in a variety of ways. She might want to buy mortgage company certificates that generate between 11 and 13 percent interest per annum. Or, she could choose Canada Savings Bonds that pay interest at slightly less rates, perhaps 10½ to 12½ percent. She might even want to buy gold and silver, and avoid having to pay income tax because no interest would be received.

9. Aunt Minnie owns her home, receives government pensions and generally manages comfortably by herself.

10. The most recent, condensed, financial statements of BCTVL show:

Bosomworth's Cable TV Ltd.
Balance Sheets
June 30, 19x4 and 19x5

	19x5	19x4
Current assets	$ 280,000	$ 197,000
Equipment	2,060,000	2,038,000
Accumulated depreciation	(1,040,000)	(980,000)
	1,020,000	1,058,000
Other assets	75,000	70,000
	$1,375,000	$1,325,000
Current liabilities	$ 135,000	$ 125,000
Common shares	400,000	400,000
Retained earnings	840,000	800,000
	1,240,000	1,200,000
	$1,375,000	$1,325,000

Bosomworth's Cable TV Ltd.
Income and Retained Earnings Statements
Years ended June 30, 19x4 and 19x5

	19x5	19x4
Revenue	$ 860,000	$ 845,000
Expenses	470,000	465,000
Income before income taxes	390,000	380,000
Income taxes	190,000	185,000
Net income	200,000	195,000
Retained earnings—beginning of year	800,000	765,000
	1,000,000	960,000
Dividends	160,000	160,000
Retained earnings—end of year	$ 840,000	$ 800,000

11. PIC currently pays a quarterly dividend of 10¢ per share on its common shares.

Aunt Minnie has established a procedure of staying at your home for exactly 10 days each August. She therefore will be leaving in three days, although she has not officially informed your wife as yet. Since it typically takes two days to convince her about the 'wisdom' of your financial advice, conclusions and recommendations, you will have to come to a definite decision by tomorrow morning. What are you going to tell Aunt Minnie to do about the registered letter?

* * * * * * *

Act VII (Classroom, two days later):

INSTRUCTOR: "Let's discuss the 'Entertaining Aunt Minnie' case. But first, are there any general questions?"

STUDENT 047: "That case was unfair; it was expecting too much; we don't have the knowledge to cope with it."

INSTRUCTOR: "When will you be ready to cope? Are you suggesting that we should use cases only when you have acquired all the accounting knowledge that exists? If so, do you really think that once you have acquired *all* the knowledge in existence the 'right answer' will be obvious to you in an instant, and be painless?"

STUDENT 047: "Can't you ease us into cases later?"

INSTRUCTOR: "The professors I have spoken with tell me that there is no, one, easy time to introduce analytical and judgment cases. They say that if you wait until next year the students complain that 'it is too late,' and that they should have received better case instruction in the previous year. . . . There certainly are some positive effects of teaching knowledge and case analysis side-by-side. Instructors are not insensitive; they know that you are not ready to thoroughly handle all facets of some cases.

Look at the issue from another angle. You may know little income tax law and practice at the moment, and therefore may have had trouble advising Aunt Minnie in this regard. But, think of the motivation benefits that you will receive if you take a tax course. We have created a curiosity or built-up enthusiasm for you to learn the tax law as it affects Aunt Minnie type investments. We have shown you a realistic possible application; quite likely you'll approach your study of tax law with greater motivation because you know that the tax law as it affects investment income is highly relevant material.

Have you ever studied a section of a course and wondered whether you'd ever see or need the knowledge again? Be honest. . . . Sure you have. There are pros and cons to every issue. The mark of an educated person is that he keeps an open mind. . . . You have enough knowledge to begin the process of coping with 'Entertaining Aunt Minnie.' Make the most of what you have.

Let's work our way through the case. Stop me when you have a question.

First, let us 'size up' the case. Although there isn't a 'required' section in the case there is plenty of direction. You are told that a main problem is whether Aunt Minnie should: (1) keep her shares in BCTVL; (2) sell the BCTVL shares for $120,000; or (3) sell the BCTVL shares and receive PIC's in exchange. If you missed this, go back to the case and find the direction. Note that if she is willing to receive the $120,000, you must decide what to do with it.

Where does the case fit, in terms of Exhibit Two—4? Is it mainly concerned with problem identification, with analysis, with making suitable recommendations, or with a balance of all three? In short, where do you think the marks are, and what skills do you think are being tested?

Clearly, one skill that is being tested is whether you can identify with the investment needs, and methodical personality, of Aunt Minnie. *Accounting* must somehow link up the needs of users with the viewpoints of preparers; if accounting does not, it fails to meet an important objective of being a 'language of business.' In order to understand accounting, the user-preparer interface must be probed. The Aunt Minnie case helps us to be aware of the importance of receivers of financial statements and recipients of accounting advice. In brief, can you *analyze* the problem from Aunt Minnie's point of view?

Rephrasing the previous paragraph, the case seems to have a number of marks allocated to linking up recommendations to the objectives or needs of Aunt Minnie. Some qualitative and quantitative analysis of alternatives is required, but the main problem is fairly obvious. Thus, in terms of Exhibit Two—4, the case seems to break down to something like this:

Problem identification	10%
Data analysis	30-25
Recommendations	60-65
	100%

A second skill that is being tested is your knowledge of the factors that should be considered in making an investment. Do you *comprehend* the significance of interest and dividends? What gives an asset, such as BCTVL, value or worth? Just the future dividends? How relevant are financial statements of past periods in helping to predict future profitability of BCTVL? Do the past financial statements recognize future events such as 'pay TV' movies? To repeat, we do not expect you to have all of the knowledge and answers at this point in your career. But, we want you to start thinking about these issues, and motivating yourself to acquire the knowledge and assess where it applies.

A third skill that is being tested might be called common sense *evaluation* of where accounting can help and where it may be useless. Maybe Aunt Minnie will refuse to sell her shares as long as any one of Uncle Chester's old 'partners' wants to keep his shares, for sentimental purposes or for some other reason. Maybe before he died, Uncle Chester made Aunt Minnie promise to hold onto the shares unless she badly needed money, which is not her present circumstance. You might think that this is a far fetched or obscure point; or, that if it were true you would already know about it. . . . Well, let us just say that you can waste a lot of time on computations that will be ignored unless you know Aunt Minnie's 'ground rules.'

I once remember my marketing professor asking the class on an examination to develop a plan to sell diet soft drinks in a particular African county. What he didn't tell the class, but was common knowledge if you read a newspaper or listened to television news, was that starvation was widespread in that region. Persons who said that 'no marketing plan would be successful' and explained the starvation reason were given full marks.

Accounting does not exist in a vacuum, in other words. Any questions? . . . None? . . . Well, let's press on.

What are Aunt Minnie's objectives, or purposes, or desires? She is well on in years and will not last forever. She is comfortable, and does not seem to need more cash. Is she willing to sell the shares? An assumption is required and we should *state it in writing;* and not just keep it to ourself. (By stating the assumption we make the marker aware of our skill in spotting the missing information.) Let us assume that she *is* willing to sell the shares.

Aunt Minnie seems to be straightforward, methodical, and capable for her age. Maybe she is stubborn (the case mentions a two day 'convincing' period), but that is not unusual for a person her age.

Why include all of the preamble? The reason is that we want to see if you consider that Aunt Minnie may 'not care in the least' to *maximize* her investment and profits. That is, we *may* have designed the case to catch the 'memory regurgitators' who start with the automatic belief that everybody wants to maximize their profit. The latter view may be the farthest thing from Aunt Minnie's mind, and you may have no hope of convincing her otherwise.

We appear to need another assumption. We cannot make assumptions that are contrary to evidence in the case. There is an indication that Aunt Minnie listens to you, the accountant. In all probability you want her to maximize her income from BCTVL. Thus, the most reasonable assumption to make is that your aunt in reality wants you to pick the most profitable alternative for her.

Note clearly that you do not have to make a 'profit maximization' assumption. You are *not* 'wrong' if you fail to make a 'profit' assumption, but choose something else instead. You have simply chosen another route to follow, and as long as you display your skills logically you will receive a passing grade.

Profit cannot be considered by itself. You also have to consider the *risk of loss* of her investment. Maybe you have a *chance* of tripling her investment by betting all of her $120,000 on a particular horse at the local racetrack. You could lose the entire $120,000 if the horse is merely out for a stroll that day. Hence, it first appears that you must have some understanding of what risk Aunt Minnie is willing to consider. But, of the alternatives mentioned in the case BCTVL seems the 'riskiest.' Thus, on second glance you may not have a real problem with her in regard to risk. If she is willing to keep BCTVL shares, the risk inherent in the other choices would probably not bother her.

What is the next step? Analysis of the qualitative (non-numbers) and quantitative data is necessary. Aunt Minnie gets more dividends from BCTVL than she would get from shares in PIC. *If* she needed the annual cash receipts, then she would probably keep her BCTVL shares. But we know that she doesn't need the money. Maybe through holding onto its cash PIC will be able to reinvest and be very successful some day. Its shares might then be worth $20 per share or more instead of $12 or so. This willingness to invest for the future may appeal to your aunt. We encounter the same issues with Canada Savings Bonds and mortgage company certificates. All of these alternatives, incidentally, have income tax implications. But we will ignore income tax until another day. (Chapters Six, Eight and Nine of this book.)

Perhaps sooner, perhaps later, you will recognize that Aunt Minnie must, or should, have a 'will.' Who will receive her money when she passes on? What would the beneficiaries like: shares in BCTVL? shares in PIC? gold? silver? bonds? certificates? something else?

As her nephew you face a problem. Can you ask Aunt Minnie what her 'will' says? Probably not. What can you do instead? One approach would be to prepare a list of pros and cons of each of the alternatives available to her. She can then interpret in light of her 'hidden' objectives.

For example, *if* 'pay TV' is coming and *if* cable TV companies are permitted to handle a pay TV system, additional investment dollars would be needed by BCTVL. Where would this money come from? Would the dividends be reduced? Would money have to be borrowed from the bank? Would Aunt Minnie be asked to supply more money? This uncertainty may not be appealing to Aunt Minnie because she *may* intend to leave her shares to a child. She may, therefore, feel that the child would be better off with PIC shares, which seems to have a more stable future.

At this point you probably are thinking that I could go on and on, forever perhaps. Not really. The case boils down to one of explaining the options to your aunt, and helping her meet her objectives.

In a real situation, as you explain matters she may tell you more, thereby eliminating some options. In a case you do not have the benefit of her additional comments. Therefore, you have to *anticipate* her reactions and be prepared for them. Your 'report' has to say '*if* this occurs, *then* I must respond this way.' This is much like the preparation needed by a courtroom lawyer. What will the opposing lawyer say? (If . . . then; if . . . then; etc.)

Notice that we are *not* saying that you should handle this case merely by dumping out a laundry list of pros and cons of the alternative investments that are available. At some point you should prepare such a list, but only after you have explained its relevance, significance, importance or whatever. You will be given marks for your reasoning process *and* for the list. The list by itself is not worth that much; all it shows is memory or recall of knowledge and not the application, evaluation and similar skills.

Obviously there are many other approaches to this case than the one I have talked about. The more open the case the more alternative approaches there are. You must pay attention to direction the same way that you heed traffic lights.

No doubt you are feeling let down at this point because your approach was different from the one I took. A 'let down' feeling is normal, I'm told; don't worry about it.

Those who were expecting one correct answer may feel bewildered at this point. You may wonder what you should do next. I would suggest that you go back over what I have said and compare it to the approach that you selected. What is the same? What is different? Did you miss something? If so, file it away in your mind so that you don't miss it next time.

Any questions? . . . Probably not, because you are exhausted.

. . . Think of some questions for next class. Remember, what you need most is practice. . . . Let us take a five minute break, then I want to talk about common errors in case analysis."

* * * * * * *

COMMON ERRORS

INSTRUCTOR: "Let us try to summarize the errors that are made in learning case analysis. Do not be discouraged by the length of the list. Ignore the points that you are handling well, and concentrate on the others.

1. Probably the most common reason why students fail any examination (aside from not knowing their subject) is that they do not read the questions and the requirements carefully. Most questions and cases provide some direction within the body of the case and also in a separate 'required' category. These portions have to be considered with care and perhaps read three or four times. Get into the habit of quickly assessing each case in terms of Exhibit Two—4. That is, determine whether you are being asked to be a physician (someone who diagnoses the problem and recommends a cure); a laboratory technician (somebody who analyzes specific items on instructions from the physician); or a pharmacist (who helps in the cure by assembling some medicine); or all three.

2. The second most common error seems to lie in attempting to respond to cases without recognizing why case learning is being employed. Accounting is a very practical subject. Accountants have to relate particular accounting procedures to improvements in resource allocation. Otherwise, they may be preparing useless or misleading reports. Know what applies where.

   It is therefore imperative that accountants identify implicit assumptions underlying their various procedures. For example, do some procedures make sense only under stable economic conditions and for a small business? Case analysis aids this process of relating techniques to decisions by requesting such a display of logic. In short, the logic process has to be set forth.

3. Assumptions are often needed in order to show your logic process. An instructor learns a considerable amount about a student by observing the type of assumptions which he or she makes. For example, suppose that information may not be available about depreciation of assets and yet some assumption has to be made in order to prepare income statements for the next five years. The simplest assumption likely would be to assume equal

annual usage, and no scrap value and no obsolescence difficulties. Why? Straight-line depreciation is easy to calculate. Some students, however, will go out of their way to complicate a simple matter, perhaps by assuming declining benefits and so forth. Sometimes complex calculations make sense. If so, proceed; if not, make the assumption which makes life easiest for yourself.

4. On the other hand do not assume away the case. For example, if you assumed that Aunt Minnie wanted to keep her shares in BCTVL for sentimental reasons, the case vanishes.

5. The next common error is to fail to put yourself in the shoes of the person you are supposed to be. If a report is requested for the president, you do not bluntly state that the president should be fired. Similarly, when a report is to be addressed to a particular person write to that person.

6. Remember to assess the case in terms of Exhibit Two—4. If the case appears to be heavy on data analysis, do not ignore the data. Some students who have been exposed to a Policy and Environment type of case course try to turn every subsequent case they encounter into a Policy case. They discuss strategy, structure, objectives and so forth but do not become involved with the numbers. Such can be disastrous in an accounting case. Use the data to clarify problems and support recommendations. Avoid saying, "Well, there is no point in deciding anything else until we first decide. . . ." The world cannot stand still. Explain the significance of your important point and then press on to other problems.

7. Avoid regurgitating facts which are known and not disputed by readers of your analysis or report. Regurgitation wastes time and bores readers.

8. If you are facing severe time restrictions on a case examination, state in words how you would solve a problem which involves substantial data analysis. For instance, state that you would prepare an income statement and if it resulted in an income figure in excess of "x" you would do such and such. Otherwise, you would do something else. Decision trees can help. Remember that you are being graded on logic as much as, or often more so than, you are being tested on arithmetic and ability to perform detailed technical computations. An amazing number of students would rather play with another technical matter than explain their recommendations which flow from performing a previous analysis. Perhaps this is because they do not know what the numbers indicate.

9. Some students have a bad habit of computing financial statement ratios and then either:

a. assume that the ratio speaks for itself, or
b. ignore the fact that accounting is not exact, and the reason for the strange ratio may be that the company has errors in its accounting system or is following an acceptable, but unusual, accounting principle. Ratios must be interpreted with care. They should not be calculated without having good reasons, and they should not be left hanging without adequate explanation.

10. Some so-called accounting cases may cover several related functional areas as well. Avoid spending all of your time on one topic or facet of a case, leaving huge portions untouched. Prepare a time budget if you are not an organized person. On case examinations it is absolutely essential that you prepare a budget and then adhere to it unless strong evidence later comes to light to show that your original budget erred.

11. On case examinations, it is advisable to have a plan ready to cover particular features on your first, your second, and other readings of the case. For instance, a first reading should take note of the direction in the case, and requirements, and be seeking general evidence of major problems. Some students try to cover too much on their first reading and 'see too many trees instead of a forest.'

12. Many students try to fit the main problem of a previous case into the case they are currently analyzing, regardless of the facts. It is common, for example, to have students see potential bankruptcy in several subsequent cases after an instructor assigns a case where pending bankruptcy has indeed been the prime problem. Presumably this tendency is a direct result of requiring students to do problems at the back of each chapter as they study a book chapter by chapter. If chapter five of a book covers accounts receivable the student comes to expect only problems on accounts receivable until the next chapter is read. Some instructors do not assign problems which integrate several chapters; the outcome of this approach becomes obvious in later case courses.

13. A few students misuse assumptions by either:
a. Stating assumptions when they are not necessary, or stating them and forgetting about them in subsequent analysis; or
b. Stringing together several assumptions which completely change the direction of the case. Do not write your own case and avoid responding to the one in front of you.

14. Be alert for the fact that some case problems are best solved in a particular order. That is, a negative decision regarding a building expansion automatically rules out having to worry about how to finance the expansion. If you are not certain that your arithmetic is correct in arriving at the conclusion of not expanding the build-

ing, then you may wish to discuss financing. However, do the expansion computations first in those situations where they can be separated into individual problems.

15. Avoid rewriting your report in better handwriting when you are doing case examinations. You can often save time by including some elaborate calculations in exhibits—which you write once— and cross-referencing them to your main report.

16. Try not to panic during case examinations. Generally the examinations are intentionally far too long to allow you to comment on everything that you encounter. The reason for the length is to force you to separate the important from the unimportant. Do not worry; no one else will have discussed everything in the case.

17. Do not dump out everything you can think of when you are running out of time on examinations, or in other settings. Memory dumping merely irritates an instructor or case marker and convinces him/her that you have missed the educational philosophy underlying case learning. Naturally, it is always possible that you will encounter an instructor who will permit you to dump from memory. However, this instructor has not learned how to use the other class members to discipline memory dumpers. Other instructors and case markers will know better. Thus, do not acquire bad habits such as dumping.

   Any questions? . . . Next day we can cover some other ways of helping you improve your skills."

SUMMARY

At this point it is important that you do not think that the task that lies ahead is too challenging for you. Most other students have nicely survived the process. You will too.

CHAPTER FOUR

Improving Your Skills

INTRODUCTION

This Chapter provides two quite different opportunities to improve your full range of accounting skills. The first opportunity may seem too unusual to merit your full attention. But we are quite serious. We want you to change roles and place yourself in the shoes of a marker. By adopting a different viewpoint you can assess your evaluation and communication ability and be forced to evaluate application, comprehension, and related skills of others. In short, you can learn to assess your own work a little more thoroughly.

The second opportunity involves doing another short case and checking your response. Chapters Five and Six provide longer cases that are useful to advanced students. The situations in this Chapter can be handled by students who have had only a few weeks of introductory financial accounting.

The chapter concludes with a reprint of an article that the author prepared for students studying introductory management accounting. The article, "Tailoring Accounting Techniques to Management Decisions," should be read before proceeding to Chapter Five. It describes which accounting procedures and techniques appear to be useful for several different management decisions. A main theme is that unless you know what judgment management intends to make you should not provide any cost or revenue figures. You may be providing data that lead to a bad decision! Like a doctor, you must know what medicine to prescribe for different illnesses. An all-purpose medicine does not exist.

COULD YOU REPEAT THE QUESTION?

We have told you that we intend to "turn the tables" on you. The precise way in which we do the "turning" involves giving you three different answers or responses and asking you to make your best guess as to the wording of the questions that each respondent was asked, including the body and the "required." By reversing the usual process you can gain greater insight into techniques of responding to questions. Learn to review your response in terms of the question that is being asked. Are you on target? Have you made the most of your opportunity to reply to the question?

Response A: "Revenue should be recognized when the goods are delivered (because costs are known accurately at this point) and cash receipts and revenue can be estimated accurately. This would occur in February or March 19x2 when the buyer expresses an intention to pay the seller's final invoice price."

Required: What is the question?

Response B: "The important facts in this situation are: (1) the buyer is a new company with no proven credit or payment record, *but* they have already paid a deposit of 50 percent of their estimated purchase price to the seller; (2) only 25 percent (at retail price) of the goods that are being shipped can be returned, unless some prove to be defective (and this does not seem likely because the seller has been manufacturing the products for several years); and (3) any selling price adjustments downward from the date the goods are ordered until they are received by the buyer are not likely to occur in a period of inflation such as we are currently experiencing. Therefore, if I were the seller I would recognize revenue when the goods were manufactured.

If I were the buyer I would show the 50 percent payment as a deposit, and would not record the purchase until I received the goods in my warehouse. The timing does not affect my income, anyway; so this is not an important issue."

Required: What is the question?

Response C: "The question is not sufficiently clear to give a definite response. It is necessary to make some important assumptions or to gather more information about the situation. The assumptions that I am making are:

1. What is the purpose or use to be made of the financial statement? If the sole purpose or use is to aid in postponing income tax I would wait as long as the facts permitted before recognizing revenue and the accompanying costs. I would try to figure out what attitude or position an income tax assessor would take and choose a revenue recognition point that would be acceptable to the assessor. However, if the sole purpose of the financial statement was to

meet a request from the company's banker I probably would recognize revenue earlier than for income tax purposes. If the financial statement was to be used for the banker and income tax assessor I would compromise and choose an in-between point.

2. How reliable is the buyer? What is the quality of the manufacturer's product? If the buyer can easily sell the manufacturer's
product because of its high quality and the buyer's marketing
skills, I would be inclined (subject to the objectives in 1 above) to
recognize revenue when legal title to the goods passes to the
buyer. This would be when the goods are delivered to the public
warehouse that is storing goods on behalf of the buyer. At this
point all of the costs of manufacturing are known, as are most of
the selling costs. The only uncertainty is whether the entire
amount of sales proceeds is collectible. (I assume that storage costs
are not large, can be estimated accurately and will be accrued as an
expense to match to the revenue.)

If the sole use of the financial statement is to aid the company in
postponing income tax for a year or so I would delay revenue recognition until greater certainty exists with regard to cash receipts of revenue. But, if we are preparing the standard stewardship accounting report I would recognize revenue when title passes, under the set of
assumptions that I have made.

If there is greater uncertainty about, (1) the product line's quality,
(2) the financial stability of the buyer, (3) the ability of the buyer to
sell, rather than return goods, and (4) future selling prices of the
product, I would delay revenue recognition until most of the cash
revenue is received from the buyer (ran out of time)."

Required: What is the question?

WILLPOWER TIME

As with several portions of this book, you should not proceed with
this section until you have made a solid attempt at phrasing the questions that each of A, B, and C were probably asked to "answer." By
going backwards from the response to the questions you are performing a check on the quality and depth of the response. No marks are
given for answering your own question instead of the one that was
asked.

Let us now attempt to reconstruct the questions that might have
been asked. From A's response it seems possible to assume that a
buyer orders goods that are to be delivered a few months later, in
February or March 19x2. There must be something in the question
about the buyer having to inspect the delivered goods and "express
an intention to pay." The "required" part of the question probably
asks: "when should revenue be recognized?"

The question seems to be what might be called a "knowledge recall, with a straightforward application." That is, the purpose of the question is to see whether the student can remember the general criteria for revenue recognition under stewardship accounting. If she can, then she is asked to apply this knowledge in a mythical situation that has few facts. The question is a *starting point only* for testing purposes. Why? Although some may say that there is a general rule for revenue recognition, others would say that there are too many exceptions to be able to claim that there is a general rule. In short, from an education point of view it becomes necessary to point out the nature of the "exceptions" to the "rule" (regardless of whether one believes that such a rule exists). It is most important that educators *not* leave students with the impression that exceptions are few or do not exist.

The question that B is answering appears to require greater skills in analysis and application, and is not a straightforward recall or memorization question. The question seems to contain certain facts that are not subject to other interpretations: 50 percent cash deposit; 25 percent of the cost of goods can be returned; and selling price is subject to a downward revision. However, B has placed a particular slant on these facts when he uses words such as "only." He may also have made assumptions, such as "a period of inflation."

Quite likely the "required" has asked B to consider the situation from both the point of view of the seller and of the buyer. B has done this and has tried to explain his conclusions and, in the case of the buyer, the significance of the conclusion. Without knowing what the question was, it is not possible to assess B's response. But, we might have a general feeling that B has displayed several skills: knowledge, assessment, application, and so forth. B's question seemed to give him more freedom to display skills than did A's.

From the response provided by C we might conclude that the question was less directive than those given to A and B. For instance, C has to make some assumptions about who are the readers or users of the financial statements. In contrast, B seems to have been told (or he might have unwisely assumed) that the financial statements were those of a large company that had to comply with Corporate and Securities Legislation and generally accepted accounting principles. Somehow B appears to believe that the amounts are not material. Maybe the question tells him the amounts and their relative importance; maybe he merely assumed, without stating it, that the dollars were not significant. In any event, B moved quickly towards a conclusion, and did not seem to be troubled by any uncertainty about dollar amounts.

Seemingly faced with a different situation than B's, C feels obliged to clarify the objectives of financial reporting and the "facts." She qualifies her response in terms of different interpretations of the facts, but particularly in terms of different possible purposes or uses. She, in effect, selects more than one answer. In so doing she displays an ability to think out the importance of different facts and different purposes of accounting on a recommended accounting treatment.

Without seeing the question that she was asked, we cannot mark her response. As a minimum we have the impression that she understands the subject better than A does. We are not sure by how much, though, because A may have been given a very restrictive question.

We tend to feel more certain that it would be harder to reconstruct the question given to C than it would be to assemble A's and B's. For instance, C does not list the facts as well as B does. Accordingly, we would have to guess in many places at what they might have been.

YOU TRICKED US!

Act VIII: (Classroom)

INSTRUCTOR: "Have you now tried your best to reconstruct each of the questions given to A, B and C?"

STUDENT 035:   "It's hard. We've never done this before. You're asking too much."

INSTRUCTOR: "I'm asking a lot, but I certainly wouldn't say that it is too much. When you graduate, your employer will certainly expect you to be able to follow instructions, to communicate effectively, to be able to reason . . . ."

STUDENT 050:   "We've tried. Let's see the three questions."

INSTRUCTOR: "Would you believe that all three people were given the *same* question!"

STUDENT 075:   "I thought so."

STUDENT 020:   "You set us up. You tricked us! That's not fair."

INSTRUCTOR: "What's not fair about it? It wasn't an examination. It's a learning experience."

STUDENT 040:   "It's intimidating. . . . why don't you give us things that we feel comfortable with. . . ."

INSTRUCTOR: "Let's not get into that again. Sooner or later you have to mature and learn to accept comments as being helpful, and not as being ego-destroying. You will not learn what you need if you expect to be complimented on everything you do and say. . . ."

STUDENT 050:   "Let's see the one question that they were given."

INSTRUCTOR: "O.K. When I'm finished handing it out (Exhibit Four—1), I want you to play the role of marker and grade each of the three papers. When you are finished we'll compare impressions."

STUDENT 020:   "This is a course in gimmicks, not accounting."

INSTRUCTOR: "Now, just a minute. What do you mean by "account-ing"? What do you think accounting involves? (Class time is dis-covered to be used up). . . . Let's take up your impressions about marking next day."

*   *   *   *   *   *   *

EXHIBIT FOUR—1

A Ltd. manufactures a standard line of goods that it has successfully sold for many years. B Ltd. has reached an oral agreement with A Ltd. to acquire many products in the line and distribute them in a new region. The terms of sale are that B Ltd. makes a cash deposit of 50 percent of the estimated purchase price when an order is placed. When the products are manufactured they are to be transported to a public warehouse until needed by B Ltd. Title to the products passes to B Ltd. when the goods enter the public warehouse, but all storage costs are to be paid by A Ltd. (A Ltd. wants to produce the goods in slack periods and is therefore willing to pay storage costs). When B Ltd. withdraws the products from the public warehouse A Ltd. renders an invoice for the purchase price less the deposit. Selling price is to be based on the lower of the usual selling price on the date of order, or on the date of withdrawal. After the products are with-drawn from the public warehouse B Ltd. has 30 days to pay the in-voice. Up to 25 percent of the goods, using selling price, may be re-turned to A Ltd. if they cannot be sold by B Ltd. Defective products can be returned at any time for full credit.

In November 19x1, B Ltd. placed its first order with A Ltd. and paid the 50 percent deposit. The products were manufactured in No-vember 19x1 and placed in the public warehouse; B Ltd. expected that it would require the goods in February or March 19x2. A Ltd.'s year end is December 31.

Required:

A. When should A Ltd. recognize revenue on its contract with B Ltd.?

B. When should B Ltd. record purchases for the above?

THE NEXT CLASS

INSTRUCTOR: "What was the point of the exercise in which you guessed at the question and acted as a marker?"

SEVERAL STUDENTS: *(laughter; some groaning).*

INSTRUCTOR: "I assume then that all of you see the point of the exercise. Now, student 090 who gave the best response? A? B? or C?"

STUDENT 090: "I had a little trouble deciding between B and C. Neither did a terrific job. C's answer showed greater understanding of the purposes of accounting and how you can and should tailor your accounting principles and methods to fit facts and purposes. But C didn't budget her time too well and did not answer the second part of the 'required.' Also, she did not make full use of the facts in the question. . . . You didn't tell us how long they had to answer the question so it's a little hard to say. . . ."

INSTRUCTOR: "It was a homework assignment so they. . . ."

STUDENT 032: "But, did it count in their final grade in the course?"

STUDENT 090: "Oh? Why did student C run out of time then?"

SEVERAL STUDENTS: Hiss.

STUDENT 090: *(blushing):* "Anyway, B needs more work on purposes of accounting, and A does not understand how to respond to questions that test more than memorization of knowledge."

INSTRUCTOR: "How would you have responded to (Exhibit Four—1)?"

STUDENT 090: "Probably a combination of B and C."

INSTRUCTOR: "O.K. Sounds reasonable. Any other remarks?"

STUDENT 099: "I enjoyed this exercise."

STUDENT 011: "That figures."

INSTRUCTOR: "For practice, why don't you prepare a response to Exhibit Four—1?

ANOTHER OPPORTUNITY?

INSTRUCTOR: "Let us assign another short case, and make it due for next week. This should give you a good opportunity to apply the additional insight that you obtained from our previous exercise. Remember:

1. Read the question carefully; try to pick out the key words and study the 'required' so that you know exactly what is expected of you.
2. Make logical assumptions whenever important information is missing.
3. Explain your reasoning, especially why you rejected alternative 'x' and selected 'y.' Try to provide a balanced response.
4. Make the most of the opportunity and show the markers your full range of skills, especially assessment, application, and so forth.
   I'll hand out the case now (Mark's Market). Are there any questions?"

STUDENT 011: "How long of an answer do you want?"
INSTRUCTOR: "I'll ignore that remark."

Mark's Market

Mark's Market (MM) is owned by Mr. Mark Lawrence. MM was acquired many years ago and consists of a ground floor "24 hours a day, 365 days a year" retail grocery and produce store, plus three floors of apartments above the store. Mr. Lawrence paid off the mortgage on the building five years ago, and has been saving his money to acquire a second building and store.

The fiscal year that has just finished (January 31, 19x6) has been a hectic one for MM. In early 19x3 the city in which MM is located served notice that they were intending to widen the street and to remove six feet from the front of the four floors in MM's building. This came as a surprise to Mark even though when he bought the property and building he knew that this might happen some day. After all, his building was constructed over 60 years ago and stood six feet closer to the street than the other buildings in the neighbourhood. Fortunately, the city was willing to pay for the cost of putting a new front on the four floors plus arranging a settlement for expropriating the six feet of MM's property that was needed for a sidewalk and some of the parking space lane in non-rush hours.

After several discussions with the city and MM's banker it was agreed that the new front would be built in the summer of 19x5. Mark decided to seize the opportunity and completely renovate the building, adding 20 feet to the back on all floors. The renovations were to be financed by a mortgage, funds that Mark had saved, the settlement from the city and a bank loan.

Since every apartment in the building was affected by the alterations Mark served notice on the tenants that they had to vacate by April 30, 19x5. Most tenants were paying on a month-to-month basis but the notices still caused difficulty, and many tenants did not buy groceries from MM in the months prior to April 30, 19x5. Since Mark and his family used one of the apartments they had to find accommodation elsewhere, at a much higher rental than they wanted to pay.

The renovations were completed in October 19x5 and Mark managed to lease the apartments for one and two year periods commencing November 1, 19x5. None of the previous tenants returned to the building, but Mark's family moved into a large apartment on the second floor.

The widening of the street and alterations to MM's store had a serious effect on sales and lowered them about 30 percent from the year ended January 31, 19x5. Extra labour costs were necessary to move grocery shelves here and there to stay out of the way of carpenters and other tradesmen. During some periods certain types of goods (lettuce, grapes, etc.) could not be stocked because they would have been covered in dust from construction activity in the store.

Mark has never regarded himself as much of a bookkeeper. Over the years he learned to keep books for MM, receiving some assistance from a retired public accountant, who prepared Mark's income tax return. Unfortunately, the retired accountant died last summer. Until last week, when he received a call from his banker, Mark was too busy to be concerned with financial statements. The banker reminded him that the loan agreement had conditions, one of which was that financial statements had to be filed with the bank every six months.

During the period of construction Mark opened a ledger account called "Renovations" and posted everything "that I did not know what to do with" in it. The first entry is dated April 19x5 and the last is December 19x5:

Payment to Mrs. Gibbins, to terminate her lease	$ 300.00
Moving costs—Mark Lawrence family (April)	318.50
First payment to Stonewall Construction, Mark's contractor for all of the renovations	45,000.00
Receipt from city—first installment for new front to building	(40,000.00)
Six months' rental for new apartment for Mark Lawrence family	4,200.00
Deposits refunded to "old" tenants	2,400.00
Property tax installments—second half of year	5,217.20
Receipt from city re expropriation	(30,000.00)
Second payment to contractor	20,000.00
Mortgage advance of $140,000, less payment to contractor $140,000	—
Labour costs of moving items in store-estimated	4,000.00
Payment to architect—new building's plans	12,200.00
Final receipt from city re store front	(6,190.00)
New neon sign in front of store	3,950.00
Payments to customers re damaged groceries	867.32
Gifts to contractor and others	317.41
Miscellaneous	417.95
New cash registers and fixtures	36,792.43
Proceeds on disposal of old equipment	(3,250.00)
Payment to security guards hired for construction period, when windows and doors were not secure	1,800.00
Bank loan interest, to November 1, 19x5	912.44
Final payment to contractor	17,688.73
Deposits received from new tenants	(3,600.00)
Construction permits	300.00

Moving costs—Mark Lawrence family (October)	361.50
Extra heat, light and power during	
construction, estimated	800.00

Besides the "Renovations" account Mark opened a "Lost Revenue" account that contains only pencilled memo notations: "Uncollected rents, May to October 19x5 $30,000; Lost sales in store $36,000."

Mark has approached you to help him prepare the financial statements that he needs, and to close out the "Renovations" account. He also wonders "what can be done about the lost revenue."

Required:

Advise Mark.

A RESPONSE TO MARK'S MARKET

If you are an introductory or intermediate level student this is your last chance in the book to do a case and have a response provided for you. The cases in the remaining chapters are designed for those who have completed much of their accounting, auditing, income tax, and management training.

First, let us "size-up" the question. How much guidance or direction is being provided in the "required" or within the body of the question? What have we been told?

1. We know that the owner of MM has to file an income tax return and would attach the financial statements of MM. We also know that the banker wants financial statements. In previous years the financial statements were probably used only for income tax purposes. Hence, some re-thinking of accounting principles may be in order because of (a) the major changes in the business; and (b) the addition of a new user, the banker. Generally accepted accounting principles (GAAP) would probably be requested by the banker.

2. The business is unincorporated. Often this means that we have to be careful defining the entity that we are accounting for: is it just the store, or the store plus the apartments? What decisions do people want to make from viewing financial statements? Also, we have to watch for non arm's length transactions between the owner and the business. In this question, the prime needs for financial statements appear to coincide. Both the income tax authorities and the banker want to see the overall financial picture of the store and the apartments. However, both would hope that the owner excludes personal living costs, especially heat, light, depreciation and similar costs of the apartment occupied by the Lawrence family.

3. We have been given an extensive list of costs and receipts to consider. In short, we have been directed to most of the issues,

which are financial accounting in nature but with income tax overtones.

What have we *not* been told? Our primary concern has to be the needs of the bank manager. Specifically, if MM prepared the financial statements in a manner that helped minimize income taxes (through minimizing income) would the banker understand? Is the banker just "going through the motions" to please his head office, or is he keeping an eye on MM's profitability or liquidity?

Surely the banker knows what revenue will be coming in from the apartment leases. (He probably has discussed the proposed rental rates with Mark). The banker's objective may be to learn the effect that the new store will have on cash flows. Will the cash flow (receipts less disbursements) from the apartments be drained by the store? Can the bank loan be paid off as planned? (If the security for the bank loan is adequate, repayment of the loan would receive the bank's prime attention).

If cash flow is what the banker wants to keep track of, of what relevance are the items in the "Renovations" ledger account? On the surface these items are not *future* cash flows that will affect repaying the bank loan; the cash has already been spent. Thus, what the matter boils down to is whether the banker will *misunderstand* future income statements of MM. They will be based on *accrual* accounting, (including depreciation of the renovations) and he might confuse them with *cash* receipts and disbursements.

The question does not tell us how informed the bank manager is; hence, we have to make a logical assumption. Let us therefore assume:

1. The banker knows the difference between accrual and cash basis "income" statements. He also knows that Mark is intentionally lowering MM's income by expensing some items that might be assets, etc. Mark is doing this to avoid paying income tax this year, but he knows that in time the income taxes will have to be paid.

2. If the banker wants proof that the bank loan can be repaid we will prepare a "Special Report" for him based on projected cash receipts and disbursements.

Having made these assumptions (and therefore having shown the markers that we have the ability to assess situations) we can proceed with recommendations for Mark. The underlying motivation or thrust of our suggestions is to expense where possible, in order to postpone income taxes.

However, we still have to separate business expenses from personal expenses that are included in the "Renovations" account.

These are:

1. Moving costs in April ($318.50) and October ($361.50) are not part of the business of MM. Mark merely has the same problem as the tenants that were evicted.
2. The six months' rental ($4,200) is the same as 1, and is not part of the MM entity.

Let us now go through the remaining items and suggest an accounting treatment for each:

1. Payment to Mrs. Gibbins. This can be expensed against rental revenue in the early months of the 19x6 fiscal year, thereby helping to lower income tax.
2. Payment to contractor ($45,000). This would have to be capitalized, but the $40,000 from the city could be deducted for a net of $5,000 debited to "Building."
3. The deposits of $2,400 that are being refunded should be credited to assets already on MM's books ("Deposits from Tenants"). If the deposits were previously recorded incorrectly as revenue then the $2,400 can now be expensed.
4. Property taxes of $5,217.20 can be expensed because they do not enhance future income.
5. The $30,000 expropriation payment is tricky. It is for the sale of some of MM's land. Hence, MM should ascertain the value of the land when capital gains tax was introduced into Canada and the percentage of square feet that was expropriated. For example, if the value of the land was $200,000 when capital gains tax was introduced, and 10 percent of the land was expropriated, then the "tax" cost of the land that was "sold" was $20,000. Proceeds were $30,000; hence, the gain is $30,000 less $20,000 or $10,000. One-half of this gain is taxable to MM's owner, who is Mark. (Other options might exist but we need not worry about them unless we become tax accountants). In any event the $30,000 should not be in the "Renovations" account. The original cost of the land that was expropriated (*not* tax cost of $20,000) should be credited to MM's "land" ledger account. The remainder of the $30,000, less income taxes as calculated above, becomes what is called an "extraordinary" gain.
6. The $20,000 second payment to the contractor should be capitalized as "Building."
7. The $140,000 mortgage advance should be debited to "Building" and credited to "Mortgage Payable." Observe that the question does not tell us when the first mortgage payment is due. If it was due in the period October 19x5 to January 19x6 we should check the ledgers to see what Mark has done. He may be expensing the

entire mortgage payment instead of debiting the amount of principal that was repaid to "Mortgage Payable."
8. The $4,000 extra labour cost can be expensed, given our objective.
9. The payment to the architect should be debited to "Building."
10. The receipt of $6,190.00 from the city should be credited to building.
11. The new neon sign of $3,950 is too large an amount to expense and would have to be capitalized in a separate asset account and depreciated as permitted by income tax law.
12. The payments to customers, gifts, and miscellaneous can be expensed, in view of our objectives. (An income tax assessor may question some of the gifts, but we can ignore this.)
13. The new assets ($36,792.43) less proceeds ($3,250.00) can be netted and charged to separate asset accounts. In stewardship accounting we might try to compute a gain or loss on assets that were sold. However, in a small business like MM we can ignore the matter, especially given our income tax objective.
14. The $1,800 payment to the security guards could be expensed because they represent protection of the grocery store items.
15. Given our objectives, the bank interest would be expensed.
16. The final payment to the contractor would be debited to "Building." (It is possible that a thorough study of the contractor's invoice may reveal some items that could be expensed.)
17. The deposits of $3,600.00 from the new tenants are an asset to be held until they are repaid.
18. You could try to expense the $300 construction permits but might encounter arguments from a tax assessor.
19. Given our objectives the $800 extra heat, etc. would be expensed.
20. Again, given our objectives "lost revenue" can be ignored. It is an "opportunity cost" and is not recorded even under stewardship accounting.

Obviously, the foregoing is not the only approach that could have been followed. We might have concluded that the sole purpose of accounting was not for income tax postponement. If so, we might have capitalized some items that were expensed. Or, if MM has large losses this year, because of the disruption, we might have capitalized several items even when our objective is income tax postponement.

Other points could have been added. For example, we might tell Mark that additional tax savings are available when he incorporates. Many of these additional points are more appropriate when the case is assigned in advanced courses. An introductory student is not expected to pick up all of the items that we noted, including cash budgets and planning tools.

SUMMARY

Learning to assess situations, reasoning through problems, and figuring out how to apply your knowledge can be frustrating. Your ego gets bruised when you miss obvious points and get caught in what turns out to be a minor symptom of a much larger problem. But, if you want to advance past the junior bookkeeper stage, where everybody gives you orders or makes the decisions for you, it is necessary to struggle on. Pleasure comes later when you start to hit the targets frequently. If you had difficulty with this chapter try reading it again in a few days.

TAILORING ACCOUNTING TECHNIQUES TO MANAGEMENT DECISIONS*

Graduates of accounting courses in which "principles" of accounting are illustrated in terms of stereotyped merchandising examples rather than examples of operations such as mutual funds, real estate development, finance and insurance companies and banks, may eventually wonder if they have wasted their time taking these types of courses. The failure to use a wider selection of business situations is especially sad because many important accounting concepts can be more clearly communicated by using mutual funds or similar illustrations.

For example, the usefulness of current value accounting could be illustrated by showing how one method of establishing current value is effectively used in quarterly and annual reports of open-ended mutual funds. Since people want to pay only what a mutual fund is worth, based on the value of the net assets in its investment portfolio, accounting could better tailor its valuations to specific management/shareholder needs by using a current value such as replacement cost. This would result in a more relevant accounting report than one based on the historic cost of the fund's assets and liabilities. Many similar illustrations are available.

It appears that students have great difficulty in transferring their knowledge of merchandising settings to other businesses with dif-

* Reprinted with permission from *CA Magazine* (March 1974; pp. 60-64).

ferent facets of operations. For instance, it is not unusual to find a CA student one year away from his Uniform Final Examination making the following elaborate calculations when analyzing, say, a construction company case:

1. Inventory turnover
2. Receivables turnover—5-year comparisons
3. Quick net asset ratios of various forms and other like computations drawn from merchandising illustrations in his textbook.

It almost appears as if he views these calculations as some form of self-evident truth and accounting principles as having a universal validity. He does not seem to realize that certain techniques are preferable in some situations and make no sense at all in others.

Some educators adopt the attitude that the knowledge of "which accounting principle fits which situation" will come later in a person's career and is not worth worrying about at the university level. Others believe that it is important to make some attempts to tailor accounting techniques to the uses of accounting information from the very first accounting course on, particularly for nonaccountants. There is some evidence, based on responses to comprehensive cases in the Uniform Final Examination, of a large comprehension gap about the relationships between accounting procedures and actual uses of accounting. This article presents one possible way of filling parts of this gap for managerial accounting.[1]

A TAILORING FRAMEWORK

This educational gap may not be quite as prevalent in management accounting as in financial accounting because several good textbooks have stressed a "relevancy" theme.[2] However, rarely does one encounter a sufficient number of realistic management accounting illustrations where job order or process cost systems are not combined with standard cost variance analysis. Consequently, many students believe that standard costs solve all ills. It would be far better if Canadian students could work with real cases drawn from mining, forest products and similar industries where clear-cut standard cost applications may not make sense and other accounting techniques may be more useful instead. These could be balanced with some problems

---

[1] For further elaboration of a similar approach for financial accounting, see L. S. Rosen, "A Framework for Studies in Accountancy," *CCA* (July 1971), pp. 89-91; and *Current Value Accounting and Price-Level Restatements* (Toronto: CICA, 1972).

[2] A prime example is C. T. Horngren, *Cost Accounting: A Managerial Emphasis* (Englewood Cliffs, New Jersey: Prentice-Hall, Inc., 1972).

encountered by small businesses to lend some perspective as to "what accounting technique fits where."

The approach about to be discussed can be an effective beginning to such an understanding,[3] but it is only half of the total learning process; the other half involves repeated use of the specific approach to solving cases and real client problems until the application of the viewpoint becomes automatic.

Exhibits I and II form the basis of one type of decision orientation to teaching introductory/intermediate management accounting. (Explanations here are in abbreviated form due to space limitations.[4]) The aim of this approach is to encourage students to develop their own method of judging which accounting technique fits a particular management problem or evaluation.

Exhibit I (A Tailoring Chart) sets out several typical management decisions/evaluations in the left hand column. Explanations of these terms are essential for an understanding of the chart.

1. *Performance evaluation.* How well did individuals or groups perform various tasks essential to the success of the organization? What corrective action is sensible?

2. *Output decisions.* What quantity and quality of each product should be manufactured, or what service should be performed? Should some products be sold in a partially-completed state? and so on.

3. *Pricing decisions.* For products where the company is a price leader, as opposed to follower, which selling prices should be selected for the short term and which for the long term? If the company is not a price leader, it naturally does not have to make a pricing decision. Its principal decision is one of output: whether or not to produce at the expected selling price.

4. *Financing considerations.* How much cash is needed at which times and for how long? Should the cash be obtained by selling bonds or shares, through a bank loan, from internally-generated funds, or from some combination of these?

5. *Investment alternatives.* Should manual operations be mechanized? If so, with which one of various competing machines? What is the desirable balance in each asset and liability account? Can risk and

---

[3] The author has used the approach effectively on many occasions. As always, some classes are quicker than others to understand the approach and its educational philosophy.

[4] Further elaboration is contained in the following references: L. S. Rosen, *Topics in Managerial Accounting,* Second Edition (Toronto: McGraw-Hill Ryerson Limited, 1974); *Accounting for Cost Determination, Analysis and Control* (Hamilton: The Society of Management Accountants, 1973); and, to a lesser extent, in L. S. Rosen, *Cases in Accounting and Business Administration* (Toronto: McGraw-Hill Ryerson Limited, 1970).

uncertainty associated with investment opportunities be quantified?

6. *Market area considerations.* In which cities and towns should each product be sold? Which distributors should be used?

   Although all of the management decisions shown in Exhibit I are interrelated, market area evaluations are closely related—and perhaps subdivisions of output and pricing decisions. In some companies market area is limited by freight rates or laws of competition, etc.

7. *External reporting obligations.* On one level this category includes all facets of reporting to shareholders, creditors and similar "outsiders" (i.e., an examination of fair presentation and generally accepted accounting principles). On another level—the traditional narrow management accounting viewpoint—the specific problem is one of attaching a cost to goods manufactured or in the process of being manufactured. Both levels must be considered in light of the purposes or uses of accounting. Ideally, external accounting reports ought to be matched to the use to be made of accounting information; however, to this point in its evolution, accounting has opted for one general purpose set of financial statements. Yet, it is clear that external accounting is supposed to serve different audiences with different expectations, for example, those persons interested in using accounting reports for:
   (a) complying with income taxation laws;
   (b) complying with Companies Acts and government requests;
   (c) predicting (future) cash flows or various definitions of income to aid in buy, sell, or hold investment decisions;
   (d) assessing management's past efficiency to aid in prediction, which in turn is used for investment evaluation.

Each of these uses could dictate different conclusions about what should be valued, which valuation should be selected, which types of financial reports should be adopted, what additional disclosure is needed, and similar considerations. Exhibit II (Costing and Control Alternatives) touches upon some of the matters which require thought.

8. *Income taxation implications.* Income tax provisions play an extremely important role in several of the above evaluations such as financing, investing and external reporting. Business contracts are arranged in particular ways to obtain maximum benefit of taxation laws. However, income taxation is listed as a separate category in Exhibit I because taxation is the prime reason many small businessmen choose any form of combined financial-managerial accounting system. The system is set up first for income taxation needs and second to aid incidentally in some of the other management problems.

9. *Bookkeeping considerations.* A variety of paperwork is necessary in most organizations: invoices have to be rendered and paid, accounts must be collected and cash must be deposited. Obviously, some bookkeeping system is required. In charitable institutions, for instance, this could be the main problem listed in Exhibit I. In the case of a grocery store, bookkeeping and income taxation needs may be the sole reasons for having an accounting system. The system would thus be much different to that of a company with performance evaluation and pricing as its main problems.

10. *Other evaluations.* Naturally, there are many other management decisions where accounting information and systems might prove of assistance. If the problem is nonrecurring, the system probably will not be specially arranged to accommodate quick access to information. However, when there is a continuing need for, say, current market selling prices in order to make asset trades, the system must be organized to provide such data quickly.[5]

USING EXHIBIT I

The main theme built into Exhibit I is that different businesses face different management problems. A one-owner enterprise often may have little use for an accounting system which emphasizes external reporting. A price follower should not be incorporating techniques into its system which are helpful only in pricing. A very highly automated concern is unlikely to want techniques primarily designed for performance evaluation of individuals.

Thus, when one faces a system design problem—such as may appear from time to time on CA examinations—a variation of the theme of Exhibit I could be useful. First, management's problems/decisions must be ascertained and listed in order of priority. Then, the required system would be designed by reference to the next two columns of Exhibit I (Management Accounting Procedure/Technique). Although some would call the foregoing "common sense," many students tend to overlook the approach when studying and integrating their courses. For best results the Exhibit I theme should be commenced in introductory courses, expanded in intermediate courses and amended and polished in advanced courses.

The "Management Accounting Procedure/Technique" column is split into two to acknowledge that some methods are better than others for assembling needed information. For example, in row 1, "Performance Evaluation," a general idea about performance success could be ascertained by comparing accounting return on investment

---

[5] See the writings of R. J. Chambers for examples.

EXHIBIT I
A Tailoring Chart

Management: problem/ evaluation/ decision	Management accounting procedure/technique	
	Broad approach or viewpoint (only a "rough" indication is provided)	Specific or refined approach or viewpoint
1. Performance evaluation	—Accounting return on investment (income ÷ invested capital) —Fixed budgets	—Responsibility accounting (flexible budgets and analysis of variances from actual costs) —Individual variances from standard cost (e.g. several direct material purchase price variances) —Human asset accounting —A variety of other measures such as number of units spoiled, or hours worked
2. Output decisions	—Accounting return on investment —Break-even and cost-volume-profit analysis on a multi-product basis —Some types of fixed budgets —Variable or direct costing	—Contribution margin or segment margin analysis —Break-even and cost-volume-profit analysis of single product or simple situations where assumptions of the technique are not violated —Standard cost variance analysis such as for volume or capacity variances
3. Pricing decisions	—Break-even and cost-volume-profit analysis on a multi-product basis —Master budgets or overall profit budgets for an entity —Variable or direct costing —Full manufacturing cost plus selling and administrative overhead, plus profit	—Contribution margin or segment margin analysis —Break-even and cost-volume-profit analysis of single product or simple situations —Perhaps cash budgeting if a not-for-profit institution (e.g. municipality desiring to set property tax rates)

4. Financing considerations	—Industry "rules-of-thumb" (e.g. "3" times direct material cost) —Use of accrual basis "funds" statements to estimate cash flows —Weighted average cost of capital computations —Various measures of risk and uncertainty	—Cash budgeting of receipts, repayments, interest and dividend effects —Profit computations of effect of financing by various alternatives
5. Investments alternatives	—Accounting return on investment —Rule-of-thumb methods such as "pay back" —Rough portfolio effects of investment returns and risk	—Discounted cash flow capital budgeting procedures
6. Market area considerations	—Profit budget effects on the entire company	—Incremental—or differential cost/revenue computations of effects of including various geographical areas —Contribution margin analysis
7. External reporting obligations	—Emphasis on past behaviour and results; conservative application of historic cost accounting —See Exhibit II	—Perhaps published forecasts —Perhaps segment reporting —Perhaps use of different valuation methods, additional footnote disclosure, human asset valuations, et cetera.
8. Income taxation implications	—Use of accrual accounting reports which may not claim maximum capital cost allowance and various permissible benefits	—A variety of tax planning features could be listed here
9. Bookkeeping considerations	—Cash basis or modified cash basis	—Accrual basis accounting with control accounts and perpetual inventory records
10. Other specialized evaluations		—A variety of items could be listed here (e.g. liquidation values vs. going concern values in a potential bankruptcy situation; see also footnote 5)

to some bench mark of expected performance. But broad averages, like return on investment, ignore performance which is better or worse than the average. Hence, in order to pinpoint deviations from expected performance by individuals, a technique such as responsibility accounting is required. Responsibility accounting and the other techniques in Exhibit I are not explained in this article but are described in most management accounting textbooks.

Therefore, to a great extent, the approach illustrated in Exhibit I encourages people to think about the uses of a technique at the time when mechanics are first illustrated in a textbook. The "how to compile the figures" viewpoint adopted by many authors does not become an ultimate end in the education process. Rather, the resulting figures are evaluated for success by comparing them against a management problem (is the information useful?). In most courses this evaluation of each technique is vital. Dozens of techniques are described in most management accounting textbooks, but without an evaluation of each, students leave a course assuming many techniques are alternatives to each other. In time, perhaps later in a course, when relationships among management problems can be clearly seen, Exhibit I can be replaced with a more sophisticated overview.

Many organizations encounter on a regular basis only a few of the management evaluations listed in Exhibit I. Their management accounting system may thus consist of only a few "specific or refined" techniques and several broad techniques. For a company with main needs, for example, 7, 8, and 9—external reporting, income taxation and bookkeeping—a double entry system with control accounts may suffice. Standard costing, responsibility accounting and account segregations permitting contribution margin analyses are not needed. Exhibit II discusses this point in more detail.

SOME ALTERNATIVE SYSTEMS

Exhibit II, "Costing and Control Alternatives," is designed to show which of several accounting techniques are alternatives to each other and which are entirely different concepts. The main point underlying Exhibit II is that an inventory costing system must be composed of one selection (A or B or C or D) from *each* of columns 1, 2 and 3. That is, A, B, and so on are alternatives to each other whereas 1, 2 and 3 are entirely different concepts. A manufacturing company's cost system is not complete unless there is a selection from each of columns 1, 2 and 3!

A company which desires information for output, pricing, performance evaluation and investment decisions may choose a (1) (B);

EXHIBIT II

Costing and Control
Alternatives

1. *Basic characteristic of system*	2. *Which valuation?* —Actual? —Predetermined? —Standard?	3. *Include vs. exclude* fixed manufacturing overhead in inventory cost?
A. Process costing methods	A. Actual direct material Actual direct labour Actual manufacturing overhead	A. Full or absorption costing (includes fixed portion of manufacturing overhead
	B. Actual direct material Actual direct labour Predetermined manufacturing overhead	
B. Job order costing methods	C. Actual direct material Predetermined direct labour and manufacturing overhead	B. Direct or variable costing (does not include fixed portion of manufacturing overhead)
	D. Standard direct material Standard direct labour Standard manufacturing overhead	

(2) (D); (3) (B) system. Such a system would separate fixed and variable costs (Column 3) to aid in contribution margin analysis, use standard costs (Column 2) for performance evaluation, and so on. A small business needing information for external reporting and bookkeeping purposes (per Exhibit I) may be content with a (1) (A) or (B); (2) (A); (3) (A) system, as it may often be the least costly system from a bookkeeping standpoint. A company wishing to postpone tax payments may choose (3) (B) along with a selection from columns 1 and 2. Direct costing charges manufacturing overhead to expense in the year incurred rather than deferring it.

An automobile repair company may choose a (1) (B); (2) (C); (3) (A) system to aid it in pricing mechanical and body work. Past experience may have shown officials of the company that unless cash is collected from customers when the car is picked up by the owner, bad debt losses are extensive. Accordingly, the accounting system must be organized for immediate billing (pricing). Each job must be kept separate; thus (1) (B) is needed. Although actual costs of parts (spark plugs, points) can be tallied quickly and direct labour hours have to be assembled for payroll purposes, overhead must be estimated. When shop overhead is roughly related to direct labour hours, a composite labour, overhead, and profit rate per hour can be set. Hence, (2) (C) has application. Probably (3) (A) could also be used unless competition was great and price shaving from full cost was occurring. In essence, the accounting system must be kept in phase with the crucial needs of the company. Without sound and quick billing the company may become bankrupt.

Inventory cost will differ depending upon which row and column in Exhibit II is employed. As a result, income will be different for different combinations. One interesting, unanswered financial accounting question concerns the effect of different income figures on readers of external reports. For example, is direct costing better or worse than absorption costing if the desire of shareholders is to estimate future cash flows?

CASE APPLICATIONS
As always, learning can be approached from several angles. Management accounting techniques may be taught first (the traditional method) and instant evaluation of each technique may be encouraged through models such as Exhibits I and II. However, to reinforce this type of learning, it seems necessary to use the reverse procedure and assign cases where organizations have particular problems. Students can then (a) pick out the important from the unimportant management evaluations which the company faces and (b) choose those accounting techniques which aid the important management evaluations selected in (a).

This article has concentrated on (b). It is clear, however, that the main benefits of the approach described can be attained only:
1. when the approach is used from the beginning of management accounting course exposure; and
2. when reinforcement occurs through using cases.

This in part explains why practical training programs such as chartered accountancy can benefit from using "cases" in courses. Previous experience has already, unfortunately, shown that unless comprehensive cases appear on examinations, an integration theme is poorly covered in courses designed for accounting majors.

CHAPTER FIVE

Comprehensive Case: Management Accounting Emphasis—With Responses

INTRODUCTION

The case that is reproduced in this chapter, Swiftair Limited, covers management accounting and related topics. It first appeared as a national examination of the Society of Management Accountants (SMA). In terms of Exhibit Two—4 it lies somewhere between Case A and Case C in design, direction and emphasis. It should provide an excellent review for those who are taking a management accounting course. It also is a useful case to ease students away from a "knowledge recall" mode of learning and into the early stages of learning a range of cognitive skills: analysis, evaluation, synthesis, et cetera.

In order to obtain maximum benefit from this chapter, you must *try* the case before you look at the responses of four candidates who sat for the SMA examination. By "try" we mean that you should spend four hours under simulated examination conditions with a pen, a calculator, tables of present values, and your full concentration. If you do not give the case a full and fair effort it is too easy to remain aloof from what we will be writing later. You can too easily rationalize your errors by thinking that "I would have done much better if I had really treated it as an examination." It is not easy to attain the anxiety levels that you undergo during an examination. But try your best.

You have probably answered hundreds of directive-style questions in preparation for memory recall examinations. How many cases have you responded to? Do you think that you might need the practice? One more time??

FIVE RESPONSES AND ANALYSES

Five responses to the Swiftair case are provided at the end of the case. After you have spent four hours doing the case, you can, after a short break, assume the role of a case grader and assign a mark out of 100 percent to each of the first four responses. Any grade below 60 percent is a fail; between 61 percent and 74 percent is a pass; and above 74 percent is a high pass. The first four responses are in abbreviated form and are condensations of actual student examination papers. The fifth response is a more complete one that would take well over four hours to assemble.

To gain maximum benefit from analyzing the first four responses you should give full reasons why you assigned the particular grade that you did. Avoid looking at the fifth response before assigning a grade to the first four. The reasons for this recommendation become obvious later. A general indication of the actual grade (pass, high pass, or fail) assigned on each of these first four responses is given later, along with reasons for the grade.

SWIFTAIR LIMITED*

Introduction

Swiftair ("the company") is what is termed a "regional" Canadian airline. It offers scheduled air transportation services in three provinces between small cities and larger airports, thereby "feeding" passengers to the cross-Canada carriers, Air Canada and CP Air. Swiftair also has scheduled passenger service between several northern Canadian cities and charter freight services in regions for which it has government licenses. Most of its revenue has traditionally been derived from scheduled passenger services but charter freight service has been growing rapidly in recent years.

Canadians tend to travel within Canada far more in the summer than in the winter months. Thus, if Swiftair decides to acquire a sufficient number of aircraft to accommodate all of those wishing to travel by air in its region in summer, there will be an excess of seats and aircraft in winter. In order to balance aircraft utilization throughout the year the company must investigate other sources of revenue. At present management sees the following alternatives:
1. lease excess aircraft capacity to other airlines which may have charter licenses to vacation resorts "in the sun";
2. offer charter flights under Swiftair sponsorship; and
3. offer discount air fares to try to increase revenue in winter.

All airlines in Canada are closely regulated by the Federal Government—in particular by the Canadian Transport Commission (CTC).

---

* Exclusive rights to this case have been granted with the kind permission of the Society of Management Accountants of Canada.

The CTC approves air fares, grants licenses to operate between specific cities and regulates the number of charter flights to various destinations. Swiftair has been granted approval to operate several flights to the West Indies—mainly to Barbados—in the winter, but has been told by the CTC that under present government policy it should not expect any further approvals to destinations outside Canada. In the event that the company acquires additional aircraft and wishes to improve total year-round utilization on such acquisitions, it must concentrate on charters within Canada to ski resorts and winter vacation areas. In order to receive CTC approval the charters cannot be in direct competition with Air Canada and CP Air on designated cross country routes.

The company has been privately owned for many years by a small group of financiers. These financiers are hoping to sell about 40 percent of their own, presently issued, Swiftair common shares to the public as soon as public interest in the stock market returns. For the past three years the small investor has tended to shy away from common share ownership. However, some underwriters of shares expect interest to return in 1985; hence, Swiftair wishes to prepare for public ownership including a common stock listing on the Toronto Stock Exchange.

Current Operation
Management is very optimistic about the future of the company. Air travel is becoming more popular because both young and old age groups are now being attracted, whereas not too many years ago businessmen were by far the main customers. Forecasting growth is important to the company because requests must be placed well in advance for new aircraft, for approval of additional flights, for expansion of ground facilities, and so forth.

At present the company operates a fleet of eleven DC 9 jet aircraft, assorted smaller airplanes and one air "freighter." Two of the DC 9s are leased; the remaining aircraft are owned by the company but are financed heavily by debt.

Current management problems can be best summarized by quoting excerpts from the most recent meeting of management, (February 1985):

PRESIDENT: I think that unless conditions indicate otherwise, we should prepare for public ownership of around 40 percent of our common shares by our year end (December 31). We will have to decide very quickly what we should do about adding to our jet fleet. We certainly should be able to improve profits by adding another daily flight to the mining country and initiate services to the oil exploration territories. We can then rearrange our schedules and change the type of aircraft serving areas, and use larger aircraft between cities with longer airport runways. . . .

CONTROLLER AND TREASURER: Oh, we are definitely going to sell some of the presently issued shares to new owners, are we? When was that decided?

PRESIDENT: The owners decided for certain last week, and the sale of shares will take place when the stock market looks good.

VICE-PRESIDENT, FLIGHT OPERATIONS: We have an option to acquire a small DC 8 or a DC 9, which expires at the end of this month. We can take delivery in early September and have the aircraft ready for scheduled flights in early October of this year. . . . (A DC 8 would contain 150 passenger seats, whereas a DC 9 would contain 100 passenger seats.)

CONTROLLER AND TREASURER: Have we, in fact, decided to buy one of the two jets? I know that you (Vice-President, Sales) have told me that the market research has been completed (See Exhibit 3) and that the results seem favourable on the surface. . . .

PRESIDENT: We may be buying a little prematurely but we have these purchase options, for an early delivery. If we don't exercise the option now, we may have to wait some time for the next delivery. Besides we've got a good purchase price on this option.

CONTROLLER AND TREASURER: So, that means we've decided to acquire either the DC 8 or DC 9. We haven't decided how we'll finance it. We could buy it and then borrow, or issue additional common shares; or a finance company could exercise our option and we could sign a 10- or 12-year lease with the finance company, or something else could be arranged.

PRESIDENT: Yes, we've decided to acquire another jet. So far we haven't decided which one. Also we haven't looked seriously at methods of financing. And, after we have chosen which one to purchase, we'll have to make a decision as to what we'll do about keeping the winter utilization up for this additional acquisition.

VICE-PRESIDENT, SALES: I have some cost figures here on winter charters to ski resorts in B.C. and Alberta. (See Exhibit 3.) From a quick glance the ventures could be profitable. . . .

PRESIDENT: Hold on a minute. I know that there's a rush to reserve the hotel space. But first we must decide which aircraft we'll buy. Once we've decided that, we can do something on the winter utilization question.

VICE-PRESIDENT, FLIGHT OPERATIONS: . . . and I have prepared information on estimated operating costs, and so forth (see Exhibits 1 and 5) for the proposed additional aircraft purchase, whether a DC 8 or DC 9.

VICE-PRESIDENT, SALES: We have several possibilities open to us with the winter charter flights to B.C. and Alberta. For example, we could send all three flights per week to Alberta or all three to B.C., or choose some combination thereof. It seems to make sense to sell a seven-day "package" encompassing air transportation, ground transportation to and from the resort hotel, and hotel room. If we do our own advertising and sell through our regular company-owned ticket agencies we'll attract less customers than if we use travel agents. (See Exhibit 3.) But, travel agents charge us 5 percent of the "package" price, although they do pay for any additional advertising they may undertake. . . . The "new" aircraft would be available three days per week for 21* weeks in winter each year—this arrangement should fit in well with what our market research indicates. . . .

CONTROLLER AND TREASURER: We'll have to look at owning versus leasing also. We can lease the DC 8 for $90,000 per month on a 10-year lease where we pay all operating, maintenance and insurance costs. The DC 9 could be leased under the same type of arrangement for $50,000 per month. . . . If we own the jet we can claim depreciation for income tax purposes at a 40 percent rate on a declining balance basis. This may help the cash flow in the early years. . . .

PRESIDENT: Sam, (Controller and Treasurer) I think you should co-ordinate the entire "expansion" plan considering which aircraft we should buy and the other matters we have discussed. . . . Drop whatever else you are working on and prepare a report for me by next Monday.

CONTROLLER AND TREASURER: O.K. as long as the other people give me the information I need on a rush basis.

VICE-PRESIDENT, FLIGHT OPERATIONS: That's fine with me. Incidentally, Sam, we have another option available for using new aircraft in winter. It can be leased to Grafair Limited for its West Indies charter operations for the 21 weeks, three times per week. They will pay direct operating costs but we have to pay for maintenance, insurance, and other similar fixed costs. They'll pay $18,000 per week for the DC 8 and $14,000 per week for the DC 9 and sign a 5-year contract. I haven't sat down yet to see if this arrangement is profitable for us. They'll use the aircraft about 5,400 miles per day. . . . You can ignore those fuel shortage problems we were discussing the other day. I was in Ottawa yesterday and received assurances that by mid-year the whole issue of a fuel crisis and price fluctuations will be history. . . .

PRESIDENT: What's next on the agenda?

VICE-PRESIDENT, FLIGHT OPERATIONS: The stewardesses are getting

---

* The aircraft travels empty one way at the beginning and end of winter. See Exhibit 2.

angrier about their contract still not being settled. . . . It expired last September 30.

PRESIDENT: I thought that you had settled the terms. Are they still asking for a 9 percent raise and an extra week's vacation with pay?

VICE-PRESIDENT, FLIGHT OPERATIONS: No, their union representatives are now asking for 12 percent because of recent inflation. I think, if Sam agrees, I'll offer 10 percent—which I'm sure that they'll accept—and sign a 2-year contract. In about two months I'll fire the union "ring leaders" so we don't have to go through this same mess again. The stewardesses are getting too organized; besides most of the "ring leaders" are old now and aren't that attractive anymore and are getting grumpy on the job. The pilots say they've been griping at passengers about working conditions.

VICE-PRESIDENT, SALES: The stewardesses are also complaining that their new uniforms are not warm enough and are too revealing. All that women's liberation talk is affecting some of them. I told them that there was nothing that we were going to do. We asked their opinion before we bought the new uniforms; I gave them a week to let me know because I had to place the order. They couldn't make up their minds, so I confirmed the order.

VICE-PRESIDENT, FLIGHT OPERATIONS: They're also complaining about the schedules and are reporting in sick more often. I've been hiring more and more married girls with children who used to work for us to fly a day or two a week to fill gaps. . . . The union leaders are angry. . . .

PRESIDENT: Sam, this sounds very unpleasant. Could you look into this matter too and give me some recommendations?

Subsequent to the foregoing conversations, the President approached the Controller and Treasurer and requested that he expand his report on a confidential basis to include a thorough review of management policy and practice. The president desires this additional information because he has recently been ill and has been away from the office several days per month.

Accounting Reports

The company has maintained the same set of accounting reports for the last ten or more years. An annual balance sheet and income statement are prepared solely to accompany the company's income tax return. (See Exhibit 2 for comparative statements.) Formal weekly reports are prepared for the President showing tickets sold, by route or destination, operating costs, seats occupied by flight by day of the week, hours flown by each flight crew member, hours flown by each aircraft, and maintenance costs incurred. Periodic tabulations are

EXHIBIT 1

Utilization of Proposed New Aircraft Acquisition, For Regularly Scheduled Flights—Based on 275 Days' Utilization Per Year
(prepared by Vice-President, Flight Operations in consultation with Vice-President, Sales)

	DC 8 Average Per Year		DC 9 Average Per Year	
	Years 1 & 2	Years 3-10	Years 1 & 2	Years 3-10
Estimated Revenue	$4,620,000	$10,164,000	$5,390,000	$7,623,000
Estimated Costs:				
Variable:				
Direct Operating Costs	1,881,000	2,069,100	990,000	1,089,000
Long Term Maintenance of Aircraft	470,250	517,275	247,500	272,250
Ground facilities:				
9-10% of revenue				
8% (approx.)	415,800	990,990	431,200	643,720
Direct Sales:				
12-13% of revenue				
11% (approx.)	554,400	1,321,320	592,900	885,115
Other:				
Depreciation	900,000	900,000	550,000	550,000
Average Interest on 100%				
Debt Financing @ 12% Interest Rate	950,000	550,000	630,000	360,000
Fixed Direct Costs (Insurance, etc.)	400,000	750,000	350,000	500,000
	5,571,450	7,098,685	3,791,600	4,300,085
Operating Margin Before Head Office Costs	$ (951,450)	$ 3,065,315	$1,598,400	$3,322,915

EXHIBIT 2

Balance Sheets
December 31
(in thousands of dollars)

	1984	1983		1984	1983
Current Assets	$20,940	$ 19,798	Current Liabilities	$15,674	$ 13,950
Property, Plant,			Debts Payable	49,882	58,400
Equipment (Net)	66,960	76,402	Common Shares	12,000	12,000
Other Assets	3,998	4,113	Retained Earnings	14,342	15,963
	$91,898	$100,313		$91,898	$100,313

Income Statements
Year Ended December 31
(in thousands of dollars)

	1984	1983
Revenue	$118,427	$109,716
Operating Expenses	96,001	94,304
Depreciation	14,765	19,210
Interest	5,926	6,887
Income Tax	870	(5,350)
	117,562	115,051
Net Income (Loss)	$ 865	$ (5,335)

kept of cash and liquid assets. Much of the invoice processing (e.g., recording and paying payables, various expenses and other items) is performed by using bookkeeping machines. When cost and revenue analysis reports are needed, information is assembled on work sheets directly from ledger accounts or by searching for applicable invoices.

REQUIRED:
Assume the role of Sam, the Controller and Treasurer, and prepare the full "expanded" report requested by the President. Assume a 50 percent income tax rate for the company and an after tax weighted average cost of capital of 12 percent.

EXHIBIT 3

Market Research Report
(prepared by an independent Market Research Bureau, January 1985)

A. Regularly scheduled flights*** for an additional aircraft:
        Expected Number of Additional Passengers**

	First Two Years	Next 8-10 Years
DC 8	60 per day* for each year	120 per day* for each of these years
DC 9	70 per day* for each year	90 per day* for each of these years

NOTES:

   * Based on 275 days per year at an average mileage of 4,000 miles per day in the first two years and 4,400 miles per day in succeeding years. Revenue is set at 7¢ per passenger mile, which is the typical rate used in the industry and approved by CTC. (Hence, each DC 8 flight-day in the first two years of the aircraft's operations would generate revenue of 60 people times 4,000 miles times 7¢ = $16,800. $4,620,000 of revenue would thus be generated by 275 days of regularly scheduled flights.)

  ** Expected number of additional passengers differ not only because of the size of the aircraft but because the routes travelled and cities serviced by adding another aircraft would differ.

*** Recognizes (a) that scheduled flights would not operate three days per week for 21 weeks in winter due to lack of demand by passengers, and (b) that some additional days are needed each year to perform aircraft maintenance.

B. *Expected demand for winter charter flights, using the additional DC 8 or DC 9 aircraft:*

If package price is:	The likely number of ticket buyers per week is:			
	Alberta Destination		B.C. Destination	
	Using Travel Agents	Using only Company Sales Offices	Using Travel Agents	Using only Company Sales Offices
$160	450	300	600	450
190	300	200	450	300
240	210	150	300	200
280	100	50	95	80

NOTES:

(1) The number of ticket buyers is not affected by the type of aircraft used. However, the DC 8 being considered for purchase by Swiftair holds 150 people and the DC 9 would hold 100 passenger seats.

(2) The expected demand is likely to remain stable for the foreseeable future.

(3) A round trip flight to the Alberta resort is 4,000 air miles whereas the round trip to British Columbia's resort involves 4,800 air miles. Hence, only one return trip flight per day is possible.

EXHIBIT 4

Winter Charter Flights—Cost Estimates
Seven Day Package Vacation—Swiftair Sponsored
(prepared by Vice-President, Sales)

Cost Item	Alberta Destination Per Person Per Flight* (one flight per day)		B.C. Destination Per Person Per Flight* (one flight per day)	
	DC 9	DC 8	DC 9	DC 8
Per Flight*				
Direct Operating				
Costs of Aircraft	$ 36.00	$ 45.60	$ 43.20	$ 54.72
Aircraft Maintenance	9.00	11.40	10.80	13.68
Direct Sales and				
Ground Facilities	24.00	24.00	24.00	24.00
Hotel	84.00	80.50	119.00	112.00
Ground Transportation to				
and from Resort**	16.00	15.00	24.00	22.00
	$169.00	$176.50	$221.00	$226.40

NOTES:

* Costs are based on a *full load* of 100 passengers for a DC 9 and 150 passengers for a DC 8. The only cost reduction on total costs per flight which occurs is for "Hotel" charges. The hotels refund $50 per passenger per week in Alberta and $70 per passenger per week in British Columbia. Costs are based on 20 return flights fully loaded plus costs of travelling empty one way at the beginning and end of winter (i.e., the first flight at the beginning of winter returns from the resort empty and the last flight at the end of winter travels empty to the resort. Otherwise, each flight travels to the resort with a group about to stay one week and returns with the group which was transported to the resort the previous week.)
** Variable per passenger.

EXHIBIT 5

Acquisition and Operating Costs of DC 8 and DC 9
(*assembled by Vice-President, Flight Operations from information supplied by the aircraft manufacturer*)

	DC 8	DC 9
Cost	$9,000,000	$5,500,000
Estimated Physical Life	16 Years	16 Years
Operating Life for Depreciation and Costing Purposes	10 Years	10 Years
Costs:		
Direct Operating Costs:*		
@ 40% seat utilization	2.85¢	2.25¢
@ 60% seat utilization	1.90¢	1.50¢
@ 90% seat utilization	1.25¢	1.00¢
@ 100% seat utilization	1.14¢	0.90¢
Maintenance Costs Are Estimated @ 25% of Direct Operating Costs		

NOTE:

* Includes all direct operating costs such as fuel, salaries and fringe benefits of flight crew. Costs are expressed as cents per passenger mile.

EXHIBIT 6

Possible Financing Alternatives
(prepared by Controller and Treasurer)

Regardless of which aircraft is purchased various government agencies will either lend or guarantee @ 12% interest over an eight year period	$5,000,000
Short-Term Bank Loan available @ 10½%	$2,000,000
Common Shares Can be sold at approximately six times estimated 1985 earnings per share—estimated proceeds of a contemplated sale.	$5,000,000 to $8,000,000
Debt Issue first mortgage, 10-year bonds can be placed privately with an insurance company at an annual interest rate of 12½%; repayable in full at maturity.	$3,000,000

EXHIBIT 7

Formal Organization Chart

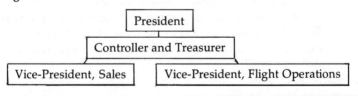

RESPONSE—CANDIDATE 1*

Report on: (1) Management Policy and Practice
　　　　　 (2) Proposed Purchase and Labour Problems
Mr. President:
　　I have undertaken a thorough review of the company's present position with regard to the above. My report presents the findings and recommendations in a qualitative manner including quantitative schedules where necessary to enhance my findings.

---

* Only slightly edited, and abbreviated to eliminate extremes in duplication of thoughts.

My recommendations are:
1. Hire a personnel director to handle the union more diplomatically.
2. Lease excess aircraft (Exhibit 1).
3. Rearrange areas of responsibility separating accounting from sales.
4. Prepare more explicit financial statements needed for going public.
5. Prepare statements comparing actual to standard, to provide a basis for comparison.
6. The company should go public but should issue additional shares and not 40 percent of existing shares, so as to increase its equity base.
7. The new airplane should be leased (Exhibit 1).
8. The DC 9 would be the best plane to obtain.

Report—Part 1—Primary Problems
A. Management Policy and Practice:
In order to do a complete review in this area I have broken my report into the following:
1. General Background of Company:
   a. Does our company fit the industry pattern?
   b. What are our policy and goals?
   c. How do we try to achieve our goals?
   d. Are our goals reasonable and attainable?
   e. Is the company's management well-coordinated toward goals?
   f. How do the various departments work together?
   g. Do we have sufficient expertise in management and proper staff training?
2. Particular Areas:
   a. Personnel problem areas.
      (i) Is employee morale good or bad?
      (ii) Problems re the union.
      (iii) Is management co-ordinated? (No, Sam does too much investigating instead of turning out proper accounting reports).
   b. Accounting problem areas:
      (i) Does our accounting area generate complete financial statements?
      (ii) Does our accounting area make use of standard costing and profit plans?
      (iii) Does our accounting area prepare meaningful financial statements for management decision making and control?
   c. Finance problem areas:

      (i) Is our company going to make proper use of debt and equity?

      (ii) Should our company go public?

      (iii) Does our company have a liquidity problem?

  d. Marketing problem areas:

      (i) Is our company making proper use of advertising?

      (ii) Is our company going after the proper market in the proper fashion?

      (iii) Is our pricing policy proper?

B. Other (page left blank)

Report—Part 2—Problems and Recommendations

A. Management Policy and Practice:

1. Problem: How does the company's overall policy fit into the industry as a whole?

   Recommendations: The company's policy at the present time is one of expansion. This being the case, and since the airline industry as a whole is expanding, there does not seem to be a problem.

2. Problem: How is the company attempting to achieve its goals?

   Recommendation: A decision has to be made at the present time on the method of expanding for (a) leasing excess aircraft, (b) offering charters and (c) offering discounts.

   In order to answer this problem I have prepared pro forma financial statements showing what we might expect in these areas (see Exhibit 1). I recommend to lease the aircraft.

B. Particular Areas—Major Problems:

1. Personnel problems: Is morale good or bad? and, Do we have a problem with the union?

   Recommendation: The answer to both of these problems is that the situation is bad. Although their primary grievance is money, I do not believe that this is their real complaint. Therefore I recommend:

   a. hire a full-time personnel director and do not let the vice-president of flight operations deal with unions;

   b. use married part-time stewardesses as little as possible;

   c. give the stewardesses a 10 percent raise and allow them to wear pant suits.

2. Problem: Is management coordinated?

   Recommendation: Flight operation and sales seem to control more than they should, e.g. union and personnel, and preparing budgets.

C. Accounting, Finance and Marketing:
1. Accounting problems: Does accounting turn out meaningful reports for management decisions?
   Recommendation: Accounting does not turn out meaningful reports. I recommend standard costs to give a basis for comparing to actual costs so as to direct expansion and pricing policy.
2. Finance problems:
   a. Is the company making full use of leverage?
   b. Does it have to go public?
   c. How do we finance additions?
   Recommendation: The company should go public at $10 per share but should sell additional shares to increase the equity base, and not sell issued shares.
3. Marketing problems:
   a. If the company is going into the charter business, is this the proper business to be in, and how is the advertising?
   b. Is the company's pricing policy for leasing aircraft proper?
   Recommendations: The company must look at its pricing policy on leasing planes and air fares.
   I trust that you will find my report helpful.

   Yours truly,
   Sam Controller

EXHIBIT I

**Pro Forma Profit and Loss
DC8—Years 1 & 2**

	Lease	Charter	Discount
Revenue	$4,620,000	$4,620,000	$4,620,000
Lease revenue	378,000		
Charter revenue		1,491	
Discount revenue			Unknown
Costs:			
Direct operating	1,881,000	1,881,000	1,881,000
Long-term maintenance	470,250	470,250	470,250
Ground maintenance	415,800	415,800	415,800
Direct sales	554,400	554,400	554,400
Depreciation	900,000	900,000	900,000
Interest	950,000	950,000	950,000
Fixed costs	400,000	400,000	400,000

RESPONSE—CANDIDATE 2*

Report to President, Swiftair Limited
Prepared by Controller and Treasurer

The following report has been prepared by me per your request concerning use and acquisition of new aircraft at our last meeting. This report contains an analysis of the problems discussed at that meeting. These problems were whether to purchase or lease a DC 8 or DC 9, how to finance it, and how best to use it.

EXHIBIT A

PRESENT VALUE OF LEASING AIRCRAFT FOR 10 YEARS

(operating and other costs are paid by Swiftair)

	DC 8	DC 9
Monthly lease cost	$ 90,000	$ 50,000
Yearly cost of lease	1,080,000	600,000
Tax savings at 50%	540,000	540,000
Present value at 12%		
Gross (Factor 5.65)	6,102,400	3,390,000
Tax savings at 50%	3,051,200	1,695,000
	3,051,200	1,695,000

Present value of cost of
purchasing DC 8 or DC 9
and 100% financing of
the purchase:

	DC 8	DC 9
Costs	$9,000,000	$5,500,000
Average yearly interest:		
Years 1 and 2	950,000	630,000
Years 3 to 10	550,000	360,000
Tax saving on interest:		
Years 1 and 2	475,000	315,000
Years 3 and 10	275,000	180,000

	DC 8	DC 9
Cash outlay	$9,000,000	$5,500,000
Present value of interest		
Years 1 and 2 (Factor 1.69)	1,625,500	1,066,700
Years 3 to 10 (Factor 3.96)	2,178,000	1,427,600
Present value of interest tax savings:		
Years 1 and 2	(812,750)	(533,350)
Years 3 to 10	(1,089,000)	(713,800)
Present value of tax savings on depreciation (Exhibit A-1)	(3,463,779)	(2,131,125)
	$7,437,971	$4,616,025

---

* Only slightly edited, arithmetic errors not corrected.

EXHIBIT A-1

DEPRECIATION SCHEDULE
(40% declining rate; 16 years life; no salvage)

Aircraft	Year	U.C.C.	C.C.A.	Tax Savings at 50%	P.V. Factor	Present Value
DC 8	1	$9,000,000	$3,600,000	$1,800,000	.893	$1,607,400
	2	5,400,000	2,160,000	1,080,000	.797	860,760
	3	3,240,000	1,296,000	648,000	.712	461,376
	4	1,944,000	777,600	388,800	.636	247,277
	5	1,166,400	466,560	233,280	.567	132,270
	6	699,840	279,936	139,968	.507	70,964
	7	419,904	167,962	83,981	.452	37,859
	8	251,942	100,777	50,388	.404	20,357
	9	151,165	60,466	30,233	.361	10,914
	10	90,699	36,280	18,140	.322	5,841
	11	54,419		27,209	.322	8,761
						$3,463,779
DC 9	1	$5,500,000	$2,200,000	$1,100,000	.893	$ 982,300
	2	3,300,000	1,320,000	660,000	.797	528,220
	3	1,980,000	792,000	396,000	.712	281,952
	4	1,188,000	475,200	237,600	.636	151,114
	5	712,800	285,120	142,560	.567	80,832
	6	527,680	211,072	105,536	.507	53,507
	7	316,608	126,643	63,321	.452	28,621
	8	189,965	75,986	37,993	.404	15,349
	9	113,979	45,592	22,796	.361	8,230
	10	68,387	27,355	13,677	.322	4,404
	11	41,032		20,516	.322	6,606
						$2,131,125

Problem 1: Whether to purchase or lease the new aircraft and whether to purchase or lease a DC 8 or DC 9.

Recommendation: In accordance with the analysis in Exhibit A, I would recommend that we acquire a DC 9 aircraft and lease it for 10 years. The cost of leasing the aircraft will be substantially lower than purchasing it and financing the purchase. The lost revenue from the loss of the greater capacity afforded in a DC 8 will be more than offset by the lower costs of the DC 9.

Problem 2: If we purchase the DC 9 what winter operations would be more profitable—lease to Grafair or charter flight to Alberta and British Columbia?

Recommendation: Charter flights can generate $3,145 per week more than leasing to Grafair (See Exhibits B and C). I think we would be better off to charter. If we acquire the DC 9 through leasing instead of buying we will realize a cost saving of $580,000 (on the average) for years 1 and 2 and further savings of $310,000 for years 3 to 10 (See Exhibit D).

Problem 3: Management policy and practice. I think we should further study the areas of conflict and try to solve the current labour problems as expediently as possible—give 10 percent pay increase and examine our policy on uniforms and flights. (There is not sufficient information on policy and practice to be able to make any judgements.)

EXHIBIT B

LEASE TO GRAFAIR

Grafair would require the aircraft three days a week and would travel about 5,400 miles per day. Grafair would also pay for the direct operating costs, but Swiftair would pay all maintenance, insurance and other fixed costs. All costs are calculated at 100% seat utilization.

	DC 8	DC 9
Weekly rental income	$18,000	$14,000
Maintenance costs:		
DC 8—Operating cost 1.14		
—Maintenance .285		
—@ 5,400 miles and 3 day week	4,617	
DC 9—Operating cost .90		
—Maintenance .225		
—@ 5,400 miles and 3 day week		3,645
	$13,383	$10,355

EXHIBIT C

WINTER CHARTER FLIGHTS—DC 9
(Using Only Company Sales Offices)

Ticket Buyers Per Week

Price	*Alberta*	*B.C.*
$240	150	200
Cost per flight at 100% utilization	169	221
Income per flight	71	19

If we book the maximum to the Alberta destination and the balance to B.C. our income per flight would be $10,650 and $2,850 for a total of $13,500 for maximum capacity at three flights per week.

EXHIBIT D

DC 9

	Average/Year	
	Years 1 and 2	*Years 3-10*
Operating margin before head office cost	$1,498,400	$3,322,915
Add depreciation and interest	1,180,000	910,000
	2,678,400	4,232,915
Deduct leasing	(600,000)	(600,000)
Add winter charter flights	13,500	13,500
	$2,091,900	$3,614,415

RESPONSE—CANDIDATE 3*

Report to President, Swiftair Limited

Dear Mr. President:

You have asked me for a full report due to the expansion plan policy of our company in either purchasing a DC 8 or DC 9. I have also looked into other company practices that I feel should be reviewed and acted upon by management.

With regard to expansion of another aircraft we have three possibilities of keeping this aircraft in the air during winter months.

1. Offer charter flights to British Columbia and Alberta.
2. Lease to Grafair for 21 weeks.
3. Offer discount air fares in winter months.

* Edited in some places for grammar and redundancies.

If we offer charter flights we would have to decide whether a DC 8 with capacity for 150 people or a DC 9 with capacity of 100 people is needed. Studying the Independent Market Research Bureau report for January 1985, the utilization percentages are quite different for the two aircraft:

	DC 8	DC 9
First two years	40%	70%
Next eight years	80%	90%

As you can see the DC 9 has a higher utilization and thus higher revenues when in use.

Using the likely number of ticket buyers in various price groups, the DC 9 carrying 100 passengers could handle four trips weekly to Alberta or British Columbia with the normal three days off for maintenance and lack of demand by passengers. The above statement is only applicable if the tickets are sold by the company sales office. If travel agents were to be used, the DC 8 would have to be considered due to the additional seating capacity. The travel agents would also decrease revenues by 5 percent for the cost of their services.

The cost report prepared by the vice-president of sales does not accept the Independent Market Research Bureau report that the aircraft will not be 100 percent utilized by the people. The vice-president of sales has assumed that if either aircraft will be purchased it will be fully loaded each time it takes off for a vacation to either British Columbia or Alberta. Thus, his direct operating costs will all be underestimated.

In considering if the company should go to British Columbia or Alberta we will have to look at sales anticipated and cost per passenger by the company. If we went to British Columbia, the DC 9 would cost us $221 a passenger and the DC 8 would cost us $226.40 for each passenger. At this rate we would have to charge for the package deal a sum of $280 a ticket. If this was to be the case only 95 people would buy through travel agents and only 80 through the company sales offices. If we have four trips per week this would mean that the average number of passengers would be only 22. This is much too low a utilization level. Thus, the company must consider going to Alberta with charter flights.

In looking at and preparing present value Schedule 1 we can realize a great deal more revenue from the DC 9 than the DC 8. Also, when the amount of money needed has to be raised, the issuing of the common shares would easily give us enough to buy the DC 9. But the DC 8 would need additional funds from other sources. The issue of common shares would not endanger control of the company.

We could also lease one of these two jets for a period of 10 years. Over a ten-year period the DC 8 would cost $10,800,000 and a DC 9 $6,000,000 (Schedule 2). Due to the income tax saving of 40 percent, Swiftair would be better off to purchase outright.

If you leased our aircraft to Grafair for the 21 weeks during the winter this would weaken our position to make available the flight each week to Alberta. Thus, this recommendation would have to be turned down unless dire conditions would force us into leasing so as to cover fixed costs. If conditions change it is doubtful Grafair would even need the aircraft themselves.

We could offer a discount on airfare but we have already introduced the charter flight to attract more customers. I would like to recommend to you, Mr. President, that Swiftair purchase the DC 9 for $5,500,000.

The DC 9 in its third year would only be 90% utilized and still have room for additional passengers. The DC 9 could handle all additional passenger service to Alberta for lesser costs. I believe it would be in the best interests of company financing that common shares be issued. No additional interest costs will then have to be absorbed. Our company is already heavily in debt and more financing could create a bigger problem.

The president does not seem to communicate to his senior management. An example is the owners wanting to sell 40 percent of the common shares to the public. The president is always making a quick decision without first looking at the financial end. An example is the jet option.

The controller seemingly does not know beforehand about financing by the company. The vice-president of flight operations knew about the option to buy a jet before the controller. The controller should not demand information on a rush basis—especially for large expenditures when accuracy is needed.

The vice-president of flight operations has prepared a schedule of operating costs without checking their validity with the controller. Handling of union matters will get completely out of hand if he fires the ring leaders after the contract is signed.

The vice-president of sales is showing no real rapport with the stewardesses. He just went ahead and ordered.

The union problems seem to be only annoyances to the vice-presidents. The employees think that their problems are real. A cessation of work will occur if union rights are ignored.

The company has the same accounting records as ten years ago and are outdated completely. The financial statements accompany the tax return. The controller and management should be using these reports to judge and evaluate their present position and the future. The company should have monthly budgets for comparison. The president is receiving reports that his vice-presidents should be receiving:

Vice-President *Sales*	*Vice-President* *Flight Operations*
—Tickets Sold	—Operating Costs
—Route or Destination	—Hours Flown by
—Seats Occupied by	Each Flight Crew Member
Flight by Day of Week	—Aircraft Hours
	—Maintenance Costs

The senior personnel should give information in reports orally to president.

There is little or no control kept over cash and liquid assets. The biggest part of our business is passengers paying for tickets over the counter. Stringent control is needed so all cash is received.

A whole new costing system should be set up by management. A qualified cost accountant should be hired. Each plane should be set up as a cost centre. All costs and revenues should be kept by each plane. The vice-president of flight operations should have maintenance costs for each plane. Also, he needs flying hours.

SCHEDULE 1

Present Value of Purchase of DC 8 or DC 9

	DC 9	DC 8
Cost	$9,000,000	$5,500,000
Revenue		
Year 1	$(951,450) × .893 =	$1,498,400 × .893 =
Year 2	(951,450) × .797 =	1,498,400 × .797 =
Year 3	3,065,315 × .712 =	3,322,915 × .712 =
Year 4	3,065,315 × .636 =	3,322,915 × .636 =
Year 5	3,065,315 × .567 =	3,322,915 × .567 =
Year 6	3,065,315 × .507 =	3,322,915 × .507 =
Year 7	3,065,315 × .452 =	3,322,915 × .452 =
Year 8	3,065,315 × .404 =	3,322,915 × .404 =
Year 9	3,065,315 × .361 =	3,322,915 × .361 =
Year 10	3,065,315 × .322 =	3,322,915 × .322 =

Due to shortage of time I did not calculate each figure, but I can see that the DC 9 has the greatest present value.

Schedule 2

Leasing for 10 Years

DC 8	$90,000 × 12 × 10 years	$10,800,000
DC 9	$50,000 × 12 × 10 years	$ 6,000,000

The controller could be given updated financial statements monthly—including budgeted and actual comparisons. Variances can be tabulated and explained. The controller should appoint a new man as treasurer. The office has poor internal controls.

The formal organization chart should be changed. The vice-presidents should report to the president.

RESPONSE—CANDIDATE 4*

A. Some of the Problems to be Examined:
1. Strong desires to make a good profit since there are hopes to sell about 40 percent of the common shares to the public.
2. Option to acquire a small DC 8 or DC 9.
   —Method of financing: purchase or lease?
   —Which to buy?
3. Where to fly and method of acquiring travellers.
   —Option to lease to Grafair Limited
   —Winter charter to ski resorts
4. Labour problems
   —Contract with stewardesses has expired
   —Numerous problems with working conditions

B. Some of the Areas to be Examined: Personnel, Accounting, Marketing, Service, Financing and Organization.
Personnel: (Top Executives) Little is said about the backgrounds of the top executives but one suspects that it is with planes not with management. This is reflected in union negotiations and the absence of quality reports. It seems strange that the reports have not changed in ten years. The financial statements are prepared solely to accompany income tax returns. More frequent reports and analysis are needed to follow operations. Sam, the controller, definitely lacks an accounting background. The formal weekly reports on operations are excellent but should be based on standards and budgets. There is a lack of communication—especially re the owners selling their shares.

The duties of the other executives are not clearly defined. The vice-president of flight operations is more informed on costing than is the controller. He is definitely weak in personnel relations. The vice-president of sales seems quite capable in his search for better revenues. He has all the information leading up to better analyses. The president is not communicating with his subordinates.

* Slightly edited to reduce some duplication; arithmetic unchanged.

On the formal organization chart (Exhibit 7) a major flaw is evident: the vice-presidents should not report to the controller but directly to the president. The president should be informed directly by the people responsible for that function.

The major fault of the organization is a lack of responsibility accounting. A proper assignment of functions and a method to check that these are accomplished is needed.

Organization and Service: This is a simple private company offering air transportation services—passenger and freight. The company has an excellent fleet of aircraft. The future looks bright because air travel is increasing.

Marketing: Good planning is needed in getting approvals from CTC. Flights must depart on schedule. There is little competition, and advertising is light. The CTC sets rates and grants licenses to protect all concerned.

Financing: The company is presently largely debt financed. Recently, debt to equity is about 70 percent debt. This is fine when the company has large fixed assets and can easily meet interest charges. In this case it is quite risky because the firm has little revenue to offset interest (which is tax deductible).

The current ratio is 1.4 to 1.0 which is rather low. Most companies are about 2 to 1. A study should be made of other air transportation companies before forming a judgement. Ratios seem to be stable from year to year.

Accounting: There is a lack of responsibility accounting, standards and budgets. There is no contribution margin analysis or sales analysis by province. The system has not been altered for 10 years and the controller's education may be behind. Formal statements should be prepared monthly.

Personnel: This area has been neglected by the vice-president of flight operations. It should immediately be looked after if the company wants to continue without creating bad will among employees and passengers. There is a need for a better personnel manager.

FEASIBILITY OF WHICH UNIT?
(in thousands)

	DC 8		DC 9	
	1 & 2	*3-10*	*1 & 2*	*3-10*
Revenues	$9,240	$81,312	$10,780	$60,981
Variable cost				
Operating	3,672	16,632	1,980	8,712
L.T.M.	940	4,138	495	2,178
Ground	1,940	18,496	2,048	12,232
	6,642	39,266	4,523	23,122
Depreciation-tax effect @ 50%	900	3,600	2,550	2,200
Net inflows	3,500	46,000	7,000	40,000
Present Values:	1,750 × 1.7	5,750 × 3.95	3,500 × 1.7	20,000
	$3,000	23,000	6,000	6,000
		3,000		
Both are equal	$26,000		$26,000	
Payback period	2½ years		2 years	
ROI	50,000 ÷ 9,000 = 550%		47,000 ÷ 5,550 = 850%	

General impression: DC 9 is better re payback and ROI

Method of Financing DC 9
(Initial Cost: $5,500,000)

1. Short term loan:
   Inadequate sum; would have to use other sources.
   Inexpensive compared to government agency.
   No control lost.
   Tax deductible.
2. Government agency:
   Interest tax deductible.
   No control lost.
3. Debt issue:
   Interest tax deductible.
   No control lost.
   Inadequate sum available.
4. Common shares:
   Lose part control.
   New owners may not be wanted.
   Not tax deductible.
   Least expensive cash flow; only dividends.

Because of the good return on the DC 9 it would be better to use debt financing—although the company is high in debt. Short term loan and the government agency would be cheapest.

Labour Difficulties

A settlement is due in order to avoid a strike. The settlement should have come earlier when a cheaper increase was possible. Try for a two-year contract below 12 percent. More attention should be paid to working conditions and grievances. Complaints about the uniforms are probably from the older generation but deserve attention. Future contracts should be settled when they expire to avoid bad feelings. The passengers deserve first-rate transportation because that is what they paid for.

Lease or Owning DC 9

Lease—committed for 10 years
    —total of $6,000,000   P.V. @ 12% = $3,390,000
Purchase—can sell if not adequate
        —interest deductible if debt financed
        —physical life 16 years
        —can claim depreciation @ 40% rate and recover cash investment quickly

In view of the above it would seem that the purchase commitment would be the best because it would require less funds to begin with. It would be the most versatile. The planes could be sold if not needed whereas the lease is for 10 years.

Lease Plane or Charter Flights?
(1) Lease plane to Grafair:
—Five year contract $14,000 × 21 = $294,000
—We pay maintenance, insurance and fixed costs
—Miles = 5,400 × 3 × 21 = 3,402,000 miles/year
—Revenue per mile: $294,000 ÷ 3,402,000 = 9¢/mile which is excellent
(2) Charter flights:
—Sales agents advertise
—Would definitely use travel agents but there is a constraint of three days per week
—Revenue: 300 × 160 = 48,000
               300 × 190 = 57,000
               300 × 240 = 72,000 (Best)
               200 × 240 = 48,000
—Choice $72,000 less 5% agents' fee $68,400
—A marginal cost analysis of Exhibits 3 & 4 is required
   Alberta = $169   B.C. = $221
   (This does not look good for B.C.)

Conclusion
By thinking ahead the management can put the company in a viable position to sell the 40 percent interest which the owners desire. By planning, management of the company can earn money.

Social and human factors should not be forgotten. Present value must be utilized.

CRITICISMS OF CANDIDATE 1's RESPONSE

General
This candidate has elected to provide a 90 percent qualitative report. He (we will assume) has not paused long enough to evaluate the type of case under review (See Exhibit Two-4) before electing a very risky method, in this situation, of displaying his knowledge. This case has many quantitative facets. Moreover, several portions of the response style consist heavily of a format he seems to have memorized to apply

to any case. This is a form of "memory dumping" or regurgitation which is unlikely to generate many marks on an examination. It is usually too general and only by coincidence will it apply to the specific case under consideration.

The candidate's series of questions shown under Part 1 of his report ("Primary Problems") is a check-list or form of overview and, as such, shows that he has prepared for the examination. However, the style is almost solely one of asking questions in general rather than applying them to Swiftair. A considerable amount of time was thus lost in listing possible problems rather than mentally asking if the problem is serious for Swiftair. If it is serious, list it; if it is not, do not list it. If the President thinks the problem is serious and you do not, explain your reasoning. As previous Chapters have indicated, cases are utilized for various reasons, one of which is to ascertain whether or not the candidate can separate very important from less important problems.

The report is very well organized with headings, subheadings, an introduction, and in Part 2, a side-by-side comparison of problem recognition and recommendations. Notice that the important recommendations (according to the candidate's viewpoint) are shown at the beginning of the report so that the president can grasp its general thrust quickly. Unfortunately, any reasoning linking problem recognition to recommendations is absent. First, the candidate often does not provide incidents from the case to support why a particular problem has been categorized by him as important. Second, data analysis is not performed to support recommendations. Third, alternative possible solutions are not shown and evaluated. (See Exhibit Two-3.) In effect, the candidate is saying, "I have decided and you will have to take my word that my undisclosed logic is brilliant." The president is not likely to appreciate such a pompous approach.

Some Specifics
1. Organization is a strong point of the candidate's report whereas the lack of schedules is a weak point. The president has called for a report on management policy and practice as well as on current problems. The candidate's report is organized this way. Often, however, there is too much repetition of the same point.
2. Unfortunately, the report does not give sufficient time to an important cross-section of problems. Most of those requiring quantitative analysis have been ignored. The case has been treated more like a "Policy" case than an accounting case. Current problems have almost been ignored—some exceptions are the labour quarrel and acquisition of the jet. In short, the candidate repeatedly fails to ask himself where the marks are likely to be given by graders.
3. The candidate continually uses vague words such as "proper" and

"meaningful." These terms have to be explained. There is no concise universal definition of such words for all types of business situations. The president wants to know what to do in specific terms. He does not want general or silly quotes from famous Broadway musicals such as My Fair Lady: ". . . which is the right and proper thing to do. . . ." Tell the president what is "proper" in this circumstance. He knows that he should do the "right thing." What is so-called "right" in this case?

4. The present owners wish to sell a portion of their shares. When they do, they—not the company—will receive the cash proceeds. Perhaps the company might also issue shares but except for the timing of the issue, this is another matter. Rather than make this distinction clear the candidate ignores the present owners' wishes and suggests what he considers to be an alternative—let the company sell shares. This approach tends to assume away a portion of the case. Why should the present owners not sell? This is not discussed.

5. The response gives one the impression that the candidate overreacted to questionable comments of some writers on how to approach cases, and tried to stress broader aspects in all functions of the business. Part 2 in particular contains a forced discussion of pricing. Why is this here? If it is not relevant, do not bring it into view. The case clearly states the power of the government over prices.

6. This discussion of standard costing can be viewed as a sign of memory dumping. Where can standard costs be applied in the company? Should a standard cost be attached to serving "coffee, tea or milk"? The candidate's discussion is just not credible. Perhaps this shows a lack of understanding of technical accounting. But who knows? The candidate's remarks are too brief. It is vital to follow some problems through the steps of recognition, analysis and recommendations, or as per Exhibit Two-3, in order to show that you are capable of logical reasoning. When you have established your credibility with the marker, you can take some shortcuts when you are short of time. This candidate has not established his credibility and the marker then tends to pass off the standard cost comments as more memory dumping.

7. Much the same comment as in 6 applies to the discussion of personnel and finance. What is "bad"? Where did the $10 come from?

8. The purpose of Exhibit 1 is not clear. The candidate has not conveyed that he understands which accounting procedures should be used in which situations.

Many other criticisms could be mentioned. But the main weaknesses and strengths of the candidate's approach should now be clear if they were not already.

Conclusion

The candidate should not, and did not, pass the examination. Most of his marks were obtained for recognizing problems, for the earlier portions of his report format and for some analysis and recommendations concerning management conflicts. Huge losses of marks occurred for not providing data analysis, for not explaining alternative solutions and for not making supported recommendations. Major issues of selection of a jet, how to finance it, and what use to make of it in the winter were almost ignored. The candidate's decision to concentrate on only qualitative issues was obviously disastrous. Perhaps, however, the candidate does not understand technical problems and had no choice. We will never know.

CRITICISM OF CANDIDATE 2's RESPONSE

General

Candidate 2 is in a sense an opposite to Candidate 1. Many, many candidates who failed the examination wrote either a Candidate 1 or Candidate 2 style of response. Candidate 2 has concentrated almost 100 percent of (we will assume) his effort on quantitative data analysis of a very few problems. He has followed through from problem recognition to data analysis to recommendations on those problems he has faced. But he has not expanded his report into many problem areas. Easy marks have thus been lost by not at least identifying problems in other operating functions of the company. Clearly this candidate would rather do an elaborate capital budgeting analysis and prepare a very time-consuming computation such as Exhibit A-1 than look broadly at the company.

The candidate has created a failure for himself by (1) not budgeting his time to cover three or four or more areas in the company, as requested by the president, and (2) assuming away problems by stating that insufficient information is available. Exhibit A-1 is the classic example of wasting time. There is nothing wrong with calculating two or three years of the exhibit in order to show the marker that you understand the technique. However, a ten-year computation is pointless.

Candidate 2 must learn more about setting up problems without doing all of the detailed arithmetic. He should explain which accounting procedure he would use and why. Some parts of his analysis are incomplete, but it is difficult to tell whether or not he understands which figures should be used. Exhibits C and D are examples where more description of intention would be very helpful.

Some Specifics

1. The report format is good because exhibits are cross-referenced to the main report and a problem—analysis—recommendation style is employed.
2. Exhibit A seems to have unnecessary duplication. For example, net-of-tax, rather than both gross figures and tax figures, could have been chosen to save time.
3. Interest costs and cash flows are already included in the 12 percent cost of capital computation. Double-counting occurs in Exhibit A where they are used twice.
4. The following comment in all probability would upset a marker: "There is not sufficient information on policy and practice to be able to make any judgements." Instead of spending time on such a remark and in performing arithmetic exercises, the candidate could have listed several problems. In some situations, recommendations would not be wise because information might be lacking, and assumptions would be difficult to state. If so the quoted comment could be appropriate. However, as a blanket comment it is out-of-place.
5. The figures in Exhibit C could be better explained. For example, why use only company sales offices?

Other criticisms could be made. See the more comprehensive response later in this Chapter.

Conclusion

As previously indicated this candidate failed the examination through treating it as a capital budgeting question, and not as a comprehensive case. He should learn to budget his time better.

For example, he could have set aside one hour to read the case, and then made a list of possible problem areas. Then so many minutes could have been set aside for each problem. This would have helped to prevent an extraordinary amount of time being wasted on Exhibit A-1.

A REAPPRAISAL

Now that you have had an opportunity to review the criticisms of Candidate 1 and Candidate 2, you might wish to read Candidate 3's response again. The learning process is circular and consists of attempts at learning, feedback on the success of your attempts, another attempt, more feedback, and on and on. How would you revise your criticism of Candidate 3, if at all?

In particular, notice how much (or how little) each candidate was able to write in a four-hour period. Quite likely each spent about one hour reading and re-reading the case. Planning for such examinations is thus essential because some time is lost on nervous reactions and other minutes are lost on correcting errors. The importance of overviews or check-lists of matters to watch for should now be becoming clearer to you if it previously was not. How many common errors has each candidate made?

CRITICISM OF CANDIDATE 3's RESPONSE

General

This candidate seems to go out of his (again we will assume a male) way to create a poor impression. The report is not organized to sort the important from the unimportant. Subheadings are not utilized. The report switches style from being directed to the president to speaking as though the president is not going to read the remarks. The controller (the writer) is viewed as a third person. The so-called "correct" solution is often arrived at by strange logic. Unusual interpretations of case "facts" occur.

Yet, the report contains several good insights into the company's problems. Discussions about lack of communication, financial report details, and to whom reports should be sent are valid points.

What mark would this candidate have received if he had spent more time reading the case and avoided the common errors noted in Chapter Three? It is difficult to say because other errors in technical ability surface from time to time in his analysis.

Some Specifics

1. Schedule 1 is a curiosity. If the answer is obvious, why was all of the time spent writing the same numbers?
2. In a discounted cash flow analysis as in Schedule 1, accrual costs such as depreciation and interest costs must be deleted.
3. Schedule 2 is not necessary. The multiplication could easily be performed in a footnote to the body of the report, if not in the body itself.
4. The reason for not incurring debt is vague and needs more support.

5. The discussion of British Columbia versus Alberta as a charter destination is puzzling and seems to stem from a hasty reading of the case. (Four trips and three days idle.)
6. "Sentences are often not thought out before being written," to quote from a marker with a sense of humour.
7. The discussion of utilization percentages is odd because revenue effects are not tabulated and compared with costs.
8. The decision to buy instead of leasing is made lightly without computations.
9. Major recommendations are buried in the middle of the report ("purchase the DC 9").
10. Some explanations are incomplete. ("He just went ahead and ordered.")
11. Recommendations are made to hire people but full explanations are absent.
12. The recommendation to have each plane as a cost centre is unusual and requires far more explanation.
13. Who supplies reports to the controller? Who analyzes variances?
14. A sentence or two could accompany the suggestion to change the organization chart.

Conclusion
This candidate also failed for the reasons stated. Like the others his analysis is a mixture of good and bad. Most of his marks were obtained for problem identification and for recommendations concerning management and personnel changes. One suspects that the candidate is weak on technical accounting and finance matters but has some years of practical experience and, perhaps as a result, does not feel obliged to explain some recommendations. The moral of the story here may be to undertake a study of fewer problem areas, but to do them more thoroughly. Organization counts.

CRITICISMS OF CANDIDATE 4's RESPONSE

General
Although this candidate commits several of the errors noted in Chapter Three and makes many mistakes applying analytical techniques and with arithmetic, he (again an assumption) manages to consider a variety of problems and offers many recommendations, sometimes with full reasons. Notice how the first portion of his response lists the current objective of the company (to go public) and mentions immediate problems which must be solved before the current objective should be attempted. He also reviews the more serious

difficulties in each of the functional areas. As the markers noted, "He tried to touch all bases."

The analysis is packed with relevant comments, but it is somewhat light on reasons for some suggestions. For example, the discussion of responsibility accounting, standards and budgets is left hanging. Although mention is made of the need for management to make specific decisions, a full explanation of where standards may apply is ignored. The report is also strong in commenting on good features of the company. Examples are the statements that the "vice-president of sales seems quite capable in his search for better revenues. He has all the information leading up to better analyses," and "formal weekly reports on operations are excellent." Once again, reasoning is shallow or absent, but at least the points were raised.

Some Specifics

1. The analysis of which jet to select erred in neglecting insurance and income tax costs. Tax depreciation rates should have been considered as well. Later in the analysis he recognizes the importance of 40 percent capital cost allowances and modifies a previous vagueness in his report.
2. The significance of the 16-year life of the aircraft if purchased, versus the 10-year life if leased, is noted.
3. The computation of lease revenue on the Grafair option is confused as are portions of the alternative analysis concerning winter charter flights (see the response later in this Chapter).
4. The report is not addressed to the president, and the candidate seems to forget occasionally that the president will read it and act or not act upon the suggestions.
5. The remark about the current ratio of 2 to 1 is naive; however, the comments which follow recover a little credibility for the candidate.
6. From time to time there is too much regurgitation of facts which the president knows (eg., company is private, and so forth).
7. The analysis of sources of financing is good because it sets out the benefits and limitations of each method.
8. Discussions of personnel and management deficiencies are redundant.
9. Organization of the response, aside from previously noted deficiencies, is good.
10. Frequently many qualitative considerations are noted when quantitative analysis is performed. See the discussion of leasing versus charter flights, and leasing versus owning (" . . . lease—committed for 10 years"). The candidate received many of his marks for qualitative comparisons of alternatives.

Conclusion

The candidate has written a "pass" response to the case. Many marks were obtained for recognizing the various problems in several functions of the company. The main, immediate problems (such as which jet to acquire, lease versus buy, and so on) were analyzed, although not very well. Part marks were given for portions of the analysis. Recommendations were given to attempt to correct difficulties; sometimes good reasons were given to support recommendations. Hence, marks are awarded for a process of logic and for having the intestinal fortitude to offer possible solutions to difficulties.

An obvious question is: Why did he pass whereas the others failed? Several differences between Candidate 4's response and the others can be identified. The primary difference seems to be that he has established *credibility*, whereas the others have not and have instead cast doubts about their ability. The doubts took many forms, as listed previously in analyzing the response of each.

Candidate 4 initially creates a poor impression by not addressing a report to the president (as requested). However, he soon recovers credibility by informing us that he intends to address a series of immediate problems and also will analyze several functional areas of the company. Subsequent organization of the report is good and helps to convey to the reader that the candidate intends to deliver what he promised. The initial comment under "Personnel," concerning the backgrounds of the executives, is a hint that the candidate will try to sort out problems from symptoms. (The problem may be that the executives need better training in management. The symptom is poor handling of union problems). More credibility is established by displaying a logical process of problem identification, analysis, and then recommendations (see the comments under "Personnel" in the candidate's report).

Once the candidate's initial response oozes confidence or credibility, mistakes can occur, but they are not likely to be treated as being too severe. Somehow, when the candidate now makes an error, the marker is probably still inclined to believe that other parts of the report can be superb. This is just a human reaction; and case markers are human.

A second noticeable quality in the report—very closely related to the previous point of establishing credibility—is that the reader is informed of where the candidate is headed. The president is busy. He wants to know what problems are dealt with in the report and what the major recommendations are. He is not reading a long mystery novel wherein he will find out "who did it" in the final few pages.

A third feature in the response, again related to establishing credibility, is the method of noting logical qualitative considerations and alternatives in the case while sorting relevant from irrelevant matters. Notice that the candidate often performs an analysis or compiles a listing of pros and cons and later draws these into a recommendation. Deductive methodology is thus being set forth. The case marker can check the logic because it is clearly displayed. This procedure is much like submitting calculations on a directed technical-problem examination. If your answer is "wrong" the "error" may have been caused by poor addition. You would then receive 99 percent or more of full marks (unless you were being tested on your ability at addition).

In summary, Candidate 4 has displayed many qualities that the other candidates have not. Other candidates in turn wrote better reports than did Candidate 4. Which candidate's response did your analysis of Swiftair come closest to? If necessary, go back and read the four candidates' responses and assess yours. You *must* be able to recognize why Candidate 4 passed and the other three failed. If you are not satisfied that you know why, go back to the beginning of Chapter Three (or One) and try harder to establish why. It is pointless to proceed beyond the end of this Chapter (and perhaps beyond this paragraph) until you know why there is a difference between Candidate 4's response and those of the other three candidates.

A MORE COMPREHENSIVE RESPONSE TO THE SWIFTAIR CASE

General Remarks

The undernoted analysis is set out in a teaching style and not as requested in the case. The reason for this format is to aid you in marking your own analysis of Swiftair. What follows is far more complete than you would be able to accomplish in four hours. Note, however, that it does not contain every possible worthwhile remark that could be made. Indeed, you will observe that the previous four reports—especially Candidate 4's—contain valid comments not noted herein.

Where should you start? Many instructors advise students to look first at the requirements (Is a report requested? Who is it addressed to?). Second, they suggest a quick reading to give you an impression of what data exists and where the problems may lie. Third, they recommend a slower reading utilizing check lists and overviews to ensure that you keep alert and look for relevant data for subsequent analyses. On a four-hour examination these three steps may take up to one hour with a case like Swiftair. Fourth, you may choose to prepare a budget so that you cover the major problems. Avoid the fate of Candidates 1 and 2 who spent far too much time on one or two problems, bogging themselves down in detail on these and missing easy marks on other important problems.

Beyond these four steps analysis is very much a matter of personal taste. In view of the interrelated nature of quantitative material provided in Swiftair, it is fairly important to decide quickly which problems should be solved first. To illustrate, can a decision be made to acquire either the DC 8 or DC 9 without looking at net revenue from additional winter usage (i.e., lease to Grafair versus charter to Alberta and British Columbia)? The president states: ". . . after we have chosen which one to purchase, we'll have to make a decision as to what we'll do about keeping the winter utilization up. . . ." Should you accept the president's comment as an order, or challenge it? Clearly, an assumption is required. You could thus say: "I have assumed that you wish me to obey your request to recommend either the DC 8 or DC 9 exclusive of the winter usage alternatives" and proceed with your computations. If you later ascertain that the decision to purchase should be reversed after considering winter usage net receipts then say so in your report! Similarly, if you recognize that winter usage does not change the decision—which in fact is what occurs in Swiftair—then you can delete your assumption.

Financing would be another example. You should first decide which jet you will acquire. Then you must compare purchase (at a 12 percent cost of capital) with leasing. An assumption is then needed concerning the leasing contract—what rates apply to years 11 to 16 of the lease? Next, if you decide to purchase you ought to prepare a crude cash flow schedule for the next year or two. You may find, as is the situation with Swiftair, that cash flow from operations is very high and short-term financing can be utilized in part. The 40 percent tax depreciation rate (capital cost allowance) and the high return on this particular acquisition increase cash flows considerably.

Some examination candidates chose not to become deeply involved with the acquisition—leasing—winter usage—financing and related problems at the outset. They often argued very repeatedly that the company first had to attempt better equipment utilization, investigate the air freight business and improve management skills. When all of these problems were solved, management could then consider the acquisition, leasing and related problems.

Such a "policy" approach is certainly not wrong. These candidates have a valid point. The question, though, is: for how long should such a stance be taken? Some candidates made their point in a short paragraph and then continued with quantitative and qualitative analysis of other serious problems. Foolish candidates tended to drag their argument on and on as though they had to convince the whole world of the "real" (their word) problem in the case. Generally, their arguments were not written assuming the role of Sam writing to his president.

In short, there are only so many marks given to particular points. An endless argument on one point such as the foregoing does not gain you a pass on the case. Repeating a point only tends to annoy the case marker. You must always remember that cases come in three varieties—good, average, and bad. If you think that a case is poorly written you still must make the best of a situation. Make your point about quality and then press on to more fruitful problems.

Many persons who have written the case as an examination budgeted their time very poorly. It is quite acceptable, when you are short of time, to set up a capital budgeting analysis or whatever without performing the detailed arithmetic. Swiftair presented a particularly annoying example of this with respect to the effect of tax depreciation, at a 40 percent declining rate, on cash flows. As mentioned earlier, there was no need to calculate effects over 10 years as Candidate 3 may have done if he had more time. Set up the arithmetic as a formula so that the marker can see that your approach is satisfactory. Then make a quick estimate, and proceed to use this number in further analyses.

Finally, examination candidates tended to commit several of the errors noted in Chapter Three. You might want to review that Chapter to see where it would be possible for someone to make such errors while analyzing Swiftair.

Detailed Analysis

The long-term goal of the company would seem to be to attain a satisfactory return on investment. A short-term goal is to ready the company for public ownership. This involves improving management, accounting, personnel and planning as well as solving immediate capital investment and financing problems.

Specifically, the major problems in the case seem to be:

1. Which jet should be selected? A DC 8 or DC 9?
2. Should the jet be bought (if so, how should it be financed?) or leased?
3. How should the jet be utilized during the winter period (lease it? or use it for charter operations?)?
4. If charter operations are recommended, should the company use its own sales force, or travel agents?
5. Is the accounting system geared to the needs of management? If not, what changes are required?
6. Is the management competent? (Is the decision to invest in new aircraft hasty? Are other decisions made too quickly?)
7. What can be suggested to improve industrial relations?
8. Is there adequate long-range planning?
9. What improvements can be made in organization structure?

10. Is the company ready for public ownership? (If not, what changes are necessary in plans, accounting reports, and so forth?)

Most of these possible problems are well identified in the case; hence, the candidate should not expect merely to regurgitate a description of the problems and pass the examination. Rather, time must be spent analyzing data in the case to ascertain which problems are more serious than others. Then, strong recommendations must be made to help in solving the problems.

A scanning of the case should reveal that a considerable amount of data is provided about these problems:
1. Which jet should be selected?
2. Financing aspect, if the jet is bought.
3. Charter destination if the jet is to be used by the company instead of being leased.
6,8. Management competence and planning.

The existence of all of this data would often indicate that such matters should be analyzed in greater detail. This case, however, gave a considerable amount of information about various sources of financing which later proved to be largely irrelevant. Thus, a response to problem 2 had to be assembled from a variety of sources and required computing "funds from operations."

You will observe that, although very little data was provided concerning the accounting system, this aspect emerged as a serious problem through more subtle means. Officials of the company described where they were headed in future years. Also, typical decisions which had to be made by the company were described. By putting such observations and comments by executives together it is possible to suggest both an internal and external accounting system which is geared to the company's needs.

In four hours it is impossible to deal with all of these "more serious" problems in depth. Hence, in order to receive a good grade candidates have to (a) indicate that they are aware of the various problems, (b) point out which problems are more serious than others, and (c) proceed to solve a few serious problems and make strong recommendations when appropriate analysis has been completed. Often, it is wise to make reference to both quantitative and qualitative factors. The Swiftair case tended to be 55-60 percent quantitative. Other cases could be primarily concerned with qualitative factors.

Problem 1—Which Jet?

On the basis of the computation in Exhibit A, the DC 9 is clearly superior to the DC 8. It is unlikely that the winter usage aspect need initially be considered in choosing aircraft. In the final analysis, both the winter usage revenue/costs and the tax shield from capital cost allowances (assuming that the jet is purchased instead of leased) on the jet must be included in a capital budgeting justification schedule.

Problem 2—Buy vs. Lease?

A crucial assumption must be made here before analysis can be conducted and a recommendation made. Is the actual usage life of the jet 10 years or 16 years?

If the life is 10 years, leasing seems best. Alternatively, if the life is 16 years but the ownership of the jet returns to Swiftair for a nominal sum such as $1 at the end of year 10, leasing would be best.

On the other hand, if the physical life is 16 years and the lease payments would have to continue from years 11 to 16 at the year 1-10 rates, then buying is advised.

The following analysis is conducted using the 12 percent after tax cost of capital provided in the case, as well as a 6 percent rate. The 6 percent rate is pulled "out-of-the-blue" just to see what the effect would be if less risk was attributed to the tax shield portion of the asset—which is more assured of utilization if the company has other income which would otherwise be taxable. A 10-year physical life is assumed.

Once again, observe the assumption of a 10-year asset life built into the analysis in Exhibit B.

Problem 2 is in a sense a subdivision of problem 1. In turn the tax shield provided by capital cost allowance is a subdivision of both problems 1 and 2. The formula on pages 99 and 100 gives a rough measure of the tax shield. (Naturally, other methods might be used.)

EXHIBIT A

	DC 8 Average Per Year		DC 9 Average Per Year	
	Years 1, 2	Years 3-10	Years 1, 2	Years 3-10
Operating margin (Exhibit 1 of Case)	$(951,450)	$3,065,315	$1,598,400	$3,322,915
Add back:				
Depreciation	900,000	900,000	550,000	550,000
Average interest	950,000	550,000	630,000	360,000
Cash flow before tax	898,550	4,515,315	2,778,400	4,232,915
Tax @ 50%	449,275	2,257,658	1,389,200	2,116,458
After Tax Cash Flow	$449,275	$2,257,657	$1,389,200	$2,116,457

The present value of each is (ignoring winter usage):

DC 8: Cash flows:
$449,275 @ 1.69 (P.V. factor)	$ 759,275
$2,257,657 @ 3.96	8,940,323
	9,699,599
Cost	9,000,000
Excess of cash inflow	$ 699,599

DC 9: Cash flows:
$1,389,200 @ 1.69	$ 2,347,748
$2,116,457 @ 3.96	8,381,170
	10,729,918
Cost	5,500,000
Excess of cash inflow	$ 5,229,918

EXHIBIT B

	DC 8		DC 9	
A. Leasing				
Annual Lease Cost	$1,080,000		$600,000	
After tax cost	540,000		300,000	
Discount rate	6%	12%	6%	12%
P.V. of lease cost	$3,974,000	$3,051,000	$2,208,000	$1,695,000
B. Owning				
Acquisition Cost	$9,000,000	$9,000,000	$5,500,000	$5,500,000
Less tax shield P.V. on capital cost allowance (Exhibit C)	3,910,000	3,360,000	2,390,000	2,220,000
Cost of Owning	$5,090,000	$5,640,000	$3,110,000	$3,280,000
C. Net Advantage of leasing (B.-A.)	$1,115,600	$2,589,000	$ 902,000	$1,585,000

$$\text{Tax Shield} = \frac{Cdt}{r + d}$$

where c = cost of asset
d = depreciation rate of 40%
t = tax rate of 50%
r = discount rate applied

EXHIBIT C

DC 8

@ r = 12%: $\dfrac{9,000,000 \times .4 \times .5}{.12 + .4}$ = $3,360,000

@ r = 6%: $\dfrac{9,000,000 \times .4 \times .5}{.06 + .4}$ = $3,910,000

DC 9

@ r = 12%: $\dfrac{5,500,000 \times .4 \times .5}{.12 + .4}$ = $2,220,000

@ r = 6%: $\dfrac{5,500,000 \times .4 \times .5}{.06 + .4}$ = $2,390,000

From the analysis to date, it seems reasonable to assume that a DC 9 is to be acquired. If it is to be leased, there are no problems about financing. But, if it is to be purchased where will the money come from?

Some examination candidates assumed that Swiftair was on the verge of bankruptcy. Often their reasoning leading to this conclusion was sparse or non-existent. The debt-equity ratio of Swiftair may not be too unusual for the industry. In addition, the income figures for Swiftair are on an income tax basis and are based on such factors as capital cost allowance at 40 percent. Thus, a quick look at both the income figure and the debt-equity ratio is simply not adequate in formulating a conclusion on possible bankruptcy.

Accordingly, if the income figures are revised, and a computation of funds from operations is set forth on a projected basis, it will be noticed that a large sum of money is provided by "funds" generated within the company. What is more, if short term funds are used for the balance of fund needs, and the early receipt of the tax shield (@ a 40 percent rate) is recognized, there is no need to be concerned about short term financing.

Problem 3—Winter Usage

Various assumptions or interpretations were possible with this particular problem. The charter destination analysis in Exhibit D (pages 101 and 102) assumes:

a. Only close to full load trips will be made; hence, some minor demand at a particular price will not be satisfied.

b. All of the passengers will pay the required price, and revenue will not be lost through last minute illness of customers.

c. If a full load is not taken the company will receive a $70 hotel rebate in British Columbia ($50 re Alberta) and save the transporta-

EXHIBIT D

WINTER CHARTER—WEEKLY PROFITS TO COMPANY

(R = Revenue; C = Costs; CM = Contribution Margin; Neg. = Negative Figure)

A. British Columbia

Price	Passengers	Travel Agents DC 9	DC 8	Passengers	Company Sales DC 9	DC 8
$160	600	R $91,200 C 132,600 CM Neg.	R $91,200 C 135,840 CM Neg.	450	R $72,000 C 105,800 CM Neg.	R $72,000 C 101,880 CM Neg.
190	450	R $81,225 C 105,800 CM Neg.	R $81,225 C 101,880 CM Neg.	400	R $64,000 C 88,400 CM Neg.	
	400	R $72,200 C 88,400 CM Neg.		300	R $57,000 C 66,300 CM Neg.	R $57,000 C 67,920 CM Neg.
240	300	R $68,400 C 66,300 CM 2,100	R $68,400 C 67,920 CM 480	200	R $48,000 C 44,200 CM 3,800	R $48,000 C 58,720 CM Neg.
				150	R C CM	R $36,000 C 33,960 CM 2,040
280	95	R $25,270 C 21,630 CM 3,640	R $25,270 C 28,900 CM Neg.	80	R $22,400 C 20,220 CM 2,180	R $22,400 C 27,520 CM Neg.

EXHIBIT D (Continued)

B. Alberta

Price	Qty	R	C	CM		R	C	CM
$160	450	$68,400	81,200	Neg.		$68,400	79,425	Neg.
	400	$60,800	67,600	Neg.				
190	300	$54,150	50,700	3,350		$54,150	52,950	1,200
240	210	$47,880	44,760	3,120		$47,880	47,100	780
	200	$45,600	33,800	11,800				
280	150	$34,200	26,475	7,725				
	100	$26,600	16,900	9,700		$26,600	23,225	3,375

Qty	R	C	CM		R	C	CM
300	$48,000	54,700	Neg.		$48,000	52,950	Neg.
200	$38,000	33,800	4,200		$38,000	46,450	Neg.
150				CM	$28,500	26,475	2,025
150	$36,000	30,500	5,500		$36,000	27,475	9,525
100	$24,000	16,900	7,100				
50	$14,000	13,600	400		$14,000	19,975	Neg.

tion charges of $24 (DC 9) or $22 (DC 8) in British Columbia [$16 (DC 9) and $15 (DC 8) in Alberta].

In order to provide a recommendation re winter charter usage, it was not necessary to perform all of the computations in Exhibit D. In fact, very few calculations were necessary. For example, once a decision had been made to acquire a DC 9, the DC 8 computations could be deleted. Also, several of the possibilities were clearly negative contributions to fixed costs—especially those at the low sales prices. Further, a quick look should tell that in many circumstances travel agents are cheaper in generating heavy sales volume. Finally, only loads around the full capacity of the plane seemed on quick glance to be profitable.

In cases full of data it is absolutely vital to pause and think about what an elaborate computation will tell you. Some examination candidates responding to Swiftair bogged themselves down in the winter usage analysis and did not get to other parts of the case. Naturally, they did not pass the examination.

In summary, Exhibit D indicates that if the DC 9 is acquired, the winter usage contribution per week will be:

2 flights to Alberta @ $240 using travel agents	$11,800
1 flight to B.C. @ $280 using travel agents	3,640
	$15,440

Exhibit E sets out the lease option of winter usage (i.e., lease to Grafair). It indicates that winter charter operations with the DC 9 are preferable to leasing to Grafair. Hence, the charter proposal set out previously is recommended.

At this point, the season contribution margins could be included in the cash flow figures for Problem 1, and the DC 8 versus DC 9 decision re-examined. However, results of choosing the DC 9 over the DC 8 would not be affected.

Problem 4—Agents vs. Own Sales Force
This was settled in solving Problem 3.

Problem 5—The Accounting System
Candidates are often foolishly tempted to recommend a standard cost textbook system regardless of the needs of the company. The accounting system must be built around areas of crucial importance in a company (See the article reproduced in Chapter Four). In this situation, the prime judgments which must be made frequently are:

EXHIBIT E

A. Lease option to Grafair:
The only expense is maintenance, which is a function of miles travelled.

Costs:		Miles Travelled	
	4000	4800	5400
(a) Per passenger per flight			
DC 9	$ 9.00	$10.80	$12.15
DC 8	11.40	13.68	15.39
(b) Per flight			
DC 9	$ 900	$1,080	$1,215
DC 8	1,710	2,052	2,308
(c) Per week (assuming 3 flights per week)			
DC 9			$3,645
DC 8			6,926

EXHIBIT E (Continued)

B. Profit on lease option:

	Per Week		Per Season	
	DC 9	*DC 8*	*DC 9*	*DC 8*
Revenue	$14,000	$18,000	$294,000	$378,000
Cost	3,645	6,926	76,545	145,435
Contribution Margin	$10,355	$11,074	$217,455	$232,565

C. Comparison:

	DC 9		DC 8	
	Per Week	*Per Season*	*Per Week*	*Per Season*
Charter	$15,440	$308,800	$11,565*	$231,300
Lease	10,355	217,455	11,074	232,565

* assumes 1 flight to Alberta @ $240 and 1 flight to British Columbia @$240, both using your own sales force.

a. Output Decisions—add a flight; delete a flight; change times of arrival, departure and so on. (What is the contribution per flight?)
b. Performance Evaluation—who is performing well, who is doing poorly, and so forth. What changes are necessary in motivation devices?
c. Investment Decisions—add a new aircraft?
d. Financing Decisions—obtain funds from which sources and for how long?
e. Income Taxation Needs.

Any system which is recommended must keep the above foremost in mind. For example, contribution margin reports are needed for performance evaluation and output decisions. Also, cash budgets are needed for investment and financing decisions. Some cost budgets would be useful for functions such as maintenance.

Many of the reports being received daily and weekly are probably adequate for this size of company with this quality of management. The monthly profit reports seem to need more detail and some changes in the ledger system could be called for.

The company has a problem with "bootleg" systems. That is, the vice-presidents prepared some of the schedules in the case. Such is not their realm of responsibility. Hence, these people must be interviewed to ascertain their needs.

In summary, some alterations are needed in the company's system—especially with regard to ascertaining fixed versus variable costs and cash flows. However, a product costing system with standard costs is not necessary. The precise system recommended depends upon needs and personalities of specific individuals in the company. Some information can be assembled from work sheets; other information needs require changes in the ledger system.

Problems 6 to 9—Management and Organization

Most of the problems in these functions were readily apparent in the case. Some are:

—President's health.
—Poor communication.
—"Gut-feel" decisions seem to be made when information could easily have been obtained to confirm or refute decisions.
—Needless irritation of stewardesses.
—Complacency about a strike.
—Controller in position of authority over vice-presidents, instead of being a staff person. (This may not matter in this size of company.)
—Generally poor industrial relations and handling of part-time staff.

—Almost negligible long-range planning.
—Inadequate information about freight business.
—Possibly poor contacts with government.

In view of the obvious character of these problems a regurgitation of each is worth only a few marks on examinations.

The responses to the above are more difficult. It is possible to conclude that the employees are over-worked and are entering fields where they have little expertise. On the other hand they may be totally incompetent. It is at this stage of the case where a candidate should make some logical assumptions and then proceed to recommendations. Notice what Candidate 4 did. Be careful, and avoid turning this aspect of the case into too major of a problem. It is important, but it is not the entire case!

For instance, assumptions can be made (quoting whatever evidence exists) that some members of management are incompetent. Once this is done, recommendations for altering their status and finding replacements must be considered. It is quite possible that Sam has the expertise to be executive vice-president and not a controller/vice-president of finance. Yet, because Sam is writing the report, it becomes difficult for him to express such a view.

In summary, recommendations are needed about these problems. Such recommendations must flow from logical analysis of events described in the case.

Problem 10—Public Ownership

Many examination candidates confused this aspect of the case. A company can "go public" by having the present shareholders sell their shares to the general public. If this occurs, the company does not receive one penny. Buyers pay the sellers, and both of them are outside of the company.

However, once the "company" (through its owners) decides to be publicly owned, it must comply with Securities Acts of Provinces in which its shares are traded. A prospectus must be issued; generally accepted accounting principles must be followed; Stock Exchanges require timely reporting; and so forth.

Perhaps the timing of "going public" ought to be reconsidered. It may be necessary to establish a solid earnings and dividend record. If funds to finance further expansions are needed, and common shares are to be issued, perhaps such an event should be combined with any direct sales by present owners. Also, some months may be needed to clean up the company's accounting records, to prepare five-year statements, and to get ready for interim reporting.

Final Remarks

Candidates could bring forth problems in addition to those noted on the previous pages, and could use different approaches, and still pass the case examination. This "solution" has focused on several areas worth considering, but the conclusions reached are dependent upon specific assumptions noted in the textual material. The case called for a formal report; and grades are assigned to this aspect of communication. Once again, many different formats could have been chosen.

SUMMARY

Most accounting students have a feeling of disappointment after reading so-called solutions to cases and descriptions of how to do cases. The chances are high that you presently feel puzzled and slightly helpless. Why? The feeling is inevitable because much of accounting education consists of doing problems with very precise solutions. Some students feel cheated when they are not given a definite answer to a problem. They then place pressure on their instructor to relieve this anxiety. Some instructors will undoubtedly give in to this pressure and give strict guidelines on how to do a case. To some extent this book gives in to student demands for more information about "what 'they' (or he, or she) want(s)." The instructor's guidelines may or may not work—it depends upon the type of case. See Exhibit Two-4.

You may relieve some of your anxiety by scoring your performance differently. Do not compare your response to the one just reproduced and become discouraged when you miss points therein. Rather, evaluate your response in terms of "how well you played the game." Did you identify objectives of the company? Set out logical reasoning and recommendations? Establish credibility? Support your recommendations? Follow the advice in Chapters One to Four?

In short, "what they want" is a display of your process of logic and explicit comments from you concerning how you arrived at your recommendations. List any necessary assumptions, list alternatives, list preferences, and so forth. Tell the marker how you played the game as well as the final score!

The Swiftair case contains a large amount of data analysis. Thus, the last "solution" printed in this Chapter concentrated upon arithmetical analyses which the previous four responses treated lightly. A balanced response should acknowledge both the qualitative and quantitative features. For practice you may now want to assemble the "good" parts of all five responses to Swiftair and compare them to what you wrote. Again, ask yourself where you are strong and where you are weak. You may be strong in case analysis techniques but weak in technical knowledge of your previous courses. If so, go back and review your courses. However, if you are weak on case analysis press on to Chapters Six, Seven, Eight and Nine.

Students who are curious about how cases *might* be graded for purposes of professional examinations should review the Appendix to this Chapter. Some students disbelieve that they can take many different approaches to a case and still receive a mark of 80 percent, or a "high pass." Such is possible because markers often use a process sometimes referred to as "over-marking." For example, a case may have 200 marks (not 100) assigned to it because it has many facets and there are many ways of responding to it. In the time allocated, you have to receive, say, 60 marks to pass. Hence, you can take a far different approach to that of your neighbour, and both of you may end up with 60 percent (literally 60 out of 200, but it is considered impossible for a person to display features worth 200 marks, and the judgment is made that the absolute mark should be reported out of 100). A marking guide based on 200 points contains considerable flexibility.

Appendix Five—A

CASE MARKING ON PROFESSIONAL EXAMINATIONS

The following describes one possible way of marking case examinations when 1,500, 2,500 or more candidates sit for the same examination. The vast numbers create a special problem of maintaining equality of treatment for all candidates. This is because several different case markers must be employed, and differences of attitudes must be resolved before final marking occurs. Somehow the views of the case writer, examination boards, supervisors and markers have to be aired and compiled into a marking guide which all agree is fair in its relative weightings.

As noted in Chapter Five, the process called "over-marking" has proven successful in allowing freedom to individual candidates and ensuring uniformity of marking across all papers. Over-marking merely involves assembling all of the remarks made by a sample of candidates, the case writer(s), examination markers, supervisors and others in responding to the case. The relative importance of each remark (or problem, or analysis, or recommendation or whatever) is thoroughly discussed and assigned so many marks on a marking guide. In addition, a provision is made for additional marks which may be assigned for points not shown on the marking guide.

A batch of papers is marked against the marking guide, revisions are made to the guide, and another batch is marked against the revised guide. The procedure continues until full communication occurs among case markers and supervisors.

The next procedure involves setting a passing mark. In Canada the pass mark is 60 for two of the professional accounting bodies. A judgment is therefore necessary to decide whether a passing candidate will in fact attain 60 marks on the marking guide. If not, the guide must be revised again.

The undernoted is a *fictitious* marking guide for the Swiftair Limited case. It is included here to illustrate the foregoing principles—but the relative weights assigned to various analyses have been "pulled out of the air." Also, general headings only are shown, instead of very detailed points.

Two main reasons for including a marking guide in this book are:
1. To reassure examination candidates that several different ways of analyzing a case are possible, and that each could generate a passing mark. This means that some candidates in particular must resist the temptation to ask repeatedly for the "correct solution" to a case. Learn to relate accounting procedures to decision making. Appreciate that there may be many ways of solving a problem, not just one.
2. To stress the dangers of trying to write and reply to a case you make up, instead of the one at the examination centre. Although the marking guides can be made flexible they are not so flexible that you can pass by making a monstrous issue out of something which is minor. For example, in Swiftair, it is possible to argue that management should review various priorities before buying another aircraft. This is an extremely valid point. But a four-hour crusade on behalf of the point is absurd. You are expected to deal with several important problems, not one.

**POSSIBLE MARKING GUIDE
SWIFTAIR LIMITED**

(Marks assigned in guide are fictional)

	Marks, or Mark Range (*indicates minimum and maximum)
1. Presentation of report:	
Format, style, organization	5
Flow of logic	8
Use of exhibits	2

2. Selection of a jet aircraft:
   Recognition of problem's importance   3*
   Cash flow computations: Handling of:
      Depreciation   3
      Interest   3
      Income taxes   3
   Winter revenue considered   2*
   Present value computation   6
   Qualitative factors   5
   Recommendation:
      Quality   2
      Logic employed   3
3. Lease versus purchase:
   Recognition of problem's importance   2*
   Cash flow computations   3
   Assumptions required   3
   Recommendation:
      Quality   2
      Logic employed   2
4. Financing:
   Sources of funds:
      Importance of problem   1*
      Discussion of considerations   4
      Recommendation:
         Quality   2
         Logic employed   3
   Capital cost allowance effect   2
   Cost of capital usage   2
   Taxation effects considered   2
5. Winter use:
   Grafair alternative:
      Importance of problem   1*
      Qualitative factors   2
      Revenue computation   1
      Cost computation   2
      Recommendations:
         Quality   1
         Logic employed   3
   Agents versus own sales force:
      Importance of problem   1
      Data analysis   2
      Recommendation:
         Quality   1
         Logic employed   2
   Charter destination:
      Importance of problem   2*
      Revenue computation   6
      Cost computations   6
      Demand schedule interpretation   2
      Combination of destinations   2
      Recommendations:
         Quality   2
         Logic employed   4

6. Accounting system:
   Importance of problems and techniques:
Budgets	2
Contribution analysis	2
Detail and frequency	2
Trend analysis	2
Bookkeeping aspects	2
Other	2

   Analysis and recommendations
Quality	3
Logic employed	6

7. Management and organization problems:
Management competence, health, overlapping responsibility and related matters—logic and recommendations	12
Industrial relations, scheduling, strike, morale, uniforms, personnel manager, part-time employees and related matters—logic and recommendations	12
Long range planning, participation, freight, capital budgets, oil shortage, external financing and related issues—logic and recommendations	12
Organization chart—logic and recommendations	4

8. Secondary share issue:
Listing requirements	1
Accounting principles—deferred income tax	2
Dividend policy	1
Timing of issue	1
Interim reporting	1

9. Environmental considerations — 3

10. Other — Open

11. Overall qualities
Credibility of candidate's response; realism; importance; focus	10
Candidate's grasp of issues	10
Displaying cognitive "skills" (avoided regurgitation)	10
	213 plus

The candidate may therefore choose to concentrate on various problems and receive 60, 70 or more marks in many ways.

It is important to note that professional examinations may be marked by means other than the above. However, most other methods used are merely variations of the marking guide. To a great extent the guide is a vehicle for communicating among markers. It may also be used as a teaching device.

CHAPTER SIX

A Visit To Square Lake

INTRODUCTION

The case in this Chapter is designed for persons who have taken courses in financial accounting and public accounting practice. It was used as the comprehensive case on the 1978 Uniform Final Examination of the Institutes/Ordre of Chartered Accountants in Canada. With the kind permission of the Institutes/Ordre we are able to reproduce some actual types of responses to the case that were provided by finalists under actual examination conditions. The responses have been slightly disguised and partially edited, but were specially selected to aid persons needing help with case analysis. Each finalist's response has been analyzed by the author of this book and others so that readers have a basis on which to compare their opinion of each candidate's response. Considerable learning occurs when one marks another student's paper, and compares the assigned grade and supporting reasons to that given by other markers.

In order to obtain maximum benefit from this Chapter, the following approach and order is recommended:
1. Spend whatever time that you feel is necessary to review accounting, auditing, income tax, management and other syllabus topics in preparation for a case examination.
2. Read the "Square Lake" case and respond to it under examination conditions, spending about four hours in total. You are permitted to have tables of present values during the examination. (Also see pages 135, bottom, and 136 of the Square Lake case.)
3. Read all of the student responses and place them in order from best to worst response. Then read each one thoroughly again and assign it a grade out of 100. Give reasons why you assigned each grade. List the strengths and weaknesses of each of the five responses.

4. Read the author's reactions to each student's response, and compare your grade and reasons with those provided by the author.
5. Read the "official" response to the "Square Lake" case; then use it to mark your own response. Compile a list of the "errors" that you seem to have made, separating technical errors from procedural ones. If you need more procedural or how-to-do-it practice try the cases in the following chapters. If your main problem is a weakness in some technical areas, correct your technical deficiencies before proceeding with case responses and analysis.

Remember that the "official" response that we have provided is only one possible approach, and that several other alternatives could be equally valid. Marks are provided for problem identification, reasoning, qualitative and quantitative analysis, and so forth on cases; not for just an unsupported recommendation or answer.

SQUARE LAKE CASE

CA sank wearily into a chair in her hotel room. Now that she was alone for the first time since she'd arrived in Square Lake that afternoon, she had a chance to collect her thoughts, to sort out priorities.

CA enjoyed her regular trips to Square Lake, which was about a hundred miles from the city in which her practice was located, but the trips were often hectic. This trip, in late March 1978, looked as if it would be more hectic than usual. She had arrived late in the afternoon, in time to meet one of her Square Lake clients, John Durie, for dinner. Durie, a very energetic, ambitious man, had become CA's client shortly after she entered public practice. It was a source of considerable satisfaction to CA that she had been able to be of real help to Durie and his business over the years, though he did have a tendency to act first and ask for advice later.

At dinner, Durie, who was never calm anyway, was positively bubbling over with news and plans. "CA, I'm bringing you lots of business tonight. Durie Manufacturing (his company, for which CA is the auditor) is heading for big things and I'll need your help in several things. You know Frank Erkel?" (CA had met Erkel, another local businessman, several times in the past.) "Well, Frank and I have worked out a great deal! My company is going to buy Erkel Fabricating, with some outside help I'll tell you about, and we'll reorganize and streamline the joint operation. Durie Manufacturing is really going places! Maybe we'll even go public some day."

"You'll be involved in many ways, CA, but one of the main ways is due to the outside financing. Those guys are real sticklers for detail." CA asked who "those guys" were.

"Oh, sorry. A new company we're calling Square Lake Manufacturing Ltd. will buy Frank's and my company's manufacturing operations. I'll do the group's marketing through Durie Manufacturing, which will handle all the invoicing and collecting and customer relations in general, except shipping. Square Lake Manufacturing will ship from either factory as instructed by Durie Manufacturing. My company will own the new company, but much of the financial support will come from Tri-Line Mortgages Ltd., an outfit from your city. Know them?"

CA knew something about the company, but had never had any business contacts with them.

"Well, Tri-Line wants an audit of Frank's operations and everything's to be done according to generally accepted accounting principles, whatever that means. I never did care much how you accountants did your numbers, as long as you kept my tax down. And I remember that somewhere in the draft agreement which Frank, Tri-Line, and I plan to sign next week, there was a mention of a pro-forma balance sheet number of some kind. You'll have to put all the companies together so that Tri-Line can see what everything will look like—also, they want you to give them a "comfort letter," I think they called it, about the pro-forma figures. Do a good job of it all, because according to the agreement, the final selling price of Frank's company as well as the amount and terms of the money Tri-Line will advance depend on the numbers you come up with. But don't do such a good job that I have to give Frank the shirt off my back for his company! You work for me, not for him. I have to pay all of your fees for the reorganization as well as some other things I have in mind, but Frank and I will split your fee for auditing his company. That reminds me—I promised Frank you'd tell him right away what his company's audit will cost. He's trying to assess his own cash position for the next year or so."

As Durie talked, he wrote on his napkin. The diagram in Figure 1 took shape.

Durie continued, occasionally jabbing the diagram for emphasis. "Yes, Durie Manufacturing is going to be a company to reckon with. Frank Erkel is going to run Square Lake Manufacturing in return for a share in its profits, plus a smaller share of Durie Manufacturing's profit. Frank will be out of it as far as ownership goes, but that's OK with him since he will share the profits anyway. I'll concentrate on marketing, through Durie Manufacturing, and on looking around for other investments as we grow. CA, you can help me evaluate potential investments—matter of fact, I have one in mind right now, depending on how our cash position works out after the dust settles from our reorganization. You can also help Frank get his feet on the

FIGURE 1

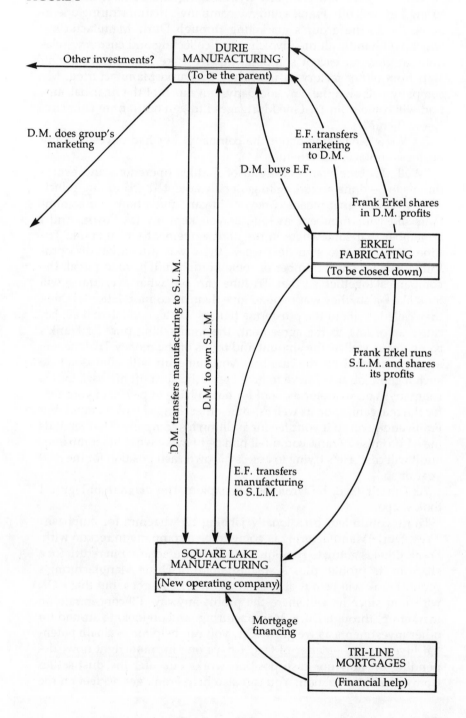

ground in managing the combined manufacturing operation, because my company's volume is more than double his. Frank is good on the production floor, but I don't really know if he'll have what it takes to run this big an operation."

When CA asked him why he was doubtful, Durie said he knew Erkel and his business well enough to feel that Erkel did not have a good history in overall production organization or, especially, cost control. It became apparent that Durie believed his company's production facilities would contribute more to Square Lake Manufacturing's profitability than would Erkel Fabricating. Durie was vague about how the new group would separate the profit contributions by marketing (Durie Manufacturing) from that by manufacturing (Square Lake Manufacturing), referring to such separation as "only a bookkeeping problem."

After dinner, Durie asked CA to accompany him to his office. "I've been so anxious to see how this deal will work out that I've collected all the data I could about my company and Frank's and I thought you might be able to give it a look, and then give me your comments on the draft agreement (see Schedule A). Frank and I drew the agreement up one night down at the club and while we knew what we wanted we'd both like your views as to how the deal should be structured so that we don't give too much to the tax man. Also, we'd like to make sure we've covered everything in the agreement that should be covered and that it's clear so that we won't be having arguments later. Frank's company has never been audited, but he's had accounting and tax help. His financial statements look pretty good, so we could use them to get a sort of rough idea of things. Maybe while you're reviewing them you could tell me if I'm paying a fair price for the company. This is a pretty big deal for me, so I'd really appreciate some ballpark figures, especially on our cash situation after I've paid Frank and how much money I'm going to get from Tri-Line Mortgages. While I eventually want you to prepare whatever pro-forma statements Tri-Line requires, I don't think we'll need these for our next meeting so don't worry about them for now."

CA and Durie talked and read the draft agreement and various other items for several hours. It was late when CA got back to her hotel, only to find a message from Frank Erkel, marked "urgent— please call tonight." When she returned the call, Erkel said he just wanted to ask CA to conduct a "fair audit" of his business and to be sure to discuss with him any "adjustments" affecting Erkel Fabricating's financial statements. He seemed concerned that CA would tend to "see things Durie's way" and might damage Erkel's interest or his tax position in some way. "After all," he said, "don't forget that I'm giving you lots of business in this deal, too, since you'll be auditing my company. And if we get along, I'll probably want you to look after my personal tax affairs. So don't forget Frank Erkel when you're working out the numbers!"

When CA hung up the phone and finally relaxed in the only comfortable chair in the room she had much to think about, including her own role in the situation and those audit problems she could foresee. Because she knew that Durie and Erkel were very anxious to see the best deal go through she wanted to sort out all of the issues very carefully before talking with them again.

REQUIRED:

As CA, organize and document your thoughts, analyses and tentative recommendations about all aspects of the situation which are of concern to you, to Durie and to Erkel, including those matters raised by the two businessmen.

INDEX TO SCHEDULES

SCHEDULE A

EXCERPTS FROM THE DRAFT AGREEMENT AMONG FRANK ERKEL, DURIE MANUFACTURING LTD., AND TRI-LINE MORTGAGES LTD.

1. All calculations are to be done from, and all references below are to, *audited* financial statements up to and as at December 31, 1977, *prepared according to generally accepted accounting principles.* Operations from January 1, 1978 forward will be presumed to have taken place within the structure being created in this agreement.

2. All outstanding shares of Erkel Fabricating Ltd. are to be sold to Durie Manufacturing Ltd. as of January 1, 1978 for a price to be specified below (item 6). In addition, the amount owing by Erkel Fabricating Ltd. to a shareholder is to be paid in cash by June 30, 1978.

3. A new company, Square Lake Manufacturing Ltd., is to be incorporated as a wholly-owned subsidiary of Durie Manufacturing Ltd. The initial capitalization of Square Lake Manufacturing Ltd. is to be $80,000 in common shares, paid for in cash.

4. Square Lake Manufacturing Ltd. is to acquire, as of January 1, 1978, the land, building, trucks and automobiles, other production assets and inventories of Durie Manufacturing Ltd. and Erkel Fabricating Ltd., in exchange for non-interest-bearing notes, at prices equal to the book values of the assets involved as at January 1, 1978. Square Lake Manufacturing Ltd. is also to acquire the Scarpel Inc. production-distribution agreement from Erkel Fabricating Ltd. at a price equal to that agreement's value in computing the selling price of Erkel Fabricating Ltd. (items 6 and 10 below).

5. Durie Manufacturing Ltd. is to acquire, as of January 1, 1978, the accounts receivable, marketing and office equipment of Erkel Fabricating Ltd., at their book value January 1, 1978. Erkel Fabricating Ltd. is then to be expeditiously wound up.

6. The selling price of the Erkel Fabricating Ltd. shares is to be computed according to the following formula which reflects the company's recent earnings trend:

Price = (a) 6 times the company's average annual net income since the company's inception January 1, 1973
PLUS
(b) 3 times the average of the annual *increase (decrease)* in net income between 1975 and 1976, and between 1976 and 1977.

Except that the price may not exceed 105 percent of the sum of the December 31, 1977 fair values of the company's net assets, where fair values are computed as:
(a) fair value of working capital = book value;
(b) fair value of fixed assets and Scarpel Inc. production-distribution agreement = amounts as set out below (item 10);
(c) fair value of non-current liabilities = book value.

7. For the shares of Erkel Fabricating Ltd.—Durie Manufacturing Ltd. is to pay 60 percent in cash, by June 10, 1978, and the remainder in four equal annual instalments beginning January 1, 1979, plus interest at 8 percent also payable annually beginning January 1, 1979.

8. In return for first and chattel mortgages (see also item 11), on all the land, buildings, machinery, automobiles and trucks of Square Lake Manufacturing Ltd., Tri-Line Mortgages Ltd. is to advance funds on April 30, 1978 according to the following formula:

Funds to be advanced = 80 percent of the fair value of Square Lake Manufacturing Ltd. fixed assets transferred from Durie Manufacturing Ltd. and Erkel Fabricating Ltd. (see item 10 below); except that the funds advanced may not exceed 175 percent of the pro-forma consolidated shareholders' equity of Durie Manufacturing Ltd. as at January 1, 1978, assuming all provisions of this agreement have been given effect in the accounts of Durie Manufacturing Ltd. and its two subsidiary companies.

The mortgage is to carry interest at 9⅞ percent per annum and is to be repaid in 120 equal monthly instalments, *plus* interest, commencing July 1, 1978 and ending June 1, 1988. Interest is to be paid at 9⅞ percent per annum for the period between the advancement of funds and July 1, 1978.

9. Square Lake Manufacturing is to use the funds advanced by Tri-Line Mortgages Ltd. to settle, as much as possible, the notes payable to Durie Manufacturing Ltd. and Erkel Fabricating Ltd. Those companies in turn are to use the funds to discharge those obligations as necessitated by this agreement.

10. For purposes of this agreement, the fair values of the Durie Manufacturing Ltd. and Erkel Fabricating Ltd. fixed assets as of January 1, 1978 are:

	Durie Manufacturing	*Erkel Fabricating*
Land	$100,000	$60,000
Building...........................	90,000	45,000
Equipment	100,000	50,000
Trucks and automobiles.......	20,000	10,000

The fair value of the Scarpel Inc. production-distribution agreement is to equal its future contribution to net cash flows (discounted at 10 percent), assuming that the historical growth trend continues.

11. The first and chattel mortgages to be held by Tri-Line Mortgages Ltd. on the assets of Square Lake Manufacturing Ltd. shall be considered to be in default if: (a) two successive mortgage payments are missed or delayed, or (b) the company's working capital is reduced to less than $10,000.

SCHEDULE B

Condensed (Audited) Balance Sheets of Durie Manufacturing Ltd.
(Incorporated under the Laws of Canada)

ASSETS

	As at December 31	
	1977	1976
Current		
Cash	$ 14,080	$ 16,955
Trade accounts receivable	61,269	60,016
Inventories (average cost)		
Raw materials	49,030	41,683
Finished goods	56,040	63,909
Prepaid expenses	3,160	2,885
	183,579	185,448
Fixed (cost)		
Land	38,000	38,000
Building	156,027	131,210
Accumulated depreciation	(67,631)	(60,450)
Equipment	162,608	138,992
Accumulated depreciation	(52,125)	(44,585)
Trucks and automobiles	70,156	62,316
Accumulated depreciation	(44,221)	(34,286)
	262,814	231,197
	$446,393	$416,645

LIABILITIES

	As at December 31	
	1977	1976
Current		
Bank loan	$ 56,000	$ 63,000
Trade accounts payable	20,997	24,532
Wages payable	3,848	3,616
Payroll deductions	3,611	3,560
Corporate income tax	7,757	(1,407)
Accrued mortgage interest	5,200	6,100
Current portion of mortgage	22,500	22,500
	119,913	121,901
8% Mortgage, less current portion	107,500	130,000
Deferred income taxes	21,112	15,028
SHAREHOLDERS' EQUITY		
Preferred shares	10,000	10,000
Common shares	1,000	1,000
Retained earnings	186,868	138,716
	197,868	149,716
	$446,393	$416,645

SCHEDULE B (continued)

Condensed (Audited) Income Statements of Durie Manufacturing Ltd.
(Incorporated under the Laws of Canada)

	Years Ended December 31,	
	1977	1976
Sales	$631,788	$567,851
Cost of goods sold:		
Cost of goods manufactured:		
Opening raw material inventory	41,683	36,019
Purchases	186,928	163,048
Closing raw material inventory	(49,030)	(41,683)
Materials used	179,581	157,384
Direct labour	164,910	161,751
Overhead—depreciation	21,814	20,163
—other	28,112	31,346
Cost of goods manufactured	394,417	370,644
Opening finished goods inventory	63,909	74,450
Closing finished goods inventory	(56,040)	(63,909)
	402,286	381,185
Gross margin	229,502	186,666
General expenses:		
Marketing—depreciation	1,952	1,850
—other	91,906	76,721
Office and general—depreciation	890	845
—other	53,917	49,816
Interest—mortgage	10,850	12,650
—other	5,784	6,136
	165,299	148,018
Income before income taxes	64,203	38,648
Income taxes:		
Current	9,967	2,206
Deferred	6,084	7,456
	16,051	9,662
Net income	$ 48,152	$ 28,986

8% mortgage payable

Original principal (July 1, 1975), $175,000
Payment of $11,250 plus interest due January 1 and July 1 of each
   year
Final payment ($6,250 plus interest) due July 1, 1983
Prepayment allowed on penalty of the next 3 months' interest
Secured by land and building.

Depreciation policy

Group straight-line method used
Annual rate for building and equipment = 5% of cost
Annual rate for trucks and autos = 15% of cost
Additions and disposals depreciated at half the annual rate in the
   year of addition or disposal.

SCHEDULE C

March 16, 1978

Mr. Frank Erkel
Box 2150
Square Lake, Canada

Dear Frank:

As you requested, I have prepared and enclosed the following summary information for Erkel Fabricating Ltd. since its inception:
1. Summary balance sheets;
2. Summary income statements;
3. Capital cost allowance information;
4. Summary income tax return figures;
5. Mortgage and equipment notes schedule.

The information has been compiled from copies of the annual financial statements, tax returns, etc. in my files and therefore accurately
summarizes the company's affairs for the last 5 years.

I would remind you, however, that I prepared the annual financial
statements and tax returns from your records without audit, so the
enclosed information is, of course, also unaudited and I can express
no opinion as to its fairness. Note also that the 1977 income tax return has only recently been filed, so the Tax Department has not yet
made the 1977 income tax assessment.

Please advise me if I may assist you further. Good luck in your new
venture. Of course, I'll be pleased to continue advising you on your
personal tax affairs.

Sincerely,

A. B.,
Chartered Accountant

SCHEDULE D

Summary Balance Sheets of Erkel Fabricating Ltd.
(Incorporated under the Laws of Canada)

	As at January 1 1973	As at December 31				
		1973	1974	1975	1976	1977
ASSETS						
Current						
Cash	$ 31,300	$ 4,046	$ 10,869	$ 9,896	$ 9,011	$ 11,943
Accounts receivable	—	29,769	38,911	42,009	37,618	46,119
Inventories (cost):						
Raw materials (FIFO)	11,200	17,962	21,615	28,401	28,760	23,358
Finished goods (average)	—	17,115	24,886	32,049	29,616	31,020
Prepaid expenses	—	860	1,401	1,380	712	1,843
	42,500	69,752	97,682	113,735	105,717	114,283
Fixed (cost)						
Land	46,250	46,250	46,250	46,250	46,250	46,250
Building	90,750	90,750	90,750	95,691	95,691	95,691
Accumulated depreciation	—	(9,075)	(17,243)	(25,067)	(32,108)	(38,445)
Equipment	54,000	73,314	83,080	116,942	124,642	124,069
Accumulated depreciation	—	(10,868)	(42,923)	(69,047)	(95,889)	(98,688)
Automotive	23,500	29,293	29,293	29,293	34,070	34,070
Accumulated depreciation	—	(617)	(9,220)	(15,242)	(20,890)	(24,844)
	214,500	219,047	179,987	178,820	151,766	138,103
Unamortized goodwill	25,500	22,950	20,654	18,588	16,730	15,056
	$282,500	$311,749	$298,323	$311,143	$274,213	$267,442

LIABILITIES					
Current					
Bank loans	$ —	$ 24,000	$ 18,000	$ 12,000	$ 10,000
Accounts payable	26,804	28,842	26,401	10,381	18,879
Wages payable	248	418	841	1,414	1,525
Payroll deductions	1,874	1,949	2,096	2,211	2,190
Corporate income tax	—	902	3,387	1,605	5,305
Current portions:					
Equipment notes	14,946	14,946	24,338	24,338	9,392
Mortgage	21,202	21,202	21,202	21,202	21,202
	36,148	92,259	96,265	73,151	68,493
Non-current					
9% equipment note	45,054	24,221	12,317	—	—
11½% equipment note	—	—	17,565	10,930	3,491
8½% mortgage	111,298	101,559	90,363	78,177	64,914
Loan from shareholder	50,000	50,000	50,000	50,000	35,000
	196,950	175,780	170,245	139,107	103,405
SHAREHOLDERS' EQUITY					
Common shares	30,000	30,000	30,000	30,000	30,000
Retained earnings	(1,275)	284	14,633	31,955	65,544
	28,725	30,284	44,633	61,955	95,544
	$282,500	$298,323	$311,143	$274,213	$267,442

SCHEDULE D (continued)

Summary Income Statements of Erkel Fabricating Ltd.
(Incorporated under the Laws of Canada)

			Years Ended December 31		
	1973	1974	1975	1976	1977
Sales	$208,819	$258,961	$284,641	$292,689	$306,874
Cost of goods sold:					
Cost of goods manufactured:					
Beginning raw material inventory	11,200	17,962	21,615	28,401	28,760
Purchases	83,669	83,323	95,054	83,871	84,723
Ending raw material inventory	(17,962)	(21,615)	(28,401)	(28,760)	(23,358)
Wages	61,707	71,128	69,433	63,815	67,008
Overhead	10,319	12,553	16,321	16,734	20,480
	148,933	163,351	174,022	164,061	177,613
Opening finished goods inventory	—	17,115	24,886	32,049	29,616
Closing finished goods inventory	(17,115)	(24,886)	(32,049)	(29,616)	(31,020)
	131,818	155,580	166,859	166,494	176,209
Gross margin	74,001	103,381	117,782	126,195	130,665

General expenses:					
Interest:					
Notes	4,996	4,063	4,695	4,682	2,657
Mortgage	11,750	10,915	10,006	9,016	7,939
Other	1,411	2,296	2,409	1,668	1,327
Selling expenses	13,161	13,588	18,916	22,060	25,973
Office expenses	20,148	18,652	21,182	24,396	26,604
Depreciation	21,260	49,110	41,060	39,531	20,298
Goodwill amortization	2,550	2,296	2,066	1,858	1,674
	75,276	100,920	100,334	103,211	86,472
Income before income taxes	(1,275)	2,461	17,448	22,984	44,193
Income taxes	—	902	3,099	5,662	10,604
Net income	$ (1,275)	$ 1,559	$ 14,349	$ 17,322	$ 33,589

SCHEDULE D (continued)
Capital Cost Allowance Information For Erkel Fabricating Ltd.

	Building Class 6	Equipment Class 8	Equipment Class 29	Automotive Class 10	Total	Eligible Capital Expenditures
Undepreciated capital cost, Jan. 1, 1973	$90,750	$54,000	$ —	$23,500	$168,250	$12,750
1973: Additions	—	340	18,974	8,293	27,607	—
Disposal proceeds	—	—	—	(1,800)	(1,800)	—
Capital cost allowance	(9,075)	(10,868)	—	(1,317)	(21,260)	(1,275)
Undepreciated capital cost, December 31, 1973	81,675	43,472	18,974	28,676	172,797	11,475
1974: Additions	—	1,648	8,868	—	10,516	—
Disposal proceeds	—	(466)	—	—	(466)	—
Capital cost allowance	(8,168)	(8,931)	(23,408)	(8,603)	(49,110)	(1,148)
Undepreciated capital cost, December 31, 1974	73,507	35,723	4,434	20,073	133,737	10,327
1975: Additions	4,941	—	36,012	—	40,953	—
Investment tax credit	(210)	—	(1,311)	—	(1,521)	—
Capital cost allowance	(7,824)	(7,145)	(20,069)	(6,022)	(41,060)	(1,033)

Undepreciated capital cost, December 31, 1975	70,414	28,578	19,066	14,051	132,109	9,294
1976: Additions	—	1,380	6,320	4,777	12,477	—
Investment tax credit	—	—	(316)	—	(316)	—
Capital cost allowance	(7,041)	(5,992)	(20,850)	(5,648)	(39,531)	(929)
Undepreciated capital cost, December 31, 1976	63,373	23,966	4,220	13,180	104,739	8,365
1977: Additions	—	6,401	4,316	—	10,717	—
Disposal proceeds	—	(2,390)	(1,692)	—	(4,082)	—
Investment tax credit	—	—	(216)	—	(216)	—
Capital cost allowance	(6,337)	(5,595)	(4,412)	(3,954)	(20,298)	(837)
	$57,036	$22,382	$2,216	$9,226	$90,860	$7,528

SCHEDULE D (continued)

Summary Income Tax Return Figures For Erkel Fabricating Ltd.

	1973	1974	1975	1976	1977
Income before tax, per income statement	$ (1,275)	$ 2,461	$ 17,448	$ 22,984	$ 44,193
Add back:					
Depreciation	21,260	49,110	41,060	39,531	20,298
Goodwill amortization	2,550	2,296	2,066	1,858	1,674
	22,535	53,867	60,574	64,373	66,165
Deduct:					
Inventory tax credit—3%	—	—	—	—	(1,751)
Capital cost allowance	(21,260)	(49,110)	(41,060)	(39,531)	(20,298)
Eligible capital expenditure amortization	(1,275)	(1,148)	(1,033)	(929)	(837)
Taxable income	$ —	$ 3,609	$ 18,481	$ 23,913	$ 43,279
Income tax before investment tax credit	$ —	$ 902	$ 4,620	$ 5,978	$ 10,820
Less investment tax credit	—	—	1,521	316	216
Income tax payable	$ —	$ 902	$ 3,099	$ 5,662	$ 10,604

Erkel Fabricating Ltd.
Schedule Of Mortgage And Equipment Notes

	Mortgage	*Note #1*	*Note #2*
Date signed	Jan. 1, 1973	Jan. 1, 1973	July 1, 1975
Date due	Dec. 31, 1982	Dec. 31, 1977	June 30, 1979
Monthly payment due ...	month-end	month-end	month-end
Principal.....................	$142,500	$60,000	$30,000
Security	Land & Building	Equipment	Equipment
Interest rate	8½%	9%	11½%
Monthly payment	$1,677.80	$1,245.50	$782.67
Annual payment...........	$21,201.60	$14,946.00	$9,392.04
Prepayment penalty	next 3 months' interest	none	none

Principal balance:

	Mortgage	Note #1	Note #2
Dec. 31, 1973............	$133,048	$50,050	$ —
1974............	122,761	39,167	—
1975............	111,565	27,263	26,957
1976............	99,379	14,242	20,322
1977............	86,116	—	12,883
1978............	71,680	—	4,542
1979............	55,969	—	—
1980............	38,869	—	—
1981............	20,257	—	—
1982............	—	—	—

SCHEDULE E
SOME ADDITIONAL INFORMATION OBTAINED BY CA DURING THE EVENING IN DURIE'S OFFICE

1. According to Durie, Frank Erkel had been dissatisfied with his performance as owner-manager. He had little taste for the selling and administrative sides of the business (which, conversely, Durie enjoys) and preferred the production activities. He felt he was a good production manager and, said Durie, was enthusiastic about managing the combined production operation.

2. Erkel has always kept a time sheet, and on that basis, about 40 percent of each year's salary has been allocated to production wages and 20 percent each to production overhead, selling expenses and office expenses. His salary was $26,000 in 1977 and averaged about $22,000 over the previous four years. Durie's $35,000 in 1977 ($31,000 in 1976) has been allocated somewhat arbitrarily: 30 percent to production overhead, 45 percent to marketing and 25 percent to office expenses.

3. Erkel's employment contract will be for 5 years (renewable for a further 5 years). He will be general manager of the new company,

Square Lake Manufacturing, and will receive a salary of $20,000 plus a bonus of 6 percent of the new company's income before bonus and income taxes. In addition, he will receive a profit share of 3 percent of Durie Manufacturing Ltd.'s consolidated income before profit share and income taxes (but after the 6 percent bonus).

4. Durie will be president of all companies but, other than a nominal $10,000 salary from Square Lake Manufacturing Ltd., will draw all his income from Durie Manufacturing Ltd.

5. When CA asked Durie why the draft agreement specified the "fair values" of the Erkel Fabricating's working capital and non-current liabilities to be book values rather than market values, Durie replied, "Your generally accepted accounting principles provide protection as to the working capital, and the non-current liabilities are to be paid off immediately anyway."

6. The two companies' fixed assets are very similar in type and useful lives. However, when Erkel Fabricating Ltd. was incorporated, it purchased equipment and a building which had only 15 years' useful life remaining and automotive assets with only 5½ years remaining.

7. The two companies' operations are also quite similar, though Erkel involves himself more in plant-floor activities than did Durie. Erkel Fabricating also sold a considerable amount of product on a consignment basis, whereas Durie Manufacturing did not use consignments. Consignment goods carried the same mark-ups as other goods, which meant that consignees paid Erkel Fabricating the same for consignment goods as they did for non-consignment goods. Given this policy, the proportion of the company's shipments made on a consignment basis grew steadily. To keep the consignment activities straight, the company's bookkeeper credited a special sales account and debited a special account receivable when consignment goods were shipped out.

Durie does not like consignment sales and plans to eliminate them. He estimates that about 75 percent of the present consignment customers can be persuaded to take goods on a regular purchase basis instead, and is confident that the lost sales can easily be made up by attracting new customers. After some digging, Durie and CA were able to prepare the following schedule of Erkel Fabricating's consignment sales:

SCHEDULE E (continued)

	1973	1974	1975	1976	1977
Consignment sales account	$ 14,039	$ 22,089	$ 41,671	$ 70,011	$106,534
Nonconsignment sales	191,780	236,872	242,970	222,678	200,340
Total sales	$205,819	$258,961	$284,641	$292,689	$306,874
Percent consignment	6.8%	8.5%	14.6%	23.9%	34.7%
Year-end consignment receivable account	$ 7,778	$ 10,808	$ 14,171	$ 15,810	$ 25,478
Other receivables	21,991	28,103	27,838	21,808	20,641
Total receivables	$ 29,769	$ 38,911	$ 42,009	$ 37,618	$ 46,119
Percent consignment	26.1%	38.5%	33.7%	42.0%	55.2%

8. Erkel Fabricating has a production-distribution agreement signed January 1, 1973 with a foreign company, Scarpel Inc., and expiring December 31, 1981. Monthly sales of products made under the agreement amounted to about $1,000 in 1973, rising about $250 each year to the 1977 level of about $2,000 (a level that Durie expects to triple by more attention to marketing the products). Gross profit on these products is about 50 percent of sales, but out of this gross profit, Erkel Fabricating pays a royalty of 15 percent of the sales revenue on the products. The royalty is paid each March 31 on sales for the preceding calendar year; the only accounting for the agreement Erkel Fabricating does is to charge the annual payment to selling expenses. The $4,500 payment Erkel Fabricating made in 1973 to acquire the agreement was also charged to selling expenses.

9. CA estimated that if Erkel Fabricating had recorded depreciation, in a similar manner to Durie Manufacturing, and had included it in its inventory cost base, Erkel's finished goods inventory cost per labour hour would have been about 7.5 percent higher at December 31, 1976 and about 8 percent higher at December 31, 1977. CA also estimated that, if Erkel Fabricating had calculated depreciation for all assets in a similar manner to Durie Manufacturing, the annual depreciation expense for all classes would have amounted to: 1973—$11,280; 1974—$12,500; 1975—$13,780; 1976—$15,340; 1977—$16,070.

10. Quantity records for Erkel Fabricating's raw materials were very poor, but it seemed likely that that company had experienced the same price increases in raw materials as had Durie Manufacturing, so that its closing raw materials inventories would be about 3 percent higher at FIFO than average cost. Erkel Fabricating's fairly stable annual purchasing cost appeared attributable to increased efficiency in use of materials, especially after additional machinery was installed in mid 1975.

11. The proportions of the two companies' fixed assets used in production, marketing and office operations would about equal the proportions of depreciation chargeable to those activities. The depreciation for Erkel Fabricating was not allocated among activities, but various records allowed the chargeable proportions (at least for 1977) to be determined:

	Durie Manufacturing		Erkel Fabricating
Activity	Depreciation Allocated	Proportions	Chargeable Proportions
Production.....	$21,814	88%	90%
Marketing......	1,952	8%	5%
Office...........	890	4%	5%
	$24,656	100%	100%

The proportion of space taken up by non-factory marketing and office activities in the two companies was small, therefore practically all building depreciation is allocable to production. The marketing and office depreciation is about 40 percent automobiles and trucks and 60 percent equipment.

12. Both Durie and Erkel are largely intuitive managers who rely on close contact with operations for management and control. Both men have had only annual financial statements prepared for their companies. CA had managed to persuade Durie to install a reasonable internal control system and hire a good bookkeeper-office manager, but only by threatening to withhold an external audit opinion. No production control system existed and inventory control was primarily physical. The situation at Erkel Fabricating seemed considerably worse. All records were rudimentary and there had been a succession of harassed bookkeepers of doubtful competence. CA saw letters, from A.B., the chartered accountant who prepared Erkel Fabricating's annual financial statements and tax returns, pleading for improvement, but little ever seemed to be done.

13. No specific plans had been made for the dislocations and rearrangements that the new operations might bring to the two companies' employees. Durie appeared unconcerned, remarking that "Of course the employees will be looked after." Neither company was unionized, though a large union was recruiting strongly in the Square Lake area and Durie's employees had recently complained of the lack of company pension or medical plans.

FORMULA FOR THE PRESENT VALUE OF REDUCTIONS IN TAX PAYABLE DUE TO CAPITAL COST ALLOWANCE

$$\frac{\text{Investment Cost} \times \text{Rate of Income Tax} \times \text{Rate of Capital Cost Allowance}}{\text{Rate of Return} + \text{Rate of Capital Cost Allowance}}$$

**MAXIMUM
CAPITAL COST ALLOWANCE RATES
FOR SELECTED CLASSES**

Class 1	4%
Class 2	6%
Class 3	5%
Class 4	6%
Class 5	10%
Class 6	10%
Class 7	15%
Class 8	20%
Class 9	25%
Class 10	30%
Class 11	35%
Class 12	100%
Class 16	40%
Class 17	8%
Class 18	60%
Class 22	50%
Class 23	100%
Class 24	up to 50%
Class 25	100%
Class 26	1%
Class 27	up to 50%
Class 28	30%
Class 29	2 years (Maximum 50% in first year)
Class 30	40%
Class 31	5%
Class 32	10%
Class 33	15%
Class 34	50%
Class 35	7%

* * * * * * *

RESPONSE OF CANDIDATE A

Mr. Durie and Mr. Erkel,

Further to our previous conversations, I have prepared an analysis of your present situations and of your future purchase and consolidation considerations. The analysis is

A. Problem and discussion areas (Identification).
B. Qualitative discussion.
C. Quantitative analysis.
D. Recommendations.

I will be available for further discussions and clarification.

Yours very truly,
C.A.

A1: Problem Areas
1. Prepare a valuation of Erkel Fabricating Limited—comment on fairness of price.
2. Prepare a cash flow analysis.
3. Prepare consolidated statements.

A2: Other discussion areas
1. Tax—re wind up.
2. Legal—lawyers have not looked at the agreement; also mortgage.
3. Ethical—CA must remain independent of Durie and Erkel.
4. Human—will the employees want to relocate?
5. Auditing—no previous audit; first engagement and beginning investors; fee misunderstandings; report content; comfort letter problem.
6. Accounting—cost accounting deficiencies; GAAP is different between the two companies; adjustments on consolidations must be explained to Erkel; income recognition between the two remaining companies; new company initiation; ensure payments on mortgage will not default; aging list of fixed assets; contingent liabilities; disclosure of mortgages; incorporation—CBCA?

B. Qualitative
1. Tax—if to be wound up, use Sections 88.1 or 88.2; use tax values; no carry forward of capital losses.
   Section 88.1, transfer at paid up capital. If less than adjusted cost base tax values are applied against paid up capital. The greater of paid up capital and adjusted cost base tax value will be the liquidation value. If 88.2 is used, assets are transferred at fair market value, capital gains arise and Erkel could have to pay a large amount of income tax.
2. Legal—is agreement legal? binding?; reviewed by lawyers?; Get lawyers to review mortgage to ensure accuracy of interpretation.
3. Ethical—C.A. must remain independent and point out necessity of independence to Durie and Erkel. They are not permitted to influence her opinion. C.A. should not associate herself with any statements which she knows or should know are false or misleading.
4. Human—the employees may not wish to relocate; may strike if unionized; there could be a contingent liability which should be disclosed because of lack of company benefits; consider legal advice.
5. Auditing—no previous audit: no inventory count, therefore cannot give unqualified report; qualify inventory, income statement and income taxes; for first audit engagement consider independence, integrity of management, professional capability of C.A.,

effect on opinion. Send out engagement letter to make terms of engagement clear: must qualify, fee structure, statutory requirements.

Make preliminary evaluation of internal control to determine if it can be relied upon for planning nature, extent and timing of year end tests; it has been pointed out to be poor (consider compensating substantive procedures.)

Point out that fees cannot be set beforehand, contingent on amount of audit work performed; Does C.A. have professional capabilities to do work? Will this make her practice too highly dependent on this group of companies? Ensure no default on mortgage payments; get copies.

6. Accounting problems—cost accounting deficiencies; standards are not current; does not appear organized; generally accepted accounting principles are different between the two companies; different treatment (e.g., deferred tax versus no deferred tax); must have similar accounting treatment.

Adjustments to accounts receivable for consignment sales must be explained to Erkel; explain nature of consolidation; why some items must be eliminated; two companies remaining (Durie Manufacturing and Square Lake Manufacturing); why have two companies left?; there is still only one owner; Durie Ltd. won't be income-producing; it causes extra administrative and accounting problems; difficult to allocate income between the companies. If Durie is worried about splitting operations why not make two divisions and have profit center type cost accounting; two companies will cause extra tax problems.

7. Valuation—Was it a wise idea to set up the deal "down at the club"? Capitalization rates should be reviewed to determine accuracy; should have professional valuation performed; one should base valuation on future, not past, capitalization of earnings; only use past if it is an indicator of future trends; the three times net change in incomes is redundant because past incomes were already considered; should have eliminated (add back) manager's salary if too high and any other non recurring or unusually high expenses.

Fair values not book values should have been used in the calculation. Salary for Mr. Erkel is fairly high; consider lowering his salary and giving him a partial interest in the company; no add-back of redundant assets; salary for Mr. Erkel very high if you don't know if he will work out; was an outside manager considered?

Fixed assets are becoming old and may require a great amount of dollar expenditures to replace them; therefore the valuation may be too high; leverage is greatly reduced; it may be very difficult to get additional capital together. If you are considering going public incorporate new company under Canada Business Corporations Act.

8. Disclosure and accounting—purchase should be at fair values; remainder is goodwill; therefore not in accordance with GAAP; disclose for note and mortgages; (percent interest); how long; separate current portion; five years' principal repayment; only prepare comfort letter if audit work is sufficiently progressed: do not give negative assurance until then; state qualifications and restrictions on use.

Revalue inventories to FIFO for tax purposes; prior period adjustment for any changes in accounting principles, if retroactive.

C. Quantitative

Valuation—consider: capitalization rate. Adding back: redundant assets; non recurring expenses; unusually high expenses (e.g., owners' salaries). Valuation method; dates of valuation. Six times average net income.

			Incomes
1973			$(1,275)
1974			1,559
1975			14,349
1976			17,322
1977			33,589
5			$65,544
÷			5
=			$13,109
×6		Ⓐ	$78,653 plus

1975			14,349	2,973
1976			17,322	16,267
1977			33,589	
				19,240
x3	=	Ⓑ	57,720	
Value Ⓐ + Ⓑ	=		136,373	

Scarpel $ 31,544

Working capital
book value
current assets $114,283
current liabilities 68,493

working capital $ 45,790

Fixed assets	$ 60,000
	45,000
	50,000
	10,000
	$165,000
Liabilities (non current)	$103,405
Therefore	$ 31,544
	45,790
	165,000
	(103,405)
	$138,790
@ 105%	$145,730

Price computed by times earnings basis	$136,373
Therefore the lower will be used, which is the price for the outstanding shares	$136,373

Tri-Line Mortgages
80% of fair value of fixed assets

Durie	$310,000
Erkel	165,000
	$475,000
@ 80%	$380,000

Proforma consolidated shareholder's equity of Durie Manufacturing

Durie 1977	197,868
add Erkel outstanding shares	
add Square Lake Manufacturing	80,000
	$277,868*
@ 175%	$486,269

* less any inter-company eliminations which may be involved

Cash flow

Purchase price	$136,373
Cash outlays Loan from shareholder June 30, 1978	$ 35,000
Square Lake Manufacturing shares	$ 80,000

Cash	$80,000	
Capital		$ 80,000

Square Lake Manufacturing	Durie	Erkel	Total
Land	$ 38,000	$ 46,250	
Building (net)	88,396	57,246	
Trucks and auto	25,935	9,226	
Other	110,483	25,381	

Inventories:			
Raw materials	49,030	23,358	
Finished goods	56,040	31,020	
	$367,884	$192,481	$560,365
Fixed assets		$560,365	
Long term loan (no interest therefore tax problems)			$560,365
Product distribution agreement		$ 31,544	
Long term loan			$ 31,544
Durie: Accounts receivable (Erkel Fabricating Ltd.)			$ 46,119

Scarpel Inc. production distribution agreement:	
Sales to Scarpel Inc.:	*Per annum*
$2,000 per month ×12	$ 24,000
Gross profit @ 50%	$ 12,000
March payment (assume no material difference to Dec. 31)	
Royalty 15%	1,800
1977	$ 10,200

The $4,500 should have been capitalized and amortized over useful life but was written off; therefore will not include.
Assume: historic growth trend continues

1978: $2,250 × 12 =	$27,000
1979: $2,500 × 12 =	$30,000
1980: $2,750 × 12 =	$33,000

	1978	1979	1980	
Sales	$27,000	$30,000	$33,000	
@ 50%	$13,500	$15,000	$16,500	
−15% royalty	2,025	2,250	2,475	
Net	$11,475	$12,750	$14,025	
Net present value— three years @ 10%	.91	.83	.75	
	$10,442	$10,583	$10,519	$31,544

Durie Manufacturing cash flow:		
Outflows:	1978	1979
Purchase Square Lake Manufacturing Ltd.	$80,000	
Pay loan June 30	35,000	
Shares of Erkel Fabricating Ltd.		
$136,373 @ 60%	81,824	
+ 8% June 10	6,546	
$136,373− $81,824 ÷ 4		13,637
Interest		4,364

Mortgage	(380,000)	
Interest $380,000 × 9⅞	37,525	35,648
Payments 6 @ ($380,000 ÷ 120)	19,000	
12 @ ($380,000 ÷ 120)		40,000
Starting cash	(14,080)	
increasing during year; assume	5,000	
	$139,185	(93,649)
		139,185
		$45,536

Note: present values can be used for this analysis
   1978 = .91   1979 = .83
Square Lake Manufacturing:

	1977
Income of Durie per financial statement	$48,152
Erkel per financial statement	33,589
Add: salaries	26,000
	35,000
	142,471
Less: future salary	(20,000)
Durie	(10,000)
Add: mortgage interest	37,525
	75,216
Less:6%	(4,512)
	70,703
Less: interest on shares	6,546
	64,157
Less: 3% bonus	1,924
If earnings remain stable	$62,233

Consignment sales were not eliminated from sales and added to inventory (only the cost was added to inventory).

1977 Consignment accounts receivable		$25,478
Less 1976		15,810
		9,668
Gross profit 130,665 ÷ 306,874 = 42.5*		4,109
Therefore cost of goods sold		$ 5,560
Sales	$ 9,668	
Accounts receivable		$ 9,668
Inventory	$ 5,560	
Retained earnings		5,560**

* assume salary of owner is immaterial
** should enter in calculation of cost of purchase

D. Recommendations

1. Cash flow—it is bad and will get worse if more financing is required to purchase more assets; most of loan is used up in first year.

2. Tax—get tax values to check effect of wind up.
3. Legal—get lawyers to review agreement to see if legal.
4. Valuation—should have professional do proper valuation.
5. Explain necessity of independence.
6. For consolidation ensure fair values are used to follow GAAP.
7. Qualify Erkel Fabricating Ltd.'s audited financial statements.

RESPONSE OF CANDIDATE B

Mr. Frank Erkel
President
Erkel Manufacturing Ltd.

Dear Mr. Erkel:

I understand that you would like to engage my services for the audit of your company. Unfortunately, I cannot make this decision without conducting further discussions with you and reviewing your financial records. I have reviewed your financial statements for previous years and some adjustments will be necessary in order to bring them in line with generally accepted accounting principles. I will be contacting you shortly regarding our discussions and my review.

Yours sincerely,
C.A.

Mr. Durie
President
Durie Manufacturing Company

Dear Mr. Durie:

As you requested I have conducted a review of the following matters:

Appendix I: The proposed purchase of Erkel Manufacturing and a valuation of that business.

Appendix II: Your cash situation assuming the purchase.

Appendix III: Tax matters regarding the purchase.

Appendix IV: Other matters to be considered in the agreement.

At this point I have not conducted an audit nor have I decided whether or not to accept the engagement as auditor of Erkel Manufacturing. A review and discussion with Mr. Erkel will be necessary before I make my final decision.

If you have any questions regarding the attached report or any of the comments in this letter, please do not hesitate to call.

Yours sincerely,
C.A.

APPENDIX I

Proposed Purchase of Erkel Manufacturing
Valuation of Business
Schedule I—Normalized Earnings

	1973	1974	1975	1976	1977
Unadjusted income	$(1,275)	$1,559	$14,349	$17,322	$33,539
Adjustments:					
Finished Goods inventory					
8% × 31,020					2,482
7.5% × 29,616				2,221	(2,221)
Depreciation:*					
if based on Durie	(11,280)	(12,500)	(13,780)	(15,340)	(16,070)
present expense	21,260	49,110	41,060	39,531	20,298
Raw material inventory					
3% increase (closing raw material × .03)	538	648	852	862	700
3% increase effect on opening inventory	(336)	(538)	(648)	(852)	(862)
Allocation of depreciation to production as part of overhead in closing inventory accounts					
Schedule II	4,217	11,572	9,225	8,602	3,310
Effect on opening inventories		(4,217)	(11,572)	(9,225)	(8,602)
Adjusted net income	$13,124	$45,634	$39,486	$43,121	$32,624

* I am assuming that the method Durie has used would have taken into account the useful life of the buildings, equipment and automobiles at acquisition in January 1973.

Schedule II—Allocation of Depreciation to Production

	1973	1974	1975	1976	1977
Depreciation expense before adjustments	$21,260	$49,110	$41,060	$39,531	$20,298
Adjustments from Schedule I	(11,280)	(12,500)	(13,780)	(15,340)	(16,070)
	21,260	49,110	41,060	39,531	20,298
Adjusted expense ©	31,240	85,720	68,340	63,722	24,526
Note 1 © × .90 = Ⓐ	$28,116	$77,148	$61,506	$57,349	$22,073
AdjustmentⒶ × 15%	$ 4,217	$11,572	$ 9,225	$ 8,602	$ 3,310

Adjustments will affect the cost of goods sold.

Note 1—finished goods inventory at the year end represents approximately 15 percent
of cost of goods sold. Therefore of the 90 percent of depreciation to be allocated to production 15 percent can be allocated as an addition to ending inventories (finished goods).

I will base this valuation on an earnings multiple of normalized earnings. (See Schedule 1.) Since 1975 was the start-up year of the company I think that we should exclude it from our calculations of normalized, average earnings. The average earnings from 1974-1977
inclusive are ($45,634 + $39,486 + $43,121 + $32,624) ÷ 4 =
$40,200. The agreement specifies that you are willing to pay six times
earnings: $40,200 × 6 = $241,200 plus three times the average annual
increase between 1975 and 1977.

Increase 1975 to 1976	$43,121 − $39,486 =	$3,635
Increase (decrease) 1976 to 1977	32,624 − 43,121 =	(10,497)
		$6,862
	÷	2
Average annual decrease		$3,431

Since profits have declined the multiple of average increases (de-
creases) will in effect reduce the purchase price.

Payment re 6× multiple	$241,200
Reduction due to 3× multiple	(3,431)
Add redundant assets:	
Cash	11,943
Land-fair value	60,000
Price using earnings multiple	$309,712

You have specified that you are not willing to pay more than 105
percent of fair values as defined by you.

Working capital	$114,283
	− 68,493
	$ 45,790
Land	60,000
Building	45,000
Equipment	50,000
Trucks, etc.	10,000
Value of Scarpel note*	17,020
Deduct fair value of non current liabilities	(103,405)
	$124,405 × 105%
Purchase price based on 105% of fair values	$130,625

Note*— assume twenty year life; no further increase assumed because if acquisition
takes place greater increases could occur; discount factor of 10 percent for an
annuity was used 2,000 × 8.51 = 17,020.

From my analysis it seems that you would have a real bargain if you were able to purchase the company for its "fair value" as outlined in the agreement. However, if Frank Erkel is not willing to take such a low offer, I feel that you still have an excellent purchase at $309,712 as computed using the earnings multiple. The earnings multiple of six assumes a rate of return for you of 16.7 percent which is a very good return indeed. Of course these figures are based upon unaudited financial figures, and before any action is taken an audit of the statements should be performed, and any adjustments taken into account in determining the purchase price.

Recommendations:

1. Try to acquire the company for 105 percent of fair value; however, if Frank Erkel is not in agreement with this, the purchase price based upon the earnings multiple is also a good buy.
2. No action should be taken until an audit of the statements of Erkel are performed.

APPENDIX II

Cash Situation—Assuming Purchase

Advance of funds from Tri-Line Mortgages not to exceed: 80 percent of fair value of assets of Durie Manufacturing and Erkel Mfg.

	Durie	*Erkel*
Land	$100,000	$60,000
Building	90,000	45,000
Equipment	100,000	50,000
Trucks and automobiles	20,000	10,000
	$310,000	$165,000

Total funds advanced ($310,000 + $165,000) × .80 = $380,000 Ⓐ

Funds may not exceed 175 percent of proforma consolidated shareholder's equity.

Shareholder's equity of Durie Manufacturing = $197,868.
$197,868 × 175% = $346,269 Ⓑ

Therefore since the loan is the lessor of Ⓐ or Ⓑ as outlined in the agreement you can expect to receive only $346,269 from Tri-Line Mortgages.

Assuming you pay Frank Erkel an amount somewhere between the two figures previously calculated, say $200,000, the advance from Tri-Line will more than cover this amount. You should not have any trouble maintaining the working capital requirement of $10,000, nor the interest payments inherent in the loan.

APPENDIX III

Tax Matters

Frank is the individual who will suffer the greatest immediate tax consequences of the sale of the company. It is possible that capital gains will arise on the sale of his company's shares. This will depend upon what he initially paid for the company and the adjustments we make to the cost base of his shares. Another alternative may exist to minimize the tax consequences of the proposed purchase. Frank could perform a rollover of his business under section 85(1) of the Income Tax Act. However this would necessitate setting up a holding company or perhaps Square Lake Manufacturing could be used. The shares of Erkel Manufacturing would be purchased by the holding company. The common stock of the holding company would then be subscribed to by Durie Manufacturing. Durie would purchase 100 percent of the outstanding common stock of the holding company. In order for a 85(1) rollover to be effective shares must be received by Frank in the holding company. Preferred shares could be issued to Frank, so that control is still maintained by you. A note receivable would also be issued to Frank to make up the difference between the value of the preferred shares and the fair market value of the company. This arrangement as described above may alter your agreement substantially, but in order to avoid capital gains you may want to consider it.

Under the new arrangement the companies will be deemed to be associated and therefore there may be some erosion of the small business deduction. In order to maximize the use of the small business deduction you must consider paying yourself bonuses, to bring the total income of the associated companies within the allowable limits.
Recommendations:
1. Consider setting up a holding company to purchase the shares of Erkel Manufacturing.
2. Future tax planning will be necessary in order to maximize the use of the small business deduction.
3. Consider using Square Lake Manufacturing as the holding company described above.

APPENDIX IV

Other Matters to be Considered in the Agreement

Frank Erkel may want his employment contract written into the agreement. The agreement may be altered substantially if the holding company approach is taken. We can discuss this at our meeting and any necessary alterations can be made at that time.

Recommendations:
1. Possible incorporation of Frank Erkel's employment contract in the agreement.
2. Agreement should be put aside until we resolve the issue of the holding company.

Memo to myself regarding the proposed acquisition of Erkel Fabricating:

It seems that an audit of Erkel Manufacturing will be necessary before I pursue this too much further. Tri-Line Mortgages requires audited financial statements and I feel that to protect my client I should conduct an audit before he completes the purchase.

The accounting records are in poor condition at Erkel and the company has had several incompetent bookkeepers.

List of procedures to be performed before accepting the engagement of Erkel Manufacturing

1. Conduct a review of the accounting records and system of internal control.
2. Send a letter to Erkel's former accountant to see whether he knows of any reason why I should not accept the engagement; consider the competence of this former accountant; his report did not meet the requirements of section 8100 of the CICA Handbook for a review or non-review engagement; at the present time I have no idea as to the extent of his procedures; consider reporting him to the Institute for not following standard reporting practices.
3. Obtain from the former accountant any working paper he may have regarding Erkel.
4. Obtain copies of any important agreements, including details of the mortgage and equipment notes.
5. Discuss with Erkel the possible effect on his report because I have not observed the ending inventory; a qualified opinion due to scope limitations is possible.
6. Discuss with Erkel whether or not there will be any further limitations on the scope of my examination and their possible effects on the report.
7. After these procedures and reviews are complete I will make a decision as to whether or not I will accept the engagement.
8. I will have to send a comfort letter during the audit, if I should decide to accept.

Notes to myself regarding Erkel Manufacturing financial statements and GAAP

Considerations:
1. No notes to financial statements regarding the amortization of goodwill or depreciation provided.
2. The description provided on the balance sheet for notes payable is not adequate; details of whether or not the loans are secured and payment obligations over the next five years should be disclosed.

3. The statements do not show any deferred income taxes; however, according to the tax returns, capital cost allowance has been claimed in the past.
4. The shareholder's equity section does not contain an adequate description of shares authorized or issued.
5. The change in retained earnings during the year is not shown on either the balance sheet or the income statement.

RESPONSE OF CANDIDATE C

Problems in order of importance:
1. Conflict of interest re audit of Erkel Fabricating (see Appendix I).
2. Analysis and evaluation of (see Appendix II):
   a. purchase of Erkel shares; tax consequences; GAAP adjusted for valuation purposes.
   b. agreement with Tri-Line Mortgages; ability to meet covenants; cash effects.
   c. sale of assets to Square Lake Manufacturing; tax consequences.
3. Evaluation of Erkel's profit sharing; profitability of Durie Manufacturing and Square Lake Manufacturing; transfer pricing.
4. Advice for production and inventory control systems (see Appendix III).

APPENDIX I

My first concern is with the conflict of interest situation regarding the proposed audit of Erkel Manufacturing. I cannot accept this audit engagement for the following reasons:
1. Both Frank and Durie are interested in the audited financial statements to establish a selling price for the company. However, Durie is my client. Even if I could be entirely independent and objective, in fact I would not be objective in appearance.
2. I would have to meet the professional requirements of a first audit: knowledge of the business; state of the company's accounting record; discuss accounting policies used to ensure no major problems with conformance to GAAP; services required by client; are my resources adequate to serve client?; opening balances reliable?

   I know his accounting records leave something to be desired and his systems of internal control are inadeqate. I did not observe inventory at December 31, 1977 (or December 31, 1976) and neither did Erkel's accountants. It would be impossible for me to issue an opinion on Erkel Manufacturing's financial statements for the year ended December 31, 1977.
3. Even if I could accept the engagement it would be against the rules

of professional conduct to quote a fee as he requested. I could only give my normal per diem rates.
4. At best, I can assist Mr. Durie in an assessment of Erkel's financial statements as to reliability and suggest adjustments to make them conform to GAAP. Mr. Erkel should have his own accountants act for him.

APPENDIX II

Analysis and Evaluation of
Purchase Price for Shares of Erkel Manufacturing

Formula: six times average annual earnings plus three times increase (decrease) in net incomes of 1975-76 + 1976-77

Because the agreement specifies GAAP financial statements I will have to make adjustments to conform Erkel's financial statements to GAAP.

	1973	1974	1975	1976	1977
Income before income taxes	$ (1,275)	$ 2,461	$17,448	$22,984	$44,193
add depreciation recorded	21,260	49,110	41,060	39,531	20,298
deduct depreciation similar to Durie (a)	(11,280)	(12,500)	(13,780)	(15,340)	(16,070)
finished goods inventory adjusted (b)				2,221	2,482
add back portion of depreciation attributable to finished goods inventory (c)	1,158	1,555	2,004	2,086	2,166
consignment sales × (.25) × gross margin (d)	(1,263)	(2,209)	(4,271)	(7,526)	(11,452)
adjusted income before income taxes	$ 8,600	$38,417	$42,461	$43,956	$41,617

(a) Assume Durie's method better because accepted for audited financial statement purposes.
(b) Increase in finished goods inventory reduces cost of goods sold.
(c) (.9) depreciation expense × $\dfrac{\text{finished goods inventory}}{\text{finished goods inventory + cost of goods sold}}$
(d) Assume 25 percent of consignment sales are returned (Durie estimate). No change re raw material because FIFO cost is an acceptable GAAP.

	1973	1974	1975	1976	1977
Income before income taxes	$8,600	$38,417	$42,461	$43,956	$41,617
Taxes at 24% (a.a.)	(2,064)	(9,220)	(10,191)	(10,549)	(9,988)
Net income (b.b.)	$6,536	$29,197	$32,270	$33,407	$31,629

(a.a.) 46%-10% − 21% (small business deduction) + 9% (provincial) = 24%

(b.b.) Adjustment to GAAP

Average annual income	26,608
	× 6
	159,647
+ 3 ($33,407 − $32,270)	3,411
+ 3 ($31,629 − $33,407)	(5,334)
purchase price based on net income	157,724
adjust for improper goodwill amortization	(9,525)
net	$148,199
reduced to (see below)	$145,113

plus Erkel will have to pay $35,000 to shareholders

1.05 (book value of working capital + fair value of fixed assets)
= 1.05 (current assets − current liabilities − non current liabilities + fair value fixed assets + fair value Scarpel Inc. agreement)
= 1.05 ($114,283 + $2,116* − $6,370** − $68,493 − $68,405*** + $165,000 + $2,879****) = $148,113

* finished goods inventory adjustment.

** accounts receivable adjustment (.25) consignment receivable Durie's estimate of non-sales portion.

*** non-current liabilities − loan from shareholders

****	Sales	Contribution Margin	10% Discount Factor*****	Net
1978	$2,250	.35	.91	$717
1979	2,500	.35	.83	726
1980	2,750	.35	.75	722
1981	3,000	.35	.68	714
				$2,879

***** Scarpel agreement cash flow discounted at 10 percent.
Purchase price Erkel $145,113 + $35,000 (shareholder's loan) = $180,113

Quantitative factors in Erkel purchase

1. The automotive assets with an assigned fair value of $10,000 have an expected useful life of a few months and the building valued at $45,000 has an estimated useful life of ten years left.

2. The undepreciated capital cost of the building, equipment and automotive assets is approximately equal to the fair values assigned. Therefore there would be no increase in capital cost base by buying the assets instead of shares. There is no amount paid for goodwill so there will be no eligible capital expenditure to claim for tax purposes, other than the $7,528 now in Erkel.

3. Erkel appears to have acquired a business because it reflects goodwill on its books and cumulative eligible capital in its tax returns. We are not given details of this but it also seems to arise on incorporation and may not be legitimate purchased goodwill. I have not included it in my calculation based on asset values.

N.B. There should also be another adjustment to average net income = average goodwill amortization after tax $2,089 $(1 - .24) = \$1,587$. $\$1,587 \times 6 = \$9,525$.

4. The adjustments I have made to conform Erkel's statements to GAAP may not tell the whole story. There could be undetected defalcations, unrecorded liabilities etc. due to the weaknesses in the internal control systems and the lack of an audit. It will not be possible for Erkel Manufacturing to obtain a clean opinion on its 1977 financial statements at this late date even from its own accountants unless they have done work to confirm opening and closing balances on balance sheet items at the time.

Conclusion: Assuming the financial statement data as adjusted is reliable the price appears to be reasonable. There is very little discrepancy in the result of applying an income and an asset valuation approach, except for $35,000 shareholder loan.

N.B. Calculation of purchase price needs to be adjusted because I added in the finished goods inventory increase twice for 1976 and 1977. The effect would be to reduce the purchase price calculated on average net income by approximately $\$4,500 = 3 \times (2,000)$ drop in 1976 net income $\times (.74)$.

Overall Evaluation of Deal: Qualitative Factors

Erkel gets a five year management contract at $20,000 plus six percent of Square Lake Manufacturing's income before taxes and bonus. He will have no investment and he may not be as motivated as he would be if he had an ownership interest. Durie would be taking all the risk. Tri-Line has mortgages on all the assets worth anything plus a fair return on their debt investment.

Conclusion: Due to the above the agreement does not appear to be in Durie's best interests. He should negotiate to have Erkel make a capital contribution to Durie Manufacturing Ltd. (i.e., exchange of shares instead of cash purchase of Erkel Manufacturing). Durie should then consider how much debt financing he requires and alternative sources. This plan seems to be ill-conceived. The division of duties between Durie and Erkel appears to be a good idea provided they operate as one company both having common stock interests.

If the Erkel Manufacturing purchase is consummated by an exchange of shares, not as much debt financing would be required.

It would appear from the following calculations that Durie Manufacturing would have difficulty raising the capital to buy Erkel Manufacturing, pay off shareholder loan and set up a new company.

However, there would be no need to do this if the share exchange method is used to acquire Erkel Manufacturing. The combined company probably would not need Tri-Line Mortgages.

Durie Manufacturing has to come up with 60 percent of the purchase price of Erkel's share (.6) ($148,000) = $88,800 plus $35,000 in Erkel Manufacturing to pay off shareholder's loan, plus $80,000 to incorporate Square Lake Manufacturing. Total cash required is $203,800.

Durie Manufacturing: Cash flow from operations:

		(rounded)
Net income		$48,000
+ Deferred taxes		6,000
+ Depreciation:		
5% × building		7,000
15% × auto		10,500
5% × equipment		8,000
		$79,000

Required to service eight percent mortgage.

Principal:	$ 11,250 × 2 =	$22,500
Interest:	107,500 × .08	8,600
		$31,100
Bank loan:	principal	7,000
	interest	5,500
		$12,500

Net cash flow after current debt service is approximately $35,400 assuming 1978 operations and profit similar to 1977.

Funds to be advanced by Tri-Line Mortgages. Lower of:
1. Fair value assets $310,000 + $165,000 = $475,000 × .8 = $480,000

2. Proforma consolidated shareholder's equity

> Parent, subsidiary:
>
> | | |
> |---|---:|
> | Preferred | $ 10,000 |
> | Common | 1,000 |
> | Retained earnings | 186,868 |
> | | $197,868 × 1.75 = $346,269 |

Common stock in subsidiary (Square Lake Manufacturing) does not affect shareholders' equity on consolidation.

Therefore funds to be provided by Tri-Line Mortgages = $346,269.

Assets to be transferred to Square Lake Manufacturing: From Durie, from Erkel through Durie:

> | | | |
> |---|---:|---:|
> | Inventory: | | |
> | raw materials | $ 49,000 | $ 23,000 |
> | finished goods | 46,000 | 31,000 + 2,000 |
> | | | adjustment |
> | Land, building, | | |
> | equipment, | | |
> | trucks and autos | 263,000 | 241,000* |
> | Notes payable | $358,000 | $297,000 |

* $138,000 + $10,000 + $37,000 + $28,000 + $24,000 + $4,000 = $241,000—Adjustments relating to excess depreciation charges in Erkel's accounts.

Financing: Durie Manufacturing will need to raise approximately ($203,800 − 35,400) = $168,400 of capital to complete the transactions contemplated in the agreement.

Alternatives:

1. Debt—increased leverage far too risky. Already plan to get debt financing from Tri-Line. Debt service charges would be too high.
2. Common—recommend exchange of shares for Erkel Manufacturing to reduce need for cash and involve Erkel in ownership to properly motivate him.
3. Preferred—possible alternative to limit participation in earnings but has drawbacks similar to debt unless non-cumulative dividends. However, probably not marketable.

APPENDIX III

Production and Inventory Control

A budget system should be introduced to the combined operations to compel planning and consideration of all factors. This budget system should help control production planning and costs as well as other expenses of running the business.

Comparison of actual to budget should help in the evaluation of the various activities and improve internal control to detect major defalcations.

The manufacturing activity could be more closely controlled with the introduction of standard costs for direct labour and direct material with a pre-determined overhead rate applied to prevent excessive complications and costs of accounting. Each type of product could be treated as a process to reduce the cost of accumulating cost data (i.e., process costing as opposed to job order). This allocation of overhead on a predetermined rate basis will result in absorption costing useful for external reporting with adjustments for variances.

Bonuses to the two key men could be based on actual performance versus flexible budgets.

RESPONSE OF CANDIDATE D

General comments: This appears to be a very open-ended case covering every syllabus area except electronic data processing. As C.A. I am given a great deal of cause for concern. As a preliminary evaluation it seems that I am faced with two clients who do not understand GAAP, an auditor's independence, the value of an audit, the time required to perform financial services, etc.

The objectives of the two men are of some importance in my evaluation of what to do and what to do first.

John Durie: energetic and ambitious; probably has normal business objective of profit maximization and tax minimization, but has two overriding objectives that appear to be expansion and successful marketing; has a desire to go public someday but this seems at this time to be a whimsy rather than a concrete objective; he wants expansion both by acquisition (investments) and by internal building; does not appear to have much concern over employees; therefore could be future problems due to the impending threat of unionization. This impending threat of unionization is evident whether or not he expands, and will not be further considered.

Frank Erkel: does not appear to be very ambitious or have much knowledge of the financial aspects of business; his objective appears to be security and supervision of production activity.

The objectives of the two men appear to meld for the proposed venture; however, neither one of the individuals appears to have strong financial background.

The environment, with the exception of the threat of unionization, appears favourable as well. Both companies appear well below their total business limit for tax purposes and a combined effort would still retain the small business deduction. They are both currently eligible for the manufacturing and processing deduction of a further five percent; however, this would probably disappear if Durie Manufacturing became simply a marketing venture. Tax benefits abound for the companies considering the small business deduction, manufacturing and processing, class 29 assets, the manufacturing tax credit (probably either seven and a half or ten percent, since in isolated area) and if they are good bargainers, probably government assistance due to relative isolation of area. Neither of the companies report any foreign exchange gains or losses so that I can assume that virtually all purchases and sales take place in Canada and therefore will not incur the extra risk of the fluctuating Canadian dollar.

Now that I have outlined some of the objectives of the individuals and some other considerations it would seem prudent to develop some of the issues and requirements that I face.

As a C.A., requested to perform certain engagements, I would definitely think that an engagement letter is in order both to Mr. Durie and to Mr. Erkel.

I have been requested to perform an audit of Erkel and these audited financial statements will be used for a purchase. The audit considerations (including whether to accept) therefore demand a high priority.

I have been requested to prepare consolidated financial statements (i.e., put all the companies together) pro forma statements and a comfort letter. Some clarification will be required here in that:

1. a prospectus is generally prepared for a public offering of shares; and
2. a comfort letter is a form of negative assurance which may only be given after substantially all of the audit work has been performed;
3. a comfort letter is generally given only to a public securities commission upon request; and
4. in a prospectus (according to Canada Corporation Act) three years of audited financial statements are required. A set of financial statements can be provided in unaudited form providing that they are not more than 90 days away from last set of audited statements.

Conclusion: A prospectus does not seem to be in order and therefore a comfort letter cannot be issued.

I have been requested to give a price quote which is against professional ethics and will be covered in the engagement letter.

I have been requested to give my comments on the draft agreement to purchase Erkel Manufacturing. This would appear to be a very high priority item as it seems to be the main reason for the journey to Square Lake. My comment is to give particular emphasis to tax minimization.

Some tax planning for both gentlemen seems to be an undertone of their conversations and some consideration should be given for ways to minimize their personal tax bills.

Also, I have been requested to supply some idea on how to install an effective management information system should the proposed transaction take place.

Audit Considerations: (due to their nature, these would be my top priority)

1. Durie Manufacturing—assume that audit is complete for 1977 fiscal year; the requests of John Durie would fall into the realm of special services and independence must be considered. Of special consideration here is the statement "Remember you are working for me. I pay all of your fees for the reorganization;" if C.A. can manage to maintain her professional independence then the job as almost outlined can be undertaken. Not enough information is available to decide so for the sake of the case, assume that she can accept; note that there is no audit opinion attached to the financial statements, that there is no statement of retained earnings or statement of changes in financial position. These should be presented along with notes to the financial statements if audit opinion has not been released before purchase and a subsequent event note is necessary.

2. Erkel Manufacturing—to begin with an ethics problem exists. AB have given unwarranted assurance in their covering letter to Frank Erkel by saying that the information accurately summarizes the company's affairs. He does not state whether his non audits were review or non review engagements. However, I would assume that they were non review as they were for tax purposes. AB should probably be reported to the provincial disciplinary committee (especially given his knowledge of the inadequacy of Erkel Manufacturing's internal controls and record keeping system; due to the inadequacy of the record keeping and internal controls etc. and given the fact that C.A. could not have observed either opening or closing inventory.) To even attempt to perform an audit or an 8100 review for the year ended December 31, 1977 would be sheer folly.

Conclusion: An audit as requested cannot be performed. For the purpose of a valuation for purchase, the company's assets should be appraised by an independent appraiser. It would be impossible to quantify the risk apparent in relying on Erkel Manufacturing's income statements for the five year period ended December 31, 1977.

However, if it is specifically requested, known deviations from GAAP can be adjusted for. In the event that these adjustments are made C.A. can probably issue a notice to reader. She may also be requested to carry out certain audit procedures (i.e. new exposure draft) with regard to accounts receivable and cash.

Since the primary direction of testing for accounts payable is understatement she would probably not wish to become associated with the liabilities side of the balance sheet.

Conclusion: Adjust for known deviation from GAAP; suggest that appraisal of other assets be performed. The adjustment for known deviation is included as Schedule I.

Proposed Purchase of Erkel Manufacturing

There are a number of qualitative considerations with regards to the proposed purchase which should be discussed.

Most important of these is the fact that the companies' operations are quite similar. This would mean that there would be a redundancy of assets. In this situation, fair values would be disposal proceeds. This supports the suggestion that an appraisal be performed.

If the business is such that there would be increasing returns to scale then the venture becomes more viable. The reasons for beginning a new company remain unclear as goodwill associated with the Erkel Manufacturing name would be lost. It would seem more appropriate to buy the shares of Erkel Manufacturing and pay for these shares with the manufacturing assets of Durie Manufacturing.

The price to be paid for the shares of Erkel Manufacturing would be calculated by a multiplier as Erkel Manufacturing would, in this case, continue as a going concern. (The purchase price has not been established as the time involved to carry out the actual valuation is prohibitive).

Note that there are no tax surplus accounts in Erkel Manufacturing except to the extent that it has received distribution from other companies (very unlikely).

Management Considerations: If the proposed purchase is effected, the company will require a more sophisticated management accounting system. The combined companies would still be too small, probably, to make effective use of a standard cost system, but flexible budgets could and should be introduced. These would be prepared on a monthly basis.

Management remuneration should be tied to profit as proposed in order to stimulate some goal congruency between management and the company. The profit referred to above would be contribution margin less controllable fixed costs not the amount reported on the financial statements. If Erkel Manufacturing is expected to continue selling, the price to be charged to the marketing company should be market price less selling costs.

Tax Considerations: John Durie:

Take $10,000 out in salary from Erkel Manufacturing (not Square Lake Manufacturing which will not exist) and Durie Manufacturing on a fair basis. This will entitle you to be eligible for the maximum Canada Pension Plan benefit.

On this $10,000, approximately $2,000 can be deferred by using a Registered Retirement Savings Plan. The company should establish a deferred pension plan for top management thereby giving you another $2,000 in deferred tax income (i.e., relevant maximum = 20 percent of salary and bonus).

Any remaining desired remuneration should be extracted from the company by way of dividends. Approximately $20,000 can be taken out tax free and the tax on any remaining dividend considerations will be considerably lower than equivalent salary withdrawals.

The dividend will also (as would salary) keep the company's cumulative deduction account down so that the company will not be subject to the high rate of tax (Note: If house, then RHOSP is another possibility).

Frank Erkel: You should specify that your remuneration will be taken by way of $3,500 deferred pension plan and the remainder in salary and bonus. There are certain benefits that will lead to a lower tax bill that you should discuss when negotiating your contract.

1. use of company car (taxed on stand-by fee)
2. the deferred pension plan as discussed
3. expense account

In addition you can tax defer your income by purchasing a Registered Retirement Savings Plan to a maximum of the least of:

1. $3,500 any registered pension plan contributions (to the extent that any plan exists);
2. $5,500;
3. 20 percent of earned income;
4. amount contributed to plan.

Mr. F. Erkel
Square Lake

Dear Mr. Erkel:

Further to our conversation on March __ 1978 I regret to inform you that it will be impossible for me to perform an audit for your company for the year ended December 31, 1977.

If you are considering an audit for the 1978 fiscal year, I would be pleased to discuss this with you at your earliest convenience.

Yours truly,
C. A.

Mr. John Durie
Square Lake
Dear John:
   Further to our conversation on March __ 1978 I would like to set out the terms of my engagement with you, as I understand them.
1. Review the proposed acquisition of Erkel Manufacturing etc.
2. Billing will be at my standard rate and will be based on time spent on the engagement.
   If you are in agreement with the above terms please confirm this by signing in the space provided.

Yours truly,
C. A.

I have read the above terms and am in agreement.

....

Mr. J. Durie
Square Lake
Dear Mr. Durie:
   In accordance with the terms of my engagement, I have carried out certain analyses and present my recommendations to you as follows.
1. Proposed purchase of Erkel Manufacturing and establishment of company Square Lake Manufacturing   Page ____.
2. Some ideas on a management accounting system for the companies.   Page ____.
3. Some personal tax planning ideas.   Page ____.
4. etc.
   I trust this information will be of assistance to you.

Yours truly,
C. A.

Note to marker:
   If time permitted I would restate the income figures for the five years for Erkel given the information in schedule E. I would approach this valuation by projecting the income so calculated as an infinite annuity discounted at Durie Manufacturing's cost of capital (which I would calculate). The above approach would be taken since the companies are in a similar risk category. I believe the answer would be as accurate an evaluation as could be obtained.

Schedule I

	1973	1974	1975	1976	1977
Sales	$	$	$	$	$
Add consignment	205,819	258,961	284,641	292,689	306,874
Less consignment out-standing i.e. ending less beginning accounts receivable	(7,778)	(3,030)	(33,637)	(1,639)	(96,687)
Less salary charge for Frank Erkel, approximately ϕ	—	—	—	—	—
Add (less) change in depreciation policy	?	?	?	?	?
Change from FIFO to average cost	?	?	?	?	?
Income restated					
Tax provision					
Income (net)	$	$	$	$	$

5 year average × multiplier (not calculated) = approximate worth

Rough notes—client ambitious; continuing engagement; possibility of going public; outside financing proposed; audited statements required for Erkel; John Durie wants tax minimization; time limitations—next week.

Required: put all the companies together so that Tri-Line can see what everything will look like; also wants a comfort letter combined with pro forma balance sheet; we seem to be dealing with a prospectus; client a bit confused about independence rules; client asking for price quote; engagement letter definitely seems in order.

Erkel wants assessment of cash position for next twelve months approximately; management accounting implications: pricing (transfer at marginal cost); remuneration of management (i.e., Frank Erkel); objective: invest in other companies.

Required: evaluate other potential investment; proposed evaluation dependent upon outcome of reorganization, therefore, low priority probable; management information system for Frank Erkel; will be running combined manufacturing operation; no experience with big operation; help in production organization with emphasis on cost control; transfer priority between Square Lake Manufacturing and Durie Manufacturing seems essential; comments on draft agreement; views on how deal should be structured for tax minimization.

Want tight agreement; pro forma statement low priority item; perform audit of Erkel Manufacturing with discussion of adjustments; problem in that Erkel does not see C. A. as being independent of

Durie; possibly have someone else do Erkel audit? No!; valuation of Erkel Manufacturing is required, therefore will require appraisal of assets, evaluation of risk, management ability, etc.

AB is giving assurance that is not warranted; will have to inform AB that personal tax is being taken over and ask for any reasons why this should not be done; tax considerations in sale of Erkel to Durie Manufacturing; should sale be assets or shares?

Draft agreement says to acquire at January 1, 1978 which is long gone; the agreement will have to be at a prospective date and cannot be retroactively applied; no statement of changes in financial position for Durie Manufacturing; working capital does not look that good; any reports to Durie should be in layman's terms.

RESPONSE OF CANDIDATE E

Tentative approach:
1. Audit of Erkel Fabricating—requirement of mortgage company; basis for valuation of company.
2. Valuation of Erkel—requested by Mr. Durie.
3. Structure of reorganization—requested by client; terms of agreement; price paid; accounting; legal and tax.
4. Financing of reorganization—determination of cash position.
5. Other matters—employees' union; production and cost control; accounting matters; share of profits and purchase agreement.

Audit of Erkel:
Audit considerations:

First audit: internal control weak; large turnover of bookkeeping staff; doubtful competence.

Aspects of audit: since poor internal control, audit will consist mainly of substantive tests; confirming assets and liabilities wherever possible; year end inventory count; verify consignment inventory; adopt GAAP policies; adjustments to financials includes statement of changes in financial position; unable to attend year end inventory count; may be difficult in verifying cost of sales and year end inventory, therefore, possible qualified opinion; adverse opinion may affect amount of financing available from mortgage company; client to be informed of this possibility; engagement letter to be obtained from Erkel advising of high chance of adverse position.

Audit fees: based on time required to perform audit plus out of pocket; cannot be immediately established due to multitude of inherent audit problems.

Problem areas to be considered:
Reliance to be placed on audit by: mortgage company; Durie for valuation; high degree of reliance by third parties thus degree of liability to these parties.

Conflict of interests: as responsible both for independent audit as well as valuation of company; audit fee shared by Erkel and Durie heightens independence problem; should consider co-audit of Erkel with other C.A. firm to establish independence.

Reliance to be placed in part on work of another accountant: no audit performed; little reliance can be placed on previous financial statements; this will likely result in qualified opinion re opening numbers; ask Erkel's accountant if any working papers may be reviewed.

Tentative adjustments to Erkel's financial statements; adjustment required for consignment sales in all years.

Conclusion:
1. Joint undertaking in audit of Erkel with another C.A. firm.
2. No reliance to be placed on opening numbers of Erkel; must verify.
3. Inform client qualified opinion likely; discuss effect on financing.
4. Audit mainly substantive in nature; internal control is weak.
5. Financial statements to be completely reviewed and additional disclosure added.

Valuation:

SCHEDULE A
Price to be paid by Durie for Erkel: approximate
Price is six times average annual net income since 1973.

	Annual income		
1973	$(1,275)		
1974	1,559		
1975	14,349		
1976	17,322		
1977	33,589		
	$65,544	÷ 5 = $13,109 × 6 =	$78,654

plus three times average annual increase (decrease)

Net income	*1975-6*	*1976-7*		
Increase	$ 2,973	$16,267	=	19,240
	= 19,240			
Average	$19,240	÷ 2 = 9,260 × 3 =		28,860
				$107,514 Ⓐ

Price to be paid for Erkel will be approximately $107,514. i.e. lesser of schedule Ⓐ and Ⓑ per point six of draft agreement.

Note: Assume that adjustments to financial statements will not materially affect the price.

SCHEDULE B

Price to be paid for Erkel cannot exceed _____.
Fair value assets
Erkel:

Fixed assets:	
Land	$60,000
Building	45,000
Equipment	50,000
Trucks	10,000
Fair value	$165,000

Scarpel
Future net cash flows discounted at 10 percent:
Expires 1981

Estimated* sales approximately 1978-1981	$2,500
	50%
Gross margin	1,250
Royalty 15% sales ($2,500 × 15%)	375
Net cash average	$ 875

Present value of Ⓐ $875 at 10 percent for four
years: $875 × 3.17 = $2,774

* based on historical

Working capital

Current			
Assets	$114,283		
Liabilities	(68,493)		
Non current liabilities	(103,405)	$(57,615)	
100% of fair value per agreement		$110,159	
105%		$115,667	Ⓑ

Square Lake cash required re Erkel purchase:

Cash position and cash required	
Purchase of Erkel approximate	$107,514
Mortgage payments 1978-1982	
Present value of (A) $21,201 for five years at 5%*	
$21,201 × 4.33 =	91,800
Equipment note 2 1978-1979	
Present value of (A) $9,392 for two years at 5%*	
$9,392 × 1.86 =	17,469
Total cash required	$216,783**

* Assume after tax cost of capital 10% × 50% tax rate = 5%
** The above calculation is the amount required to pay to outside parties.

Conclusion: Durie would need this amount from mortgage company not necessarily all at once.

Durie to consider requirements re: mortgage coming due.

Term 8 of purchase agreement:

Financing:
Funds to be advanced
Mortgage company

Erkel			$107,514
Durie			
Fixed assets			
	$100,000		
	90,000		
	100,000		
	20,000	$310,000	
		417,514	
		× 80%	
Funds to be advanced by mortgage company			$334,011

Conclusion: These funds should be sufficient for Square Lake to purchase Erkel based on forecasted requirements subject to 175 percent of consolidated shareholder's equity of Durie.

Purchase price of Erkel:

Considerations:

Problems: employees may join union and force higher wages; consider in purchase price; machinery obsolete and may have to be updated; tax assessment may be substantial influence on purchase price.

Other Matters:

Purchase agreement drafted at club. Advise client to have it carefully reviewed by lawyer for legality of clauses.

Accounting Policies of Consolidated Group:

Consolidation: Durie and Square Lake will have to be consolidated as Square Lake is a wholly owned subsidiary; year ends should coincide; accounting policies should be brought into line between two companies for ease of consolidation; detailed records of inter company transactions will be required; improved internal control; both companies to obtain unqualified reports required by mortgage company.

Structure and Organization of Square Lake

Notes: Internal control system should be clearly established at Square Lake including: performance measurement components; i.e., budgets since bonus to be based on this; inventory control budgets; economic order quantity calculations; possibly perpetual inventory.

Square Lake and Durie purchase agreement: allocation of marketing costs will have to be resolved as salaries and bonus based on profits of each company.

Rough notes:

Role of C.A. (the auditor): document to client Durie and businessman Erkel.

Required: tentative recommendations all aspects of concern; matters of two businessmen; what will audit cost Frank Erkel's company; evaluate potential investments; cash position after reorganization; advise management; increase size of operation; comments on draft agreement; goals and objects of Durie Manufacturing; buy Erkel Manufacturing; low tax; marketing; other investments.

Strengths—weaknesses: Erkel not good history in overall productions; cost control.

Problems:

1. Reorganize and streamline joint operations—Erkel.
2. Financing; go public?
3. New company Square Lake Manufacturing.
4. Audit and GAAP for Tri-Line Mortgage.
5. Pro forma not immediate; balance sheet for purchase; comfort letter.
6. Effects on final selling price.
7. Amount advanced.
8. Conflict re valuation.
9. Split audit fee. Cash position for next year of Erkel.
10. Separate marketing profit contribution between Durie and Square Lake re profit share of Erkel.
11. How deal should be structured re tax.
12. Agreement—lawyer.
13. First audit.
14. Fair price to pay.
15. Cash position after payment and money required from Tri-Line.
16. Conflict of interest; fair audit; personal tax business.

   Organize, document, analyze, and recommend thoughts:

A. Reorganization: streamline; structure to minimize taxes; legal.
B. Financing: go public; amount required from mortgage company.
C. Audit: review prior work; mortgage company requirements; audit fee split; Erkel salary allocation; conflict of interest; adjustments. Who pays for audit?
D. Valuation of Erkel: reliance of mortgage company; Erkel reliable?; possible tax assessment.
E. Cash position: audit fee.
F. Accounting system: separate profits of Square Lake and Durie; Erkel's share of profit.
G. Production and cost control: Square Lake: increased volume; cost control; organization for production.

H. Employees' union.
I. Durie's new investments.

AN ANALYSIS OF CANDIDATE A's RESPONSE

General

Of the five candidate responses, Candidate A probably provided the second best answer, although it is still not a good effort, being marginal overall. The prime reasons why the candidate did not perform better are not known for certain, but we can make a few observations that are probably not too far off target:

1. Too much attention has been given to technical matters, almost to the exclusion of broader effects that, in the end, could overrule his (we'll assume) technical conclusions and recommendations. Maybe the candidate has a broader viewpoint and knows where accounting and auditing fits the overall business picture, and has merely not shown it in this particular case. If so, greater practice with cases is essential so that non-technical issues and implications are more forcefully brought out.

   However, if the candidate has studied the subject of accounting too narrowly, immediate steps must be taken to improve his perspective. The role of accountancy has to be thought of as being within the field of business. Accounting is an information system to aid persons who have to make business decisions; accounting is not an end in itself. In short, the candidate is giving markers the impression that he is a "technician," unable to see a broader picture.

2. The candidate did not appear to prepare a budget on how he would spend the four hours that were provided to respond to such a case. Instead, he used a simple, yet convenient, analytical framework (problem identification; qualitative and quantitative analysis; and recommendations), but pushed its use too far. For instance, he even included the framework in a covering letter to the client. This tends to show an overworship of or over-reliance on, technical frameworks and not enough common sense in communicating with clients.

   In addition, the framework that he used tends to be used in accounting courses, especially cost accounting. This places too much emphasis on accounting and not enough on other business disciplines. When such an accounting framework is employed it ought to be counterbalanced by thinking about another simple analytical model such as functions of business: marketing, policy and environment, production, financing, and so forth. Or, one could think about strategic planning, policy formulation, and so on. A combination of frameworks kept at the front of one's mind during case analysis will help to prevent having a technician's outlook. The written report can then be organized by each type of major problem, or another time-saving style.

3. We suspect that the candidate did not evaluate the case in terms of its direction (highly directive; non directive; or in between). Since the Square Lake case was towards the highly directive side, the candidate was saved possible failure because most of the material had some relevance to CA. On a less directive case, or one with considerable amounts of irrelevant data, he could have been in considerable trouble. He appeared to seek out quantitative matters without giving thought to how many marks would be awarded to computations. Maybe a computation could take an hour to complete, yet because of its minor importance it could be worth only five or six marks.

Before we proceed with our comments on Candidate A's response, one other major point is pertinent. Candidates must estimate where the markers likely would award marks, and how many would be allowed in different, relevant categories. The Board of Examiners of the Institutes/Ordre of Chartered Accountants employ an "overmark" system on cases like Square Lake. The purpose of overmarking, or marking out of more than 100 percent is to allow candidates the freedom to pursue several aspects of the case and still be able to attain passing marks.

The Square Lake case was actually marked out of 231 but not all of these could be attained because the pursuit of one approach may have excluded you from other possible marks. The 231 was made up of:

		Marks
1.	General considerations, such as the personal qualities of the parties, and their motivations.	6
2.	The role of CA and her professional relations with the client(s).	18
3.	Possible audit of Erkel.	41
4.	Evaluation of the existing agreement.	77
5.	Income tax consequences.	35
6.	Alternatives open to Durie.	14
7.	Professional characteristics, such as perspective of the candidate, usefulness of the answer, ability to communicate, and overall skill displayed.	40
		231

Naturally, you do not know the precise marking system that will be used by markers. Thus, you must guess. Your guesses will improve if you write enough cases and see how competent markers have graded you. You can also read previous Uniform Final Examination cases and observe how they were graded. The worst approach to follow is to *not* make these guesses. If you do *not* plan your response and tie it to your best guess of where the marks might be, you are taking a larger risk. As a general rule you should have depth in one or two areas of crucial importance to the client organization, plus some breadth. Determine the areas which cause success or failure (perhaps bankruptcy) in the organization and go into depth. In the Square Lake case note that 77 marks were allocated to the "purchase agreement." This is because a poorly handled agreement could cause major problems for Durie, possibly leading to serious losses and even to eventual bankruptcy.

Some specifics

A paper like Candidate A's would receive slightly better than average marks in one area: an evaluation of the existing agreement. The paper is very weak on income tax, general considerations, the role of CA, and alternatives open to Durie.

The main strengths of the paper are the candidate's organizational ability in trying to place material under headings and subheadings, and his decision to go into depth on the existing agreement. The former strength shows the beginnings of a readiness to practice; the latter shows a grasp of ascertaining what is important in a somewhat confused business setting.

The paper has one potentially serious flaw and several minor flaws. The candidate has chosen to adopt what is called a "memory dump" style. That is, he is aggressively pursuing a strategy of chasing points worth one mark each. Some cases lend themselves to this type of one point marking, and some non UFE markers adopt such an approach to grading. But other cases are designed to test the logic of analysis, or the soundness of recommendations, and not just problem recognition. When logic and reasoning marks are being provided a "memory dump" style will receive some problem recognition marks and a few recommendation marks, but will *not* be eligible for logic and reasoning marks. Hence, a "memory dumper" will fail cases that are heavy in the logic and reasoning areas.

Candidates should try to track the nature and direction of the Uniform Final Examinations (UFE) and determine the type of cases that lend themselves to memory dumping, and those where credit is given for logic and reasons for, or justification of, your answer.

UFE cases test the candidate's ability to perform at a professional level with regard to: problem identification, qualitative data analysis, quantitative data analysis, willingness to make recommendations, and quality of recommendations. Accounting education should focus upon knowledge, comprehension, assessment, evaluation, application, synthesis, and similar skills. A candidate who memory dumps is not showing the markers that he can assess, evaluate, synthesize and apply. He is hoping that the markers do not award marks for such skills and do not take away marks for irrelevancies. Knowledge regurgitation, or memory dumping, can be tested by other types of questions at a lower cost. It is a mistake to think that a memory dump strategy will prove successful. Accounting educators hope that "memory dumpers" are rarely able to pass cases or questions that test evaluation, application, and similar traits.

When we review the sample response to the Square Lake case, reproduced at the end of this Chapter, it becomes clear that Candidate A did not tie all of the parts together and make convincing recommendations. Most of his writing consists of isolated points, some of which are on target, but many of which are not labelled as to their importance. In the Square Lake case, the requirement lets analysts avoid writing directly to the client. This does not mean that candidates should avoid evaluating the significance of each issue to the client. The significant issues deserve attention on examinations because more marks are potentially available, and the professional quality of an answer depends on them.

Conclusion

Candidate A did not provide a credible response, overall. He may have been fortunate to have encountered a case that enabled someone with a technician's outlook to score points. The approach that he followed is not a good one for the Uniform Final Examinations of the Institutes/Ordre of Chartered Accountants.

AN ANALYSIS OF CANDIDATE B's RESPONSE

General

Candidate B's response is in third, or perhaps, fourth place out of the five. One suspects that the candidate does not really understand the educational objectives that underly case analysis. She (we will assume) seems to have the impression that accounting examinations test either knowledge regurgitation or number crunching applications of the knowledge and nothing else. While such examinations may be adequate for those who aspire to be bookkeepers, limited regurgitation testing is not sufficient for professional accountants.

The candidate has made little attempt to convey to markers that she can soundly assess a situation, by grasping what is important, and make credible recommendations that solve the issues in the larger business context. She has to display a readiness to practice, and not just an ability to play with some of the numbers in the case. In effect she has not given herself much of a chance to pass.

In several respects Candidate B's paper is just a poorer version of Candidate A's. Both show major deficiencies, probably caused by inadequate preparation for the Uniform Final Examination. They may have taken many accounting and auditing courses that used narrow examination procedures. For example, the examinations that they sat for could have: (1) tested only the material covered since the previous examination; (2) included only relevant facts in the body of the question; (3) given only explicit instructions or high direction; (4) excluded the environment of accounting, especially the behavioural and policy considerations; and (5) been graded on a point by point basis, and not also been assessed for overall credibility and quality.

If you have been exposed only, or primarily to, the type of testing described in the previous paragraph you will have to take corrective action immediately. Appropriate action consists of: (1) doing cases and having them graded by competent graders (who do more than use a point form approach); (2) doing previous Uniform Final Examination cases and checking to see how they were graded (to the extent that this is possible); (3) perhaps, registering for short courses on how to do cases (but being careful to avoid those that advocate "memory dump" or "easy formula" approaches); and (4) devising analytical frameworks for cases so that you can be planning your response in your head while you are reading the case for the first time. See the earlier chapters of this book.

Some specifics
Candidate B has made nearly all of the errors that were described for Candidate A. Time budgets and analytical models or frameworks were not considered. A decision, probably by accident or through lack of awareness, was made to pursue a few quantitative matters and exclude large portions of the case. In short, a single subject answering style was applied quite inappropriately to a case question. A single subject style does not easily permit a candidate to display the skills thought necessary for qualified chartered accountants.

Let us choose a few phrases from Candidate B's paper and comment on them. We will begin with the covering letter to Frank Erkel. This took the candidate perhaps 10 minutes of thinking and writing time. What does it say? Would you give it any marks if you were the grader?

The letter could mention the important ethics issue in the case. It could also state exactly what CA wishes to know in order to be able to reach a conclusion or make recommendations. It could explain the significance, if any, of GAAP. But, it is a strange mixture of words, some of which illogically assume that Erkel understands, but at the same time does not understand, accounting and related issues. The letter simply is not worth any marks. It was a waste of time and effort, that could have been better spent on reading and thinking.

The letter to Durie is in the same category. Unless a letter or report is specifically asked for do not squander time. You do not receive marks for repeating the case, especially the insignificant parts of the question. Candidate B might have received some indirect marks under "professional characteristics" for the organization of her response, as outlined in the letter to Durie. But, this organization could also be provided by using suitable headings and subheadings on the subsequent pages.

Observe that Candidate B probably has not carefully read the "required" in the case. It should be read four or five times until it is absolutely clear in your mind. By not reading carefully, the candidate has wasted much time with phrases such as: "I will base this valuation on an earnings multiple of normalized earnings." The single word "normalized" would suffice when you are making notes to yourself. If you are short of time use abbreviations on schedules, but not in formal letters to the client.

Her discussion on income "tax matters" is somewhat strange, partly because of the conflict of interest issue in the case. In a letter to Durie CA is giving income tax advice to Erkel. There is nothing wrong with telling Durie that Erkel's financial advisers may ask for revisions in the agreement between the parties, and why. But the wording must fit the context of the receiver.

Theoretically, if CA had rightfully concluded that it was a conflict of interest to handle Erkel's affairs at the same time that she was employed by Durie, she should cease unnecessary communication with Erkel. This approach of ignoring Erkel's problems could close off many marks to the candidate unless she could explain why she was examining matters from Erkel's point of view. In the Square Lake case it is possible to rationalize that Durie can better understand negotiations if he is told how Erkel's financial advisers may behave and why they may want revisions to the agreement. Lacking the rationalization, it seems out of place to deal with Erkel's income tax problems when Durie is paying CA's fee.

There is a moral to the previous paragraph. Do not spend time going beyond your terms of reference unless you can satisfactorily explain your position. You may not receive marks.

Finally, much of the "Memo to myself" section is a collection of needless words. Often one or two descriptive words, such as "inventory observation," could replace sentences, thereby saving time.

Conclusion

Candidate B's response did not display an ability to analyze, apply, synthesize, recommend, and handle similar skills needed by a chartered accountant. The candidate somehow had the impression that knowledge regurgitation, especially number manipulation, was all that was being tested. While her approach may prove successful in a case devoted to quantitative data analysis, it is not likely to be fruitful for most other types of cases.

AN ANALYSIS OF CANDIDATE C's RESPONSE

General

Candidate C's response is the best of the five. She obtained a large number of marks evaluating the existing purchase agreement and a good base of marks in two other areas: professional characteristics and CA's role. The paper is weak in income tax considerations and in an overall assessment of the qualities of the parties to the agreement.

Some specifics

What makes this response better than those of the other candidates? Is it greater recognition of potential problems, greater ability to handle quantitative and qualitative analysis, well supported recommendations, or something else? Let us analyze the candidate's response.

Note that Candidate C *begins* the response with a listing of the "order of importance" of problems. This impresses clients and markers. In order to prepare such a list she would have to think about the entire case, weigh the relative importance of issues, decide on the order, plan her attack of the problems, and commit herself in writing. This shows confidence; as a client you would feel that you are "in good hands."

Contrast Candidate C's approach with those chosen by A and B. You will recall that A and B tended to list everything in sight and it was hard to tell what they regarded as of greater importance. Think of your most recent visits to your doctor. What impression would you have if the doctor told you that your broken finger nail was as serious as multiple breaks to the hand you write, and do your accounting-auditing, with? What if the doctor recommended two aspirins when you need open heart surgery? Would you want your doctor to be trained the way that Candidate A and B apparently have been?

A second positive characteristic of Candidate C's paper is that she *explains why* she has adopted a particular position. Notice the explanation that accompanies the ethical issues affecting CA. Although some marking guides may inadvertently give few direct marks to the "why," indirectly such comments indicate to the markers that the candidate has depth, which earns marks in the "professional characteristics" section of the marking guide. That is, the candidate is not groping, and has not resorted to memory dumping when she finds out that her poor preparation has placed her "over her depth."

A third positive characteristic of the response is that Candidate C makes *logical* assumptions when such are needed. As with real life, cases do not provide all, and only, relevant information. You have to know the "right" questions to ask; otherwise, you will miss important facts. The cases are testing whether you can proceed with analysis without having to be held by the hand. Can you diagnose and recommend? A good diagnosis results from having investigated possibilities, eliminating those that are unlikely, and pursuing those that might bear fruit. Again, think of a visit to your doctor, and the questions he asks while trying to pin down the cause and cure of a problem.

Candidate C's assumptions and accompanying reasoning vary in their nature and purpose. Some may help to simplify computations, yet they tell the marker that she understands the situation. ("Assume Durie's method better because accepted for audited financial statements.") Others show that she is aware of a potential problem, such as a previous business acquisition, but will not pursue it because additional assumptions are required. ("We are not given details . . . but it also seems to arise on incorporation and may not be legitimate purchased goodwill. I have not included it . . . .") As a general rule, if you have to string *together* two or three assumptions in order to perform a computation, do not bother. The particular part of the case would be testing problem recognition, and not data analysis. The marking guide would tend to allow marks primarily for problem recognition.

A fourth strength of the paper is that the candidate has displayed depth where the case allows such. In the Square Lake case, the existing agreement is a potentially major issue, and plenty of facts are provided to allow extensive analysis. Before you go into depth be sure that the issue is crucial to the success or failure of the organization. Do not chase red herrings. In some cases students have prepared a consolidation when none was required or had any bearing on the problem. Other students have prepared GAAP financial statements when the client wanted cash flow or liquidation schedules.

Towards the end of the response the candidate begins to memory dump. But, by this point she has established reasonable credibility with the markers. In a small business standard costs and budgets can easily be out of place. Maybe she has dumped because she is uncertain whether all syllabus areas have to be covered in a case. They do not. The point of case testing is to ascertain a candidate's skills in comprehension, analysis, application, synthesis and so forth. Knowledge dumping out of place can destroy credibility.

Conclusion

Candidate C has clearly spent sufficient time reading the case so that she knows what is required and what is important. For most of the response she has not resorted to desperation dumping of knowledge, in the hope that some of it fits the Square Lake case.

Her computations are clearly labelled so that the markers can follow what she is attempting. Not all of the computations are correct, within her assumptions, but the direction is obvious. Her response merits a passing grade.

Time for Reflection

Now that we have analyzed three papers and you have compared your opinion of them to those in this book, it seems appropriate to call for a pause. In order to increase your learning, go back and read the responses of Candidates D and E. Check your previous assessment of their papers, and revise your grade as necessary. This revision process allows full use of the learning feedback loop created when we analyzed papers A, B, and C.

It requires some internal strength to go back to reading candidate responses D and E. But remember, you learn by doing, receiving feedback, redoing, and so forth. Why miss a first class opportunity to assess your grasp of what the markers are looking for. Is E better than D? If so, precisely why? Can you list the strengths and weaknesses of each? Is A better than D? If so, in what respects?

AN ANALYSIS OF CANDIDATE D's RESPONSE

General

Candidate D's response is worth roughly the same number of marks, or perhaps a few less, than Candidate B's. In most other respects the responses are quite different. Candidate D chose to avoid many quantitative aspects of the case. Whereas we labelled Candidate A the "technician," we could label Candidate D as a "generalist," perhaps, a "vague generalist."

Some Specifics

Let us try to list the deficiencies in Candidate D's response, thereby explaining why the paper was judged overall to be unacceptable. The candidate obviously failed to follow two steps that we have stressed:

1. "Size-up" the case on your initial reading. Is it *primarily* concerned with problem identification, or data analysis, or recommendations? Does it seem to favour a qualitative or a quantitative approach to identification and analysis? Does it give equal attention to all of these? Where is the direction: in the body of the case, or in the required? What are you being asked to do? This "sizing-up" is no different from real life, which requires you to clarify the terms of your engagement, to gather evidence, to assess it, and so on.

   If you do *not* take the time to evaluate your role and the situation that you face, recognize what you are doing to yourself. You are *gambling* that the markers will give points to the words in your response that apply to this case, and ignore the many irrelevancies that come from a shot-gun dumping of everything in your memory. You are a doctor who prescribes two aspirins to everybody who comes into your office. In short, you are *failing* to show the markers that you can assess the situation, synthesize the important parts, apply those parts of your knowledge that fit this particular case, evaluate alternatives, and so forth.

2. Prepare a budget that gives recognition to how you have sized up the case. What are the issues that are critical to the success or failure of the company? Where is there sufficient quantitative data to go into depth? Where are the irrelevancies and blind alleys? In brief, where are the marks?

   You can always revise your budget as you proceed as long as new, previously unappreciated, information becomes available. Without the budget you can spend many minutes chasing something that is worth few marks. It is too easy to lose sight of your target.

   Failure to take the above two steps has caused Candidate D to resort to a series of unwise moves:

1. There is no order to the response. It certainly does not begin with what is important, dig into these crucial issues, and provide supported recommendations. For example, the existing agreement is given little attention. Instead, there is a note to the marker: "If time permitted I would restate the income figures. . . ." Such a note may be worth a problem recognition mark but is not worth any analysis marks. If the analysis is crucial, find the time to do it.

2. Through reliance on a scattergun memory dump, the candidate has chosen to seek out problem recognition marks, *but little else*. He has not displayed depth of understanding or analysis in any area. Trivial income tax issues (". . . approximately $2,000 can be de-

ferred by using a Registered Retirement Savings Plan") are given prominence. This tells a marker that the candidate either does not know what is important, or has little income tax knowledge. Either way the comment is damaging when given treatment equal to that of important issues. If you must list the point, put it under the heading of "less important matters." Otherwise, you convey the impression that you cannot see the entire situation described in the case. You can see an arm here, and ear there, but not the entire body.

3. The candidate has wandered into areas he is unsure of. With all of the freedom allowed in a case there is no reason why you should go out of your way to display your ignorance of some technical subjects. For instance, the candidate apparently knows little about prospectuses. Securities laws are provincial; not federal. They are in special, separate Acts, not "according to Canada Corporation Act." The 90 day ruling pertains to filing a preliminary, not the final, prospectus with a Securities Commission and has nothing to do with the date of audited financial statements.

If you are unsure, then state that you will have to check into the matter. Cases are testing your judgment, not just your ability to memorize. Show your strengths and minimize your weaknesses.

4. In a vein similar to point 3 Candidate D should avoid expending his nervous energy by paraphrasing the case. Much of the first eight or so paragraphs could be said in a few sentences. The last section, "rough notes," would appear to have taken 20-30 minutes to write. As a minimum Candidate D should have divided the notes into two headings: "important"; and "less important." A better idea would have been to build the important points into a note to "yourself." See the "required" in this case; a note to yourself answered what was required!

Conclusion

Candidate D has not communicated with the markers. Rather than attempting to display a full range of knowledge, assessment, application, evaluation, and similar skills he has dropped the ball. He has a better idea than Candidate B about the purpose of case analysis, but both are deficient and show inadequate sense or readiness to practice their chosen profession.

The reality of practice is that clients will come to you in a confused state, or wanting particular accomplishments. You have to work with them in moving from problem recognition to suitable conclusions and recommendations. Knowledge regurgitation skill is a small part of being ready to practice.

Candidate D has not provided a clear trail for the markers. He may be a better judge of the role of accounting in this situation than both Candidate A and B. Inadequate reasoning in his response and the weaknesses previously mentioned caused his downfall. A generalist approach makes sense in some types of cases. Generally, though, in accounting cases some number crunching is allocated marks.

AN ANALYSIS OF CANDIDATE E's RESPONSE

General

Candidate E's response is the worst of the five. The paper shows a few vague ideas about the purpose of cases or learning methods that test application, analysis and similar skills. However, Candidate E may be the victim of bad advice. He appears to be following a cliché of "do a little of quantitative and qualitative." The result is a scattergun something like Candidate D, but with less effective communication. What is E saying? Often we can only guess. Where is E headed? Overall, the response does not make you, as a client, feel that you are "in good hands."

Some specifics

The response has many of the same weaknesses as have been indicated for the other candidates:

1. An incredible amount of time has been wasted on rough notes and cryptic comments. Instead of explaining a point clearly only once, the same point is raised directly or indirectly three or more times in a confused manner (e.g., audit fee). Candidate E must answer the "so what"? What is the significance of what he is trying to say?

2. The candidate obviously does not have a framework or understanding of the boundaries of accounting, auditing, and income tax. He does not seem to know what to look for on an *initial* reading of the case (e.g., crucial success and failure factors; important versus unimportant issues, etc.). The rough notes are a laundry list of past, present and future points, seemingly, in the eyes of the candidate, of equal importance.

3. Candidate E has either not sized-up the case and prepared the necessary time budget or is lacking skills necessary to be a chartered accountant. One line is particularly shocking: "Note: Assume that adjustments to financial statements will not materially affect the price."

   What was going through E's mind while making such a comment? Did he think that the purpose of the case was to test problem recognition, or recommendations, or what? The problem was given to him on-a-platter, or in a directed style. Hence, it is worth few marks. The recommendations are obvious once you do the computation. Again, few marks are available. If the computation was not thought to be relevant it should not have been attempted! In all, a marker can only shake her head and conclude "try again; same month next year."

Assumptions have to be logical and fit the context of the case. When you assume that the adjustments are not material you in effect assume away a large portion of the case. The chances of assuming away many marks are considerably lessened when you have made a serious attempt to size-up the case.

4. Markers do their best to try to figure out what a candidate is attempting. Candidate E's poor labelling of computations, especially the various "A" and "B" lettering, test a marker's patience. Candidate E should have spent a few seconds explaining the purpose of the computations in order to be eligible for logic and reasoning marks. Why risk misinterpretations?

Conclusion

Most of Candidate E's response looks like preliminary analysis, much of which should have taken place in his head during an initial reading of the case. He definitely must prepare more cases and receive more exposure to other than knowledge regurgitation questions. He might even need practice in making up his mind, identifying important issues, and in general, learning the skills that chartered accountants need. Candidate E also has some glaring knowledge deficiencies, such as in income tax. In total, he requires considerable improvement.

A SOLUTION TO SQUARE LAKE

The "solution" that follows has been reproduced with the kind permission of the Institutes/Ordre of Chartered Accountants in Canada. It is *one* solution and is *not* the only possible solution to the case. By their nature cases allow for different interpretations and assumptions. One correct answer does not exist!

Assume that you are a marker and mark the response that follows. This should help you in at least two ways:

1. You will better understand marking if you place yourself in the role of a marker. Learn to recognize important points.
2. You will be forced to read every word in the response and check it back to the case. This will help you recognize direction and key facts.

General

John Durie has been my client for several years and I believe I know him well enough to describe his motive in wanting to purchase Erkel Fabricating as ego-related—he wants to be a "big" businessman. He seems to have the management ability and experience to make the purchase work, but he does have a tendency to undertake things on the spur of the moment. For example, he has done no planning with respect to combining the operations of Erkel's company and his own in such matters as product lines, market outlets, personnel or physical assets.

Despite this lack of planning, combining the two firms might be beneficial. The acquisition may lead to a more efficient use of assets and, with Durie and Erkel each concentrating on his own area of expertise, to an improved market share. Also, the financing conditions laid down by Tri-Line Mortgages Ltd. may offset any planning problems. If the motive I ascribe to Durie is correct, there will be no urgency about finalizing the agreement which will give me sufficient time to perform the necessary work.

Professional Considerations

Representing Erkel as well as Durie (who asked me to undertake the investigation) would create a conflict of interest. I could not be objective, or appear objective, particularly since Erkel, during our telephone discussion, suggested the possibility of future business if he is satisfied with my conduct of this investigation. I'll have to write to Erkel to tell him that I cannot act on his behalf in this matter and that he should retain another accountant to look after his interests.

I have the necessary competence and proficiency to do the audit work requested in the draft agreement; to do it in the time available will not be easy. A week isn't really long enough for me to gain a knowledge of the business and to check out the reputations of Erkel and Tri-Line. The records are in poor condition and the lack of internal control and the time limitation will make it extremely difficult, if not impossible, for me to:
—establish the existence of the inventory—we weren't at the count;
—effect an accurate cut-off for all assets or to roll back the figures based on work that could now be done;
—confirm consignment inventories, accounts receivable and accounts payable;
—establish the cost of assets and their existence.
Auditing a five-year time span is very difficult, if not impossible. AB appears to have undertaken a review engagement, but when I consider the many departures from GAAP that exist, I'll have to consider

very carefully whether or not I can place any reliance on his work. In fact, I should probably check for signs that AB's work is sufficiently substandard to warrant bringing it to the attention of disciplinary authorities.

Based on this information, there is a strong possibility that I would have to give a qualified report. This would considerably lessen the report's value to Tri-Line and, in fact, might cause them to withdraw their financing. I doubt that a qualified report would justify the time and cost involved in an audit.

I must send an engagement letter to Durie setting out that I will undertake a purchase investigation for him, that he will be responsible for the fee and that Tri-Line is an interested third party. I will explain that any assistance to Erkel or any systems or control work will be done as a separate, post-reorganization assignment. And I must make it clear that under the present circumstances I cannot estimate the time that will be required to perform the investigation and that the fee will be based on actual time.

Since Tri-Line is a known third party, all work must be done according to GAAS and GAAP, or the inadequacies that prevent this pointed out. Because of the difficulties I foresee in conducting a complete audit, I must check to see if Tri-Line's requirements are flexible and if they would be satisfied with something less. Tri-Line want a comfort letter, but I must make sure that they understand that such a letter is not a substitute for an audit. Perhaps a comfort letter or an investigation into the actual existence of certain assets may be acceptable to them.

There are several alternatives that may be satisfactory to Tri-Line and I'll discuss these with them and the other parties to the agreement:

1. Change the effective date of the agreement to a later date to give me time to perform an audit. This would reduce some of the audit problems but a reserved audit opinion will still be necessary.
2. Change the investigation requirement to a review engagement rather than an audit. This would eliminate the necessity for a reserved audit opinion and unaudited statements would be available.
3. Perform a purchase investigation on a basis that mainly, or only, requires the confirmation of the existence of fixed assets; neither an audit opinion nor financial statements would be needed.

Since Tri-Line appears really only interested in asset coverage of its loan, I'll recommend number 3 on my list of alternatives. I must ensure that Durie, Erkel and Tri-Line all agree to and approve any changes to the agreement.

Evaluation of agreement

Before I can determine a price for Erkel Fabricating, I'll have to make a number of adjustments to their net income for the past five years in order to conform it with GAAP:

1. Consignment shipments have been included in sales revenue although the income from these sales is still unrealized, thus overstating income (see Schedule 2).
2. Income has also been overstated because royalty expense was not accrued in the year in which it was incurred (see Schedule 2).
3. The Scarpel agreement was improperly expensed. It should have been capitalized when it was implemented and amortized in the years following, so income was understated in 1973 and overstated in 1974 through 1977 (see Schedule 3).
4. Erkel charged depreciation on a capital cost allowance (CCA) basis rather than according to a GAAP policy, thus understating income. Depreciation expense must be calculated according to a GAAP policy, although the policy used for Erkel doesn't have to be the same as that used by Durie.

These adjustments will change their five-year net income to $132,920, so valuation of Part 1 of the price is $159,636 (see Schedule 5). The agreement terms limit the price to $126,284 (say $127,000).

The six-times multiplier seems reasonable considering the company has been operating for only five years and that earnings have been flat for the past three. Caution should be exercised in applying this multiplier to present earnings because they may not actually represent future earnings if the placing goods on a consignment basis policy is discontinued. This total earnings figure is also vulnerable to undisclosed liabilities that could reduce its value. The agreement should specifically detail this possibility.

Once we determine a value for Erkel Fabricating, I must do a careful assessment of its cash position to ensure that cash will be sufficient to satisfy the terms of the agreement and the combined firm's foreseeable needs. (Schedule 8 indicates a shortfall.) If 1978 earnings remain at the 1977 level, funds generated from current operations in the first six months added to the funds advanced by Tri-Line should be sufficient to satisfy the terms of the agreement. But will sufficient cash be available for additional needs such as the corporate reorganization, for contingencies, replacement of fixed assets (autos) and, perhaps, for the other investment opportunities Durie alluded to?

If the draft agreement is adopted, the existing financing arrangements and the known and possible needs for cash could create a real risk of defaulting on the mortgage.

Sufficient or supplementary funds may be available from sources other than Tri-Line, perhaps even at a lower cost than is being offered

by Tri-Line. Government grants or incentives may be available for re-
locating to the Square Lake area, or employees could be offered
equity. Erkel might take preference of shares for part of the consideration and/or a note for part or all the consideration. Banks often offer
competitive rates for short term financing. All of these sources should
be investigated before the agreement is signed.

   I must also take the following points into consideration:
1. Unless clear provisions exist in the agreement for establishing and
   operating transfer prices between the various parts of the organization, there could be a manipulation of Erkel's bonus. We could
   avoid this potential problem by putting Erkel on a straight salary,
   but this would probably affect his motivation. Better that Erkel
   have an equity position in Square Lake—to encourage positive
   motivation and reduce cash requirements. Unless Erkel is given
   equity in the parent company rather than in Square Lake the
   agreement should include a provision for a clear transfer pricing
   mechanism.
      Since Durie has doubts about Erkel's abilities, the agreement
   should also include a provision that would enable the company to
   terminate Erkel's management contract without penalty; for example, five years' salary.
2. Careful planning is required for the transition period. The physical
   transfer of assets will be difficult and production will be disrupted.
   And employees may not want to move to the new location. The
   company must carefully consider developing a comprehensive
   scheme of employee benefits and perhaps tie it in with the move. It
   must also be aware that it is probably vulnerable to potential union
   activities.
3. Management control systems must be improved. A standard cost
   system should be considered; a reporting system by segment
   seems desirable; asset control systems require improvement and
   good budgeting principles should be introduced, perhaps with
   variance analysis and follow-up as key elements.

Tax Considerations
If Erkel sells shares in his business, he will be liable for tax on capital
gains. Taking the sale price per the agreement as $125,000 his ad-
justed cost base is $30,000 and his capital gain would be $95,000. He
would be liable for tax on half of this in the year of disposition. He
could, however, claim a reserve for the 40% balance receivable or
purchase an income averaging annuity to defer taxes.
   If Erkel sold the assets of Erkel Fabricating instead of shares,
the fair market value minus the tax amount of assets disposed of

would give rise to taxable income for Erkel Fabricating Ltd. For land, there would be a taxable capital gain of $60,000 − $46,250 =$13,750 × ½ = $6,875; for building, a terminal loss of $45,000 − $57,036 = $12,036; for equipment, a recapture of $50,000 − $24,598 = $25,402; and, for automotive equipment, a recapture of $10,000 − $9,226 = $774. For the Scarpel agreement, the capital gain would be $26,000 less the original $4,500 cost or $21,500 of which half ($10,750) would be taxable. The CCA recapture would be $4,500 less $2,000 or $2,500, assuming that tax returns can be amended. Otherwise it would be $4,500. The total tax to Erkel Fabricating Ltd. would be $34,265 × 25% or $8,566.

If Durie Manufacturing Ltd. buys Erkel Fabricating shares, this $8,566 tax can be totally eliminated by making proper elections under Section 85(1) in the year in which transfer of manufacturing assets is made from Erkel to Square Lake Manufacturing. To allow election under 85(1) Square Lake would have to issue $63,926 of preferred shares as part of the considerations given for assets received, i.e., the otherwise taxable income excluding the terminal loss on the buildings. Thus, when Square Lake buys back its preferred shares, Erkel Fabricating will realize a capital gain (therefore converting CCA recapture into capital gain). This discussion ignores the problem of splitting assets between marketing and manufacturing (under the present agreement), since the roll-over mechanism is similar (sub to parent) and the total tax amount (TTA) is the same either way. The same comments apply to the transfer of assets from Durie Manufacturing to Square Lake Manufacturing. I cannot establish precisely the tax payable if proper elections are not made since the adjusted cost base (ACB) of land sold is unknown. An estimate of potential capital gain or recapture can be made, working backwards for the latter from the CCA taken to date:

	Tax Cost	FMV	Capital Gain or Recapture
Land (depending on ACB)	38,000	100,000	very significant
Depreciable assets 224,000			
(NBV) less timing difference			
of 84,000 (21,112 × 4)	140,000	210,000	70,000 × 25% = $17,500 (recapture)

A Section 22 election (Form T2022) should be made for accounts receivable purchased by Durie from Erkel, to protect against possible future loss of receivables transferred.

The tax department should be consulted about the plan to transfer, retroactively in effect, assets as at January 1, 1978. While the companies will be all associated and it is unlikely the department will object, notifying it of the transfers and rearrangements is still necessary, in particular:

— The transfer of inventory from Erkel and Durie to the new company. Book value is to be used and there is a potential tax on the sale of inventory at fair market value.

— Any transfer of fixed assets from Erkel and Durie to the new company and Erkel to Durie (under the existing agreement). Such transfers would be handled under the roll-over provisions (i.e., transfers assumed to be at transferor's UCC, etc.), but as asset classes are being split up in some cases and moved in various directions, care must be taken in the asset allocation calculations (and perhaps the department's concurrence obtained). This would not be a problem if assets are not transferred (some other alternative selected).

— The wind-up of Erkel would have tax consequences, such as the remaining unclaimed eligible capital expenditure will be available for deduction by the parent Durie Manufacturing even though the goodwill is apparently not being sold by Erkel Fabricating.

Alternative Ways of Effecting the Combination

Durie should consider a number of alternative ways of effecting the combination before taking action on the engagement.

1. Durie could buy the assets of Erkel Fabricating instead of the shares.
2. Durie could buy shares of Erkel Fabricating and use Erkel as the operating company, thus avoiding the need to create SLM.
3. Durie could opt for internal growth by buying selected assets from suppliers or others and hiring staff.

On balance, purchasing the assets of Erkel Fabricating and using Durie Manufacturing as the operating company would appear to be the most beneficial alternative with the following advantages:

— Potential problems in Erkel Fabricating, such as undisclosed liabilities or legal problems, are left there.

— The tax costs triggered by selling assets are Erkel's responsibility.

— Costs to wind up Erkel are avoided.

— The remuneration problem with respect to transfer prices is avoided.

— Costs of operating more than one entity are avoided.

— The company has a higher UCC base for assets acquired.

This alternative will depend on whether Erkel is willing to sell assets rather than shares. If he is willing to take back shares (say preferred shares), the cash outlay would be minimized. Durie could then offer Frank Erkel an employment contract to run the manufacturing operations of Durie Manufacturing.

Conclusion

As can be seen in Schedule 5, the trend in Erkel's adjusted net income is not exciting. Real growth is modest; the apparent growth resulted from using CCA instead of accounting depreciation. The proposed agreement poses many problems—the earnings trend is flat, a tight cash position would result, and an audit to determine values would be difficult. I will recommend the purchase of operating assets. Provided Tri-Line financing is still needed, I will recommend that I perform a purchase investigation of these assets on behalf of Durie and Tri-Line. The agreement should be modified accordingly. I will make these recommendations, but will listen carefully to Durie and Erkel at our next meeting and accept whatever deal they finally arrive at, then offer whatever advice I can on that deal.

SCHEDULE 1
Consignments

	1973	1974	1975	1976	1977
1. Sales as a % of cost	156.1	166.4	170.6	175.8	174.2
2. Consignment A/R @ Y/E	$7,778	$10,808	$14,171	$15,810	$25,478
3. Consignment A/R ÷ (1) = average cost of consign. A/R	4,983	6,495	8,307	8,993	14,626
4. CM in consignment A/R	2,795	4,313	5,864	6,817	10,852
5. Unrealized NI & asset overstatement net of 25% tax (75%)	2,096	3,235	4,398	5,113	8,139
6. Less previous year outstanding	φ				
7. Overstatement of NI	$(2,096)	$(1,139)	$(1,163)	$ (715)	$(3,026)

SCHEDULE 2
Accrual of Royalty

	1973	1974	1975	1976	1977
1. Annual sales subject to royalty	$12,000	$15,000	$18,000	$21,000	$24,000
2. Royalty @ 15%	1,800	2,250	2,700	3,150	3,600
3. Less payment in previous year	φ	(450)	(450)	(450)	(450)
4. Before Tax NI effect	(1,800)	(450)	(450)	(450)	(450)
5. Overstatement of NI after tax (25%)	$(1,350)	$ (338)	$ (338)	$ (338)	$ (338)

SCHEDULE 3

Capitalization of Scarpel Agreement

Nine years @ cost of $4,500 previously expensed

Straight line amortization = $500

1973 NI understatement ($4,500 − $500) × .75 = $3,000

1974 − 81 NI overstatement $500 × .75 = $375

SCHEDULE 4

Erkel's CCA to GAAP

	1973	1974	1975	1976	1977
Total depreciation expense (given)	$11,280	$12,500	$13,780	$15,340	$16,070
CCA used as expense	21,260	49,110	41,060	39,531	20,298
Understatement of NI	$ 9,980	$36,610	$27,280	$24,191	$ 4,228
Overstatement of NI by deferred tax effect @ 25%	$(2,495)	$(9,152)	$(6,820)	$(6,048)	$(1,057)

SCHEDULE 5

Adjusted Net Income of Erkel

	1973	1974	1975	1976	1977	Total
Reported NI of Erkel	$(1,275)	$ 1,559	$14,349	$17,322	$33,589	$ 65,544
Accounting adjustments:						
(a) consignments-overstate NI	(2,096)	(1,139)	(1,163)	(715)	(3,026)	
(b) accrual of royalty-overstate NI	(1,350)	(338)	(338)	(338)	(338)	
(c) capitalization of Scarpel-under (over)	3,000	(375)	(375)	(375)	(375)	
(d) Erkel's CCA to GAAP-understate NI	9,980	36,610	27,280	24,191	4,228	
(e) deferred tax effect-overstate NI	(2,495)	(9,152)	(6,820)	(6,048)	(1,057)	
Adjusted net income	$ 5,764	$27,165	$32,933	$34,037	$33,021	$132,920

Calculation of Part 1 of price determination:

6 times average earnings: $\dfrac{\$132,920}{5} \times 6 =$ $159,504

3 times average increase from 1975-77

$33,021 − $32,933 = $88 ÷ 2 = $44 × 3 = 132

Valuation of price determination under Part 1 $159,636

SCHEDULE 6

Limitation

Working capital $114,283 − $68,493		$ 45,790
Corrections re: NI adjustments affecting		
W/C − consignments		(10,852)
− royalty accrual		(3,600)
		31,338
Fixed assets	$165,000	
Scarpel agreement	27,337	192,337
Non-current liabilities (current, non-current distinction		
compensate to nil effect)		(103,405)
Fair value − as defined		$120,270

105% thereof = $126,284

Selling price lower of: $159,636 (earnings) or $126,284 (fair value of net assets) = $126,284.

SCHEDULE 7
Value of Scarpel Agreement

	1977	1978	1979	1980	1981
1. Royalty annual sales	$24,000	$27,000	$30,000	$33,000	$36,000
2. Annual cash flow (50% gross margin)		13,500	15,000	16,500	18,000
3. Less royalty, paid in following period (15% of sales)		(3,600)	(4,050)	(4,500)	(4,950)
4. Net cash flow		9,900	10,950	12,000	13,050
5. Tax payment (on accrual basis) .		(2,362)	(2,625)	(2,887)	(3,150)
6. Net cash flow after tax		$ 7,538	$ 8,325	$ 9,113	$ 9,900
Present value at 10%		$ 6,860	$ 6,910	$ 6,835	$ 6,732
		(.91)	(.83)	(.75)	(.68)

$$= \underline{\$27,337}$$

SCHEDULE 8

Estimation of Cash Position in Draft Agreement

(a) Fair value of assets transferred (Schedule A #8)

	Durie	Erkel
Per schedule A #10	$310,000	$165,000
Office and marketing assets retained in Durie		
(Schedule E #11) 12% (210,000) excluding land	25,200	
10% (105,000)		10,500
Transferred to Square Lake	$284,800	$154,500
80% thereof	227,800	123,600
		$351,400

$351,400

(b) Advance of funds on 30-4-78 (Schedule A #8)

Lesser of 80% of FV assets transferred $346,268

or 175% of pro forma Durie after agreement fulfilled.

Purchase method means consol equity on 1-1-78 is equal to parent's (Durie)

equity 31-12-77 – $197,868 × 175% ....

Amount to be advanced $346,268

(c) Cash required 1-7-78:

(i) Owing by Erkel to shareholder (Schedule A #2) 30-6-78 .... $ 35,000

(ii) Pay-off of mortgage and notes (Schedule A #9) 30-4-78

	Principal 31-12-77	Accrued Interest 31-12-77	Approximate Interest Penalty 4 Month	3 Month	
Durie current – non-current	130,000	5,200	*3,166	2,825	= $141,191
Erkel current – non-current	86,116		*2,440	1,830	= 90,386

Erkel current – non-
current   12,883   * 494   —   = 13,377
                                                                                                                                  $244,954

*(130,000 − 11.250) × 8% × $^{4}/_{12}$ = 3,166
  86,116 × 8$^{1}/_{2}$% × $^{4}/_{12}$ = 2,440
  12,883 ×11$^{1}/_{2}$% × $^{4}/_{12}$ = 494

(iii) 60% of selling price of Erkel (.60) ($126,284) .... $ 75,770

(iv) Capital for new company $80,000 (Schedule A #3) .... offset
(v) First mortgage payment on July 1, 1978 (Schedule A #8)
   Funds advanced $346,268 ÷ 120 .... $2,886
   Interest accrued 1-5-78 to 1-7-78
   ($346,268) (9$^{7}/_{8}$%) ($^{2}/_{12}$) 5,699
                                                                        $ 8,585
Total required $364,309
Less advance 346,268
Shortfall to July 1, 1978 .... $ 18,041

(d) Estimated cash from operations to 1-7-78
   Durie $48,152 Reported NI + $24,656 depreciation + $6,084 (Df Tx) = $ 78,892
   Erkel $33,021 Adj. NI + $16,070 depreciation + $1,674 (GW)
   + $1,057 (Df Tx) .... = 51,822
                                                                        $130,714

                                                           50%   = $65,357
                                                                    to 1-7-78

IMPROVING THYSELF

If you disagree with the order of marking of the five responses, you should read the five responses and analyses again and again until you can follow what we are saying. Make a list of the errors that were made by the candidates and avoid them in your response to future practice cases. Some people may tell you to "memory dump" your way through cases; but this is not a wise strategy. Some cases and marking guides may allow memory "dumpers" to pass; other cases and guides will catch such people and give them failing grades.

If you agree with the ordering and marking of the five responses, yet feel that you need more practice, where do you head from here? Later chapters of this book contain cases that can be used for practice. But before you attempt them you might want to use the Square Lake case to sharpen your reading and comprehension skills.

The point of the following exercise is to improve your recognition of *direction* as well as your ability to *size-up* a case. You may approach this exercise in one of two ways:

1. Easy way: Read the case "solution" in the previous section thoroughly, then do not refer to it until you have completed the exercise.

2. Harder way: Do not read the "solution" *again*, even if you only skimmed it while reading this chapter.

The exercise involves analyzing *each* sentence in *each* paragraph and stating its *significance*. Start with the first sentence of the first paragraph and slowly work through the case. By *significance* we mean listing the relevance and importance to you. In some sentences you should pick out key words. Other sentences may be unimportant; they may merely introduce or connect thoughts.

Although you may think that this exercise is useless or insulting, it is anything but that for most candiates. We could have accused all five of Candidates A to E of not reading carefully. Many words have precise meanings and must be interpreted as intended in order to gain maximum marks.

Let us now refer to the Square Lake case. What is the most important word in the first paragraph? Full marks if you said "priorities." The word is giving you direction; it tells you that marks are awarded for a listing of important matters.

Read the second paragraph; what should be noted in your mind? Durie: energetic; ambitious; apparently long time, successful client who tended "to act first and ask for advice later."

Proceed to the third paragraph. After you have read only as far as the *third* paragraph your mind should be focused in large part on a merger-acquisition channel. You should start to *anticipate* particular kinds of accounting, auditing and income tax problems that arise when companies are "acquired." Pause for a few seconds and guess what may lie ahead. This will help you make crucial assumptions when information that you think should exist turns out to be "missing."

Anticipation is one characteristic that separates good from poor candidates. A good candidate will have figured out, in *advance* of writing the Uniform Final Examinations, the types of situations that make good cases and have designed analytical frameworks for each type. As she reads the case for the first time, a good candidate will be fitting key words and phrases into the framework. By the time she completes the first reading her mind will be exploding with ideas. She must then discipline herself to set a budget for the remaining time available, based on "priorities."

What does a poor candidate do? Refer to the responses provided by Candidates B, D and E on the previous pages. Look at the rough notes that D and E made. They had not anticipated an obvious setting for an accounting case! Where were their priorities?

The third paragraph has many key words and phrases: "buy Erkel Fabricating"; "outside help"; "reorganize and streamline"; "joint operation"; "go public some day"; as well as warnings such as "Frank and I have worked out." Notice the past tense "worked." Be on guard.

Proceed to the fourth paragraph, then the fifth, and so forth. When you have finished the entire case read the "solution" and check to see how well you have picked up the problems and flavour of the case. This exercise may be painful, but many students have found it extremely helpful in getting them out of a rut in their case writing.

Track down every item in the "solution" to some word or phrase in the case. A thorough reading pays off.

SUMMARY

Cases are used on the Uniform Final Examinations of the Ordre and Institutes of Chartered Accountants in Canada to test a candidate's cognitive "skills." Some of these skills are: comprehension; analysis; assessment; evaluation; synthesis; knowledge; and application. Those who have been exposed only to questions that test knowledge memorization have to begin to learn the other skills. These other "skills" are not just a different way of regurgitating knowledge. You must work hard at applying your knowledge, assessing a situation, and recommending sound solutions.

You can try to shorten your preparation for the final examinations by following unsound advice, and by "dumping knowledge" whether it fits a situation or not. However, this approach is obvious to a qualified marker. You may get lucky and pass. Then again, you might fail. The safest approach is to work as hard at doing cases, and some multi-subject questions, as you did with knowledge regurgitation questions. The choice is yours.

CHAPTER SEVEN

Unsolved Comprehensive Case I

INTRODUCTION

Three unsolved comprehensive cases are provided in this and the following two chapters. All are four hour cases. You are entitled to have a calculator and table of present values (and perhaps other tables) with you when you write the professional examinations. Solutions to these three cases are available from McGraw-Hill Ryerson Ltd., but only to university instructors and firms that are conducting in-house courses. If you are not using this book as part of a course you should try to compare responses to the three cases with others who have completed them, and discuss differences with competent accountants. Remember the purpose of these three cases is not to encourage you to regurgitate knowledge.

FLORIDA-BEECHY LIMITED

Florida-Beechy Limited (FBL) was incorporated under federal legislation many years ago. In 19x1 the company sold convertible preferred shares to the public. FBL has now (January 19x7) made an offer to buy back these shares, none of which has been converted, and to "go private." The offer is to be made by the company, not by the common shareholders. A bank has agreed to loan 40 percent of the funds necessary to repurchase the preferred shares, the owners of FBL will provide 10 percent in exchange for a 10 year, 12 percent debenture and the remainder (50 percent) will come from some of the proceeds on the expected sale of the subsidiary, Taylor Enterprises Limited (TEL).

When the transactions to "go private" and sell TEL have been completed the owners of FBL intend to sell their common shares to Philip Limited (PL), a publicly-owned, federally-incorporated company listed on a major stock exchange. As a public accountant, you have audited the accounts of PL for many years and have now been hired to conduct a purchase investigation of FBL. Your specific terms of reference for this investigation are to comment "on the fairness of FBL's audited financial statements for the year ended December 31, 19x6, which were audited by another public accountant, and to bring to the attention of the management of PL 'any matter which comes to your notice which may indicate that the price to be paid for all of the common shares of Florida-Beechy Limited may or may not represent fair value of the enterprise.' "

You have also been hired to conduct a second engagement of advising PL as to the suitability of the accounting system of FBL for management's needs and concerning the appropriateness of the financial accounting principles used by FBL in statements which will be consolidated with PL. If better principles or systems exist they should be recommended by you.

The purchase of FBL by PL will be retroactive to January 1, 19x7 and is to be based on the unconsolidated balance sheet of FBL after giving pro forma adjustment to:

1. The redemption premium of $4 per share being paid to the convertible preferred shareholders; and
2. The difference between the investment in TEL as shown by FBL's financial statements and the selling price received. (FBL has orally been offered $2,800,000 for TEL; its estimated value at the date capital gains tax was introduced in the country was $1,600,000; FBL originally paid $1,000,000 for TEL.)

Your purchase investigation engagement requires that attention be given to the "fairness" of the year end figures for 19x6 as well as to any other matter which affects the present and future worth of FBL and reflects on the wisdom of acquiring FBL.

You and your staff have assembled the information on the following schedules and are now proceeding to write two separate reports, one for each engagement. You have received full cooperation from officers and employees of FBL.

Required:
Assume the role of the public accountant and prepare the two reports requested by management of PL.

Note:

$$\frac{\text{Present Value of}}{\text{Capital Cost Allowance}} = \frac{\text{Cost of Asset} \times \text{Income Tax Rate} \times \text{Capital Cost Allowance Rate}}{\text{Cost of Capital} + \text{Capital Cost Allowance Rate}}$$

SCHEDULE 1

Consolidated Financial Data for FBL
Consolidated Balance Sheets

As of December 31

	19x6	19x5	19x4
	(in thousands of dollars)		
Current assets:			
Cash	$ 80	$ 5	$ 10
Marketable securities (market value $570,000)	562	—	—
Accounts and rentals receivable	199	175	155
Prepaid expenses and other	32	31	26
	873	211	191
Land, under development	5,275	6,989	9,570
Construction in progress, at cost	7,490	8,984	5,860
Land, building and equipment, at cost	7,820	7,240	6,990
Less accumulated depreciation	2,230	1,638	1,005
	5,590	5,602	5,985
Deferred charges	345	385	425
Investment in joint venture:			
Equipment and working capital	2,960	—	—
Construction in progress	338	—	—
	3,298		
Rental properties	10,955	9,200	9,200
Less accumulated depreciation	555	400	280
	10,400	8,800	8,920
	$33,271	$30,971	$30,951
Current liabilities:			
Bank loan payable	$ 5	$ 100	$ 700
Accounts payable	420	390	420
Income tax payable	320	60	200
Other	10	15	20
	755	565	1,340
Unearned revenue—billings on uncompleted contracts	7,780	9,110	7,990
Debt payable	11,250	9,455	9,760
Deferred income tax	320	280	250
Shareholders' equity:			
Common shares—authorized and issued	5,000	5,000	5,000
Convertible preferred shares— authorized and issued 50,000 shares	5,000	5,000	5,000
Contributed surplus	500	500	500
Retained earnings	2,666	1,061	1,111
	13,166	11,561	11,611
	$33,271	$30,971	$30,951

SCHEDULE 1 (cont'd)

Consolidated Income and Retained Earnings Statements

	Year ended December 31		
	19x6	19x5	19x4
	(in thousands of dollars		
Income Statement:			
Construction revenue	$18,465	$13,850	$ 8,590
Construction costs	14,280	11,575	6,085
Gross profit	4,185	2,275	2,505
Operating income from rental properties	145	90	135
	4,330	2,365	2,640
Expenses	920	765	725
Income before income tax and extraordinary item	3,410	1,600	1,915
Income tax	1,600	750	850
	1,810	850	965
Extraordinary item	895	—	310
Net income	$ 2,705	$ 850	$ 1,275
Retained Earnings Statement:			
Opening balance	$ 1,061	$ 1,111	$ 736
Net income	2,705	850	1,275
	3,766	1,961	2,011
Dividends—common	500	300	300
—preferred	600	600	600
	1,100	900	900
Closing balance	$ 2,666	$ 1,061	$ 1,111

SCHEDULE 2

Financial Data for TEL
Balance Sheets

	As of December 31		
	19x6	19x5	19x4
	(in thousands of dollars)		
Current assets:			
Cash	$ 72	$ 2	$ 4
Marketable securities (market value $570,000)	562	—	—
Rentals and accounts receivable	84	78	72
Prepaid supplies and expenses	14	12	10
	732	92	86

Fixed assets:			
Rental properties, at cost	10,955	9,200	9,200
Less accumulated depreciation	555	400	280
	10,400	8,800	8,920
Deferred charges	60	60	60
	$11,192	$ 8,952	$ 9,066
Current liabilities:			
Bank loan payable	$ —	$ 97	$ 259
Accounts payable and accruals	25	22	20
Income tax payable	12	8	10
Other liabilities	6	10	12
	43	137	301
Deferred income tax	1,040	600	350
Debt payable	9,334	7,510	7,750
Shareholders' equity:			
Common shares—authorized and			
issued 100,000 shares	200	200	200
Retained earnings	575	505	465
	775	705	665
	$11,192	$ 8,952	$ 9,066

SCHEDULE 2

Financial Data for TEL
Income and Retained Earnings Statements

	Year ended December 31		
	19x6	19x5	19x4
	(in thousands of dollars)		
Income Statement:			
Revenue	$ 1,390	$ 1,220	$ 1,195
Costs:			
Maintenance, wages and other	140	80	70
Depreciation	155	120	95
Interest	950	930	895
	1,245	1,130	1,060
Income before income tax and			
extraordinary item	145	90	135
Income tax	65	40	60
Income before extraordinary item	80	50	75
Gain on sale of property	—	—	310
Net income	$ 80	$ 50	$ 385
Retained Earnings Statement:			
Opening balance	$ 505	$ 465	$ 90
Net income	80	50	385
	585	515	475
Dividends	10	10	10
Closing balance	$ 575	$ 505	$ 465

SCHEDULE 3
Nature of FBL, TEL, and PL

1. FBL: (a) buys raw, usually farm, land, (b) develops and subdivides it, (c) sells some lots and (d) builds houses, apartment buildings and offices or factories on other lots.
2. TEL has always operated as a real estate management company, buying apartment buildings or office buildings from FBL and leasing them. Occasionally it sells an apartment or office building to third parties.
3. PL is a conglomerate with investments in many types of businesses in Canada.
4. FBL has a large inventory of undeveloped land, including farm land. Sometimes five or more years is needed between the date of purchase of land and the building of homes. This is because the population of the nearby city or town must increase and zoning and utilities must be obtained for subdivisions.
5. FBL will enter joint venture arrangements with other contractors on large construction jobs.

SCHEDULE 4
Review of Financial Data Affecting FBL

1. Your staff was able to review the working papers prepared by the auditor of FBL for the 19x6 financial year. The staff made notes of the following as they reviewed these files:
   a. Many of the parcels of property shown on the balance sheet as "Land, under development" are heavily financed by short term debt (of two or three years' duration). The audit procedures applied in verifying this account consisted of two steps: (i) agreeing the carrying value on the books to invoices or last year's working papers or other computations which allocated annual costs, and (ii) checking legal title against documents maintained by the client.
   b. FBL capitalizes interest charges on the debt incurred to acquire land and also capitalizes property taxes. Both are charged to "Land, under development" until the date of sale of the property.
   c. Transfers of property from FBL to TEL are not documented by FBL and occur whenever the president of FBL says that they are to occur. The bookkeeper makes entries on the books of each at whatever price is mentioned by the president.
   d. Similarly, some transfers of assets between FBL and third parties are not documented anywhere and the only evidence is

cheque receipts or payments and transfers of title of mortgages and property.

e. In 19x6 interest charges of $400,000 on general debt of FBL was apportioned to parcels of land under development on the basis of their carrying values, and capitalized in the accounts.

f. FBL acts as a general contractor in building office and apartment buildings for other real estate holding companies. It subcontracts some of the specialized work on these buildings. Most contracts call for FBL to repair any deficiencies for a period up to one year after the building is declared open by an independent architect. FBL does not accrue for these repair costs; the auditor kept track of them to ascertain whether any trends were developing:

Year Repair Costs Charged To Income	Year in Which Revenue Was Recognized	Amount (excluding sums paid by sub-contractors)
19x6	19x5	$185,500
19x5	19x4	151,000
19x4	19x3	120,550
19x3	19x2	98,600

g. FBL applies the completed contract basis of recognizing revenue. Contracts in progress at the end of 19x6 and 19x5 were:

19x6:

Contract No.	Costs Incurred To Date	Expected Future Costs as of December 31, 19x6	Estimated Revenue From Contract
6-009	$2,405,000	$ 600,000	$3,255,000
6-012	1,958,000	1,000,000	3,450,000
6-014	1,750,000	1,850,000	3,400,000
6-015	1,377,000	1,500,000	2,500,000
	$7,490,000		

19x5:

Contract No.	Costs Incurred To Date	Expected Future Costs as of December 31, 19x5	Actual Costs Incurred In 19x6 To Complete Contract	Estimated Revenue From Contract
5-006	$2,556,000	$ 500,000	$ 570,000	$3,200,000
5-008	1,766,800	640,000	506,000	2,000,000
5-009	920,000	1,000,000	768,000	1,000,000
5-011	844,000	2,000,000	1,890,000	3,000,000
4-017	2,897,400	200,000	165,000	3,400,000

The auditors apparently did not concern themselves with revenue recognition and merely photocopied schedules prepared by the company. Some minor checking of invoices to cost sheets occurred on a job-by-job basis.

h. For income tax purposes FBL did not defer revenue held back from it by architects and new building owners but it accrued holdbacks to subcontractors as expenses. In recent years these amounts at the year end were:

Year End	Revenue	Costs (re subcontractor holdbacks)
19x6	$2,860,000	$976,000
19x5	2,450,000	750,000
19x4	1,990,000	664,500

i. Contract 6-016 was commenced in 19x6 and was in progress at December 31, 19x6. FBL is a 40 percent joint venture contractor on job 6-016; the other 60 percent contractor uses the percentage of completion method of revenue recognition. At December 31, 19x6 $845,000 of costs had been incurred, another $6,000,000 was expected and the total contract was for $7,500,000. Both of the contractors are jointly and severally liable for $5,000,000 in connection with performance guarantees on job 6-016.

2. Your staff attempted to gather evidence of the present worth of the assets included in the "Land, under development" account. Here is what they were able to learn:

		Appraisal Data	
Description	Book Value December 31, 19x6	Date Appraised	Amount of Appraisal
Parcel 2-02	$ 640,000	July 19x5	$650,000
2-07	720,000	Oct. 19x6	700,000
3-01	510,000	Nov. 19x6	400,000
4-02	890,000	Dec. 19x5	950,000
4-04	255,000	Dec. 19x5	280,000
5-01	85,000	—	
5-04	390,000	Dec. 19x5	450,000
6-01	770,000	Dec. 19x6	765,000
6-02	490,000	—	
6-03	525,000	—	
	$5,275,000		

3. Deferred charges include the following as of December 31, 19x6:

Severance pay to three foremen who were released after a dispute (Being amortized over five years)	$160,000
Discounts allowed on finance contracts (Being amortized over life of debt)	125,000
	285,000
Deferred charges of TEL	60,000
	$345,000

4. The bookkeeper of FBL had a policy of charging 90 percent of the depreciation on building and equipment to "construction in progress."

SCHEDULE 5

Review of Financial Data Affecting TEL

1. Your staff obtained the following information from the other auditors' working papers.
   a. Rental records for TEL were not complete and the audit staff had trouble tracing from rental agreements back to cash receipts, and vice versa. The audit staff apparently gave up the reconciliation, but the working papers called for a letter to management recommending changes in the system.
   b. TEL capitalizes all interest and pre-opening costs into its real estate asset account. A building is regarded as "open" only when 50 percent or more of the total rentals are being received by TEL. Once declared "open," interest, property taxes, janitor services, and so forth are expensed instead of capitalized.
   c. Depreciation is recorded for accounting purposes on an annuity basis at 5 percent over 40 years on all real estate rental property. Maximum rates are used for income tax reporting.
   d. The other auditors did not check ownership of the assets, but relied upon cash receipts records to signify that TEL owned the property.
2. Your staff learned that the offer to purchase TEL is not yet in writing and has not been accepted by the management of FBL. Apparently TEL is being sold mainly to obtain funds to "go private" and FBL must be "private" or PL does not wish to buy FBL.
3. The bookkeeper of TEL prepared a listing of rental contracts on property owned by the company. This showed the following:

	Book Value December 31, 19x6 (Land & Building)	*Rental Revenues*	
		Lease Expiry Dates (Grouped by expiry date)*	Annual Rental*** Over Lease Period (based on 19x6 rates)
Building			
#101	$ 4,050,000	19x24	$420,000
		19x19**	100,000
		19x14**	80,000
#104	2,960,000	19x25	300,000
		19x20**	100,000
#106	1,690,000	19x25	150,000
		19x20**	60,000
		19x15**	30,000
#107	980,000	19x16**	80,000
		19x11**	40,000
		19x8**	20,000
#108	720,000	19x8**	50,000
		19x7**	20,000
	$10,400,000		

4. Each building is financed by debt to varying degrees; in all cases the debtholder does not have any other guarantee than the security of the specific asset—land and building. At December 31, 19x6 outstanding debt, by building, was:

			Debt	
Building	Principal Amount Outstanding	Interest Rate	Annual Cash Payment Required (Principal and Interest)	Expiry Date of Debt Instrument
#101	$2,668,000	12%	$280,000	19x28
	1,024,000	15%	145,000	19x23
#104	2,092,000	12½%	225,000	19x29
	643,000	15%	87,000	19x24
#106	1,321,000	13%	126,000	19x29
#107	902,000	13%	90,000	19x36
#108	684,000	13%	70,000	19x36
	$9,334,000			

* Office buildings tend to be leased for five, ten or twenty year periods and all leases expiring in a year are grouped in this table. Apartment buildings are usually leased on one or two year bases.

** Lessee has the right to renew at same rate plus an allowance for inflation set by the lessor.

*** Buildings #101, 104, 106 and 107 are fully rented; vacancies existed in 108 at December 31, 19x6 but all apartments are expected to be rented shortly.

5. Your staff was able to obtain, and roughly verify from past records, annual maintenance and other costs (excluding depreciation and mortgage interest payments) for each building. Inflation is expected to average five percent per annum over the next 10-20 years. Approximately 80 percent of the undernoted cost of buildings #101, 104, and 106 are recovered from tenants under terms of leases; only 60 percent of building #107's annual cost is recovered from tenants; none of building #108's costs can be recovered.

Building #	Annual Costs—19x6
101	$200,000
104	150,000
106	90,000
107	60,000
108	50,000

6. Your staff has been able to assure itself that all five buildings are in good locations and have been well maintained. In discussions with real estate appraisers you gained the definite understanding that TEL would have no difficulty leasing its buildings when the current leases expire. Most appraisers felt that renewals of leases would occur at yields on investment which would be only slightly less than those currently being received.

7. All of TEL's agreements with lessees who are leasing for periods in excess of five years contain escalation clauses for their share of annual maintenance and other cost increases. Annual rental rates are fixed for five years and then adjusted for the next five year period to cover expected average annual costs over that next five year period.

8. The capital cost position for income tax purposes is as follows for TEL's five buildings:

Building	Undepreciated Capital Cost December 31, 19x6	Land Carrying Value December 31, 19x6
#101	$2,624,400	$200,000
#104	2,223,450	200,000
#106	1,166,400	150,000
#107	828,000	100,000
#108	571,500	100,000

All five buildings are limited to a maximum 10 percent rate on the diminished balance.

9. The deferred charges account represents incorporation charges

and other expenditures incurred prior to "opening" the company's first "rental property."
10. TEL has agreed to acquire an office building which FBL is constructing and will complete by mid 19x7. TEL will pay FBL $500,000 and assume a first mortgage of approximately $2,000,000.
11. In 19x6 FBL sold its office building and moved into rented premises which it constructed. A gain on sale of $895,000 was credited to extraordinary income.

SCHEDULE 6

Accounting System of FBL

Your staff reviewed the accounting system employed by FBL and learned the following:
1. The bookkeeper maintains a separate ledger account for each separate parcel of land, building under construction, joint venture, and so forth. Costs which are common to more than one account are allocated on different bases as judged appropriate by the bookkeeper. For example, a piece of raw or undeveloped farm land may be split into approved subdivisions, and total cost is allocated to each subdivision.
2. Separate ledger accounts are maintained for each house that is being constructed. Usually a subdivision includes anywhere from 15 to 60 houses, and construction occurs over the span of six months to one year or more. The bookkeeper allocates costs of lumber, concrete, etc. (which is ordered for several houses at a time) to each on an equal basis unless evidence exists that some other method makes sense. Carpenters and other tradesmen are asked to keep track of which house they are constructing so that labour and subcontract work may be charged to each house.
3. For purposes of recognizing revenue each subdivision is treated as a job and all houses must be completed before revenue is recorded.
4. A junior bookkeeper handles payroll and accounts payable. Foremen are in charge of each job under construction and it is a foreman's responsibility to keep track of hours for each employee, and to initial invoices for receipt of goods and price.
5. On large jobs the engineering department maintains its own cost records. There is no attempt to reconcile these with accounting department figures.
6. Transfers of assets to TEL tend to occur at the cost shown on the books of FBL, although there have been exceptions over the years.

7. In recent years FBL has charged TEL a management fee of $100,000 for "general services rendered." This sum is netted against various expenses of FBL. You so far have not been able to learn the basis of the charge or accounting procedure. The bookkeeper said that "we've always done it that way."

8. Management of FBL gives its senior foremen and department heads a bonus for good performance. No criteria have been formally set out but employees feel that their bonus is somehow linked to net income. This has caused some grumbling in the past.

SCHEDULE 7

Details re "Going Private" and Sale of FBL

Your staff was able to learn the following about redemption of the convertible preferred shares and proposed terms of acquisition of FBL by PL:

1. The convertible preferred shares were issued with a restriction preventing the company from buying them back for a period of 10 years from the date of issue. It is possible that some holders of the preferred could convert before the redemption date of March 31, 19x7 specified by FBL. In order to minimize this possibility a $4 premium per share is being paid by FBL. If necessary FBL is prepared to pay substantially more to buy back any shares that are converted; however, it naturally is keeping this fact confidential.

2. The convertible preferred shares are widely held.

3. The debenture that is to be sold to the owners of FBL is a straight 10 year instrument secured by the general assets of FBL and bearing a 12 percent rate. The rate may increase after five years if inflation exceeds four percent per annum in the first five years. The new rate would be 15 percent.

4. PL is intending to have an "adjustable purchase price" for acquiring FBL's shares. That is, if FBL's net profits exceed a specified average sum over the *next* five years, the selling shareholders will receive a lump sum payment of 50 percent of the excess for the five years.

5. PL has made an offer of $8,000,000 for all of FBL's shares. This price assumes that the convertible preferred shares have been redeemed and TEL has been sold.

CHAPTER EIGHT

Unsolved Comprehensive Case II

INTRODUCTION

The three cases in Chapters Seven, Eight and Nine have similarities, but are also quite different. Can you identify the similarities and differences? Where is the direction located? Where are the irrelevancies? What skills are being tested by the case?

The case in this chapter, Brown Corporation, gives you a little more freedom than the previous case, Florida-Beechy Limited. However, this is not necessarily a matter to be celebrated. The client wants some specific questions answered but also makes some vague requests. Your prime problem is to ascertain where you can most fruitfully spend the four hours you have been given to respond to the case. In short, how can you best display your skills and show that you are a qualified accountant with a professional outlook?

BROWN CORPORATION

Brown Corporation (BC) was incorporated many years ago under federal legislation. Its common shares are listed on the Toronto Stock Exchange. BC is a holding company with investments in the voting shares of operating companies. Its shares tend to sell at a discount from the combined market value of BC's proportion of common shares of its subsidiaries. Since incorporation BC has acquired about 50 companies in different industries. Approximately three-quarters of the 50 were companies having financial and management crises. The remainder were thought to have above average growth potential. Forty of the 50 companies have since been sold by BC at good profits.

You have been engaged as a special consultant by BC's president. Your assignment is to conduct a purchase investigation of Sud Dorval Limited (SDL), a company that BC is considering as an investment. SDL, incorporated 20 years ago under federal legislation, has been privately-owned since incorporation. SDL has three main divisions: investments, manufacturing, and real estate. Twenty years ago SDL was strictly a manufacturer of jewelery and tourist merchandise. It has diversified over the years mainly as a result of buying "troubled" companies.

At present the investment division is trying to sell its holdings in mortgages and common shares, and may close down. The manufacturing division has three departments: jewelry and souvenir manufacturing, trading of "old" gold and silver, and custom jewelry products. The real estate division has two departments: development and management. The latter handles all property management including relations with tenants and government officials. The development department locates potentially good investments. For example, it acquires raw land, obtains necessary permits, subdivides the land, contracts with builders to construct properties and then turns them over to the management department to sell or retain.

The president of BC wants to buy a minimum of seventy percent of the common shares of SDL. BC wants to have legal control of its investments even after it may sell some shares of SDL at a later date. Any offer to the shareholders of SDL would be partly for cash and partly for shares in BC, perhaps in equal portions.

As a special consultant to the president of BC, you have been asked to respond to five questions:
1. Is the share price requested by the shareholders of SDL fair? If not, what price should be suggested? Provide reasons.
2. Should BC acquire the voting common shares of SDL? Support your recommendation.
3. Should the investment division be sold?
4. Indicate how SDL's operations could be made more profitable. Be specific.
5. Indicate matters that the auditors of BC and SDL might be concerned about. State how the matters should be treated so as to avoid an unqualified audit report and yet be in the best interests of the two companies.

REQUIRED:
Assume the role of special consultant to the president of BC. Prepare a report that addresses the five questions.

SDL—Investment Division

The investment division (ID) was started six years ago by the president of SDL for two reasons. First, the president wanted to train his son "in the ways of business" and thought that "the time had come" to let the son "swim or sink" in a division over which the son had "total control." Second, the president of SDL was curious about the profit potential of finance-type companies. The only instruction that the president gave his son was to "stay in the finance business, which means making loans to small businesses, buying mortgages, making consumer loans, and related activities; do not buy real estate or get involved in activities of the other two divisions." ID was given about $1,000,000 to commence operations.

The son began cautiously by investing in second mortgages on residential homes. These tended to yield 15 to 18 percent on the investment; but there were a few losses of minor amounts. Next, the son arranged with a pleasure craft dealer to finance consumer purchases of various types of small boats. In exchange for a finder's fee paid to the dealer, ID would be allowed to buy (at fair market value) notes signed by craft purchasers. These notes required the purchaser to make monthly payments to ID over periods up to 24 months. If the purchaser failed to make the payments ID could repossess the craft. This venture caused the son considerable problems. The winter following the first Spring-Summer of buying purchasers' notes in effect moved ID into the pleasure craft business. Repossessions were over 50 percent of the number of notes purchased. Much time was spent the following Spring-Summer selling the craft at large losses to ID.

Next, the son began making loans to small businesses. A typical loan was secured by a few business assets but was mainly secured by the personal assets (house, automobile, etc.) of the owners. All loans allowed ID an option to buy up to 20 percent interest in the companies at any time up to five years from the date of the loan.

The president's son began to exercise some of the options. By December 31, 19x3 ID owned the following shares in other companies:

	Cost	Estimated Fair Market Value
Hill Enterprises Limited	$ 50,000	$40,000
Nelson Manufacturing Corporation	100,000	—(*)
Computer Controls Limited	30,000	—(*)
Tiny Toys Inc.	30,000	20,000
Bolla Realty Inc.	24,000	30,000
	$234,000	$90,000

(*) Companies are not profitable, and market value may be minor.

ID's other main asset at present consists of mortgages on residential properties. At December 31, 19x3 these amounted to $266,000 and were yielding about 15 percent per annum on the investment.

SDL—Manufacturing Division

The manufacturing division (MD) represents about 30 percent of the assets and liabilities of SDL and in the latest year, 19x3, contributed less than 20 percent of the operating income. The three departments operate as follows:

Jewelry: The department has long-standing arrangements with a variety of jewelry stores and tourist shops to sell necklaces, charms and bracelets, and many other gold, silver, and alloy items. Recently, sales have fluctuated primarily because of large variations in gold and silver prices, and unpredictable tourist travel helped on the one hand by a lower exchange value of the Canadian dollar, but hindered by increased automobile gasoline prices.

MD just lost a major contract, that generated revenue of $800,000 in 19x3. Two years ago it purchased a special unusual metal alloy in bulk and paid $600,000. MD felt that the alloy would be used over a four year period on a special contract, two years of which were guaranteed, and two which were under an option. To MD's surprise, the customer did not renew the contract for the two year option period. The department has $350,000 of the alloy on hand at the year end just completed, December 31, 19x3. The financial statements show the alloy at cost because departmental management believes that it can use the alloy in roughly equal amounts over the next ten years for other souvenir items and contracts. The net realizable value of the metal at December 31, 19x3 was $160,000.

In view of the fluctuations in sales and other events such as the loss of the contract, departmental management has tended to budget and plan on the basis of last year's results. Management assumes that production volumes will be the same as last year, until sales orders prove otherwise. This leads to uneven production, layoffs of employees and periods of high overtime for skilled craftsman and production-line employees. The busiest months for the department are April, May and June. Funds must be borrowed from banks during peak periods to assist in financing receivables and inventory.

Departmental volume has declined in the past decade even though total sales have increased. Other countries have been producing inexpensive souvenirs and have acquired some of the department's customers. Sales promotions were attempted about five years ago, but records are not available to indicate how profitable these were. Generally departmental records are inadequate for management decision making, especially concerning profitability of customers.

All manufacturing operations are in one building in Saskatoon, Saskatchewan. Production workers are unionized, but the sales and office staff are not. Three sales offices are situated in St. John's, Toronto and Vancouver. All sales staff are paid on a salary basis. Sales orders are sent to Saskatoon for purposes of coordinating production and purchasing of raw materials. If a customer wants a special discount it must be approved by head office.

Most of the manufacturing machinery has been used for many years, and over one-half is fully depreciated. The combined head office and manufacturing building is about 20 years old but is in first class condition for a building of this age. The current selling price of the land and building is about $1,000,000.

Gold and silver trading: SDL has always had a gold and silver trading department but it operated on a very minor scale until two years ago. For years the department bought used gold and silver jewelry from jewelry stores that had accepted it as trade-ins on new items produced by SDL. Only small profits were made by refining the jewelry items into metal suitable for manufacturing. Recently, however, increasing inflation and European and Middle East purchases of precious metals has caused prices to fluctuate as follows:

U.S. dollars per ounce:
   Gold: $450 to $875
   Silver: $11 to $48

As precious metal prices rose, SDL began buying "old" gold and silver objects directly from the public. It placed advertisements in newspapers, listing the addresses of its sales offices and manufacturing plant as purchase depots. In view of the wide price fluctuations it offered only 60 percent or so of the current price per ounce of the metals. A portion of the discount was needed to pay for refining costs. In spite of the discounts, during 19x3 the public sold large quantities of the two metals to SDL, which made a good profit (roughly ten times that of the previous years) on the purchase and bulk sales to others. The trading department was also able to provide the jewelry manufacturing department with gold for considerably less than current acquisition cost. Overall, manufacturing cost was lowered eight to 10 percent from what it would otherwise have been if both metals were purchased from outsiders.

Departmental managers believe that gold and silver prices will continue to increase annually by the percentage increase in U.S. inflation, or even more. They therefore have asked management of

MD for more cash for the department so that larger purchases of gold and silver may be made, and inventories of the refined metals increased. Over the next five years departmental management wants about $2,000,000 extra per year to buy and hold the two metals. For accounting purposes the department wants to record the metal at net realizable value.

Custom jewelry products: This department is staffed by skilled craftsmen, many of whom are over 60 years of age. Sales volume has been steady over the past 10 years. Most of the revenue comes from special orders placed by wealthy persons. A secondary source of revenue is making special trophies for athletic and professional associations and service clubs. Less expensive models are made by the manufacturing department. The department has a $70,000 investment in standard types of trophies, which sell slowly over several years at fluctuating prices.

As a consequence of the increase in silver prices, sales volume is expected to decline over the next five years. Regular buyers probably will buy cheaper trophies instead of those that had previously been made of silver. Departmental managers hope that sales declines can be matched against the retirement age of craftsmen, so that employee terminations are not necessary.

Jewelry repair sales volume is steady, but not very profitable for the department. Repairs are offered more as a service to the manufacturing department than as a major part of the business. Most repairs are made by jewelers or the department's agents in various cities. The department reimburses agents for any work performed under guarantees.

Departmental contributions to sales and income before common costs are:

| | | Year ended December 31, 19x3 | |
	Manufacturing	Gold and Silver Trading	Custom Jewelry
Sales	$1,310,000	$4,675,850	$611,550
Cost of goods sold:			
Materials	381,500	3,539,350	184,250
Labour	238,700	125,500	283,400
Overhead	102,300	50,000	25,000
	722,500	3,714,850	492,650
Gross profit	587,500	961,000	118,900
Selling expenses	112,000	120,400	28,900
Administration	89,500	70,600	50,000
	201,500	191,000	78,900

Income before common costs (such as interest expense) and income tax	$ 386,000	$ 770,000	$ 40,000

SDL—Real Estate Division

The real estate division (RED) has been growing rapidly in the past few years primarily because it held land in Saskatchewan, Alberta and British Columbia prior to the latest expansion in these locations. About one-third of this land was sold in 19x2 and 19x3 at good profits. Another one-quarter was used for various construction projects by the development department. The remainder is being held for future development or resale.

Development department: As of December 31, 19x3 the department owned the following land and projects under construction:

Building	Land*	Construction Cost	Total
# 96	$260,000	$ —	$ 260,000
# 99	252,500	—	252,500
#102	304,800	91,200	396,000
#103	355,000	4,099,500	4,454,500
#105	312,600	1,877,200	2,189,800
#112	402,000	—	402,000
#113	265,000	—	265,000
#114	790,400	—	790,400

Projects #96 and 99 are major land holdings acquired 10 to 12 years ago, and that will soon become prime land as the cities nearby expand. Projects #102, 103 and 105 are apartment, office or shipping complexes under construction. Projects #112, 113 and 114 are more recent land acquisitions that will be held for future development or sale.

The estimated net realizable values of the five land parcels as of December 31, 19x3 are:

#96	$1,200,000
#99	1,300,000
#112	450,000
#113	350,000
#114	800,000

Projects #102, 103 and 105 will be completed in 19x4 and will either be sold or turned over to the management department. The president

---

* Includes original cost of acquisition plus property taxes and interest on debt incurred to acquire the land.

of BC has specifically asked you to recommend which of the two or more alternatives should be selected for each project.

#102: This project is an apartment complex. Construction activity has been very active in early 19x4 and the lower portions of the building should be ready for occupancy by September 19x4. Total construction cost is expected to be $3,200,000. Another $150,000 will be incurred in advertising for tenants, and similar occupancy costs. The department can then either sell the complex for $4,300,000 or turn it over to the management department for $4,300,000 less 10 percent (the intercompany transfer price).

Management department executives believe that they can obtain the following annual rental revenue from #102. In order to do this some annual operating costs will be incurred:

	Annual Revenue	Annual Operating Costs (excluding depreciation)
19x4	$ 200,000	$300,000
19x5 to 19x24	1,100,000	400,000

At the end of 20 years project #102 will be sold. The best estimate of the selling price twenty years hence is $3,200,000. (As of December 31, 19x3 the land had a value of $850,000.)

Since departmental management are paid a bonus based on departmental operating income, the development department managers favour selling #102 to outsiders. But management of SDL makes the final decision, and it has not said what it intends to do. It feels that a 15 percent return on investment before income tax would be necessary in order to retain #102.

#103: This project is a large shopping centre that is separately incorporated. Several investors have expressed interest in buying common shares in the separately-incorporated company. Total cost of construction is expected to be $16,000,000. Land value at the expected date of completion of August 15, 19x4 is estimated at $5,500,000, or $500,000 higher than at December 31, 19x3. Costs of leasing the stores in the complex, and other opening or promotion costs are estimated at $600,000.

The following revenue less operating expense pattern is expected for #103:

	Per Year (excludes depreciation)
19x4	$ 700,000
19x5 to 19x14	3,000,000
19x15 to 19x29	4,000,000

Investors would expect to receive a 15 percent return on investment before income tax on a project like #103. At the end of 25 years, four and one-half months (i.e., December 31, 19x29) the shopping centre would have a value of about $16,000,000 to $18,000,000. However, the stores would require a major renovation and therefore may have to be sold to another group of investors.

If any common shares in project #103 are to be sold to outsiders they would be sold as of December 31, 19x4. Departmental management of SDL is thinking of selling no more than 40 percent of the 1,000,000 common shares outstanding. Senior management of SDL are considering a price of $40 to $45 per common share for project #103.

#105: This project is an office building. Until December 27, 19x3 the department owned only 40 percent of the project; the remaining 60 percent was owned by another company under a joint venture agreement with SDL. The other company was experiencing liquidity problems and had to sell its 60 percent to SDL.

The joint venture records on project #105 were kept by the other company, because it held the 60 percent ownership. The records provide the following data as of December 20, 19x3 (before the construction site was closed down for two weeks over the holiday period):

Cost estimates:

General contractor—fixed fee	$3,200,000
—extras	70,000
Subcontractors' costs not included above	280,000
Land—acquisition cost	181,500
—clearing and excavation	100,000
Overhead at site—supervision and records	70,000
Other overhead—charged by joint venturers	100,000
Interest on borrowings to finance	
construction—during construction	80,000
—first year after completion of project	180,000
Property taxes on land—during construction	30,000
Expected total cost to complete the project	$4,291,000

The "expected total cost to complete" is for 100 percent of project #105. The figures are believed to be accurate.

The office building will be ready for occupancy on July 1, 19x4. About 40 percent of the available space has been leased to the federal government for 20 years at an annual rental of $560,000. Another 20 percent has been leased to a large corporation for 20 years at an annual rental of $270,000. Both lessees pay for electricity, cleaning and most leasehold costs. SDL would like to earn a return on investment before income tax of 15 percent. Management therefore has to decide what rental revenue per annum is needed on the as yet unleased 40 percent of the floor space. Present indications are that short term rentals generating $300,000 per year are probable. With luck the rentals could be as high as $350,000 per year. At the end of 20 years the building will be sold for approximately $6,000,000. Annual operating expenses expected to be incurred by SDL, including depreciation expense of $200,000, are about $800,000.

SDL had to pay market value of $240,000 (60 percent of total market value of $400,000) on December 27, 19x3 to acquire the other 60 percent of the land for project #105. However, the department paid only cost per the other venturer's books for the 60 percent of "construction cost" to date.

SDL can sign a contract with outsiders to sell project #105 for $4,200,000 on its completion. However, the potential buyer wants a decision within 45 days or the offer expires.

Management department: The management department spends a considerable amount of time forecasting rental and growth potential for different regions of Canada. It keeps a master file of rental and leasing rates for apartments, office buildings, shopping complexes, and industrial locations by major region within Canada. When it quotes expected rental rates to the development department it tends to use current figures and ignore expected inflationary effects. But, salvage or resale prices 20 or 25 years hence include an estimate of inflationary effects on prices.

Nearly all of the department's leases on shopping centres that it owns contain clauses that base much of the rentals on a percentage of sales in each store. This means that the department must monitor expected sales of different types of goods if it wishes to predict likely revenues from its leases with store owners. If it does not estimate likely revenues it is not able to ascertain the expected profitability and return on investment of possible projects.

The department has not yet developed a reliable system for forecasting sales for each type of store in a shopping centre. It estimates volume changes in sales by using an economic model that combines unemployment, interest rate changes in Canada, and alterations in disposal income of potential consumers. Rate changes in sales are estimated at 10 percent per annum, an expected average rate of inflation over the next 10 years.

Lease agreements that tie rent to a store's sales allow SDL to send an auditor to verify the sales figure reported to SDL. Unfortunately, most of SDL's lease agreements are not specific on how sales are to be computed. For example, they do not specify whether bad debts may be deducted from sales, whether charges made by credit card companies are deductions, and so forth. This oversight was recently corrected. To date SDL has not hired an auditor to verify sales; but recently it asked a store's auditor to send a letter attesting to the amount of sales, as outlined in the rental agreements.

The department has its own maintenance staff for all of the projects under its management. This has not proven to be successful because maintenance charges per square foot are in excess of industry averages. The department does not keep records for each team of maintenance workers or for each building.

The department recognizes revenue on an accrual basis, except for the portion of rent which is based on a percentage of sales. In the latter situations cash basis recognition is used because it is only at this time that precise figures are known. Income tax assessors have not questioned this procedure in the past, probably on grounds of materiality. But, the amounts are getting larger each year and the procedure may need alteration. Very few bad debts occur on office and store leases, but residential apartment rentals are troublesome from time to time. Occasionally, renters vacate without paying the last few months' rent. To date the department has not pursued such people by hiring collection agencies. However, losses are increasing. It will, however, report the facts about the renters to a credit bureau.

Senior departmental management are paid on the basis of part salary and part bonus tied to departmental operating profit. Included in departmental operating profit are rental revenues less rental expenses, profits and losses on disposal of rental properties, and direct overhead expenses. Excluded are head office expenses, interest, and income taxes.

Senior departmental management may recommend the sale of any rental property that is not yielding 14 percent before income taxes. They have to receive approval from senior management of SDL before a property can be offered for sale. As of December 31, 19x3 departmental management estimated that its properties are yielding about 18 to 19 percent before income taxes.

General

The shareholders of SDL appear willing to sell their shares for between $130 and $140 per share. However, they want BC to offer five year management contracts to three senior personnel or pay $200,000 in severance to each.

BROWN CORPORATION

Consolidated Income Statement
Year ended December 31, 19x3

Revenue	$139,413,000
Costs	96,993,000
Operating income	42,420,000
Income of investments reported on equity basis	2,900,000

		45,320,000
Income taxes		21,500,000
		23,820,000
Minority interest in subsidiaries		1,620,000
Income before extraordinary item		22,200,000
Extraordinary gain on sale of investments, net of $3,500,000 income taxes thereon and net of losses of $250,000 after income taxes		8,350,000
Net income		$ 30,550,000

BROWN CORPORATION

Consolidated Statement of Retained Earnings
Year ended December 31, 19x3

Balance, January 1		$ 28,270,000
Add net income		30,550,000
		58,820,000
Deduct:		
Dividends on preferred shares	$ 5,000,000	
Dividends on common shares	15,000,000	20,000,000
Balance, December 31		$ 38,820,000

BROWN CORPORATION

Consolidated Balance Sheet
Year ended December 31, 19x3

Assets

Working capital	$ 91,235,000
Investments in nonconsolidated subsidiary companies, at equity	2,144,000
Long-lived assets, at cost, net of accumulated depreciation	68,471,000
Goodwill, less amortization	12,590,000
Other assets	2,115,000
	$176,555,000

Liabilities and Owners' Equity

Deferred income tax		$ 5,958,000
Long term debt, due 19x7 to 19x17, secured		15,000,000
Minority interest		14,277,000
Owners' equity:		
Preferred shares, no par value convertible after 19x5	$35,000,000	
Common shares, no par value*	60,000,000	
Contributed surplus	7,500,000	
Retained earnings	38,820,000	141,320,000
		$176,555,000

* 20,000,000 shares are outstanding. The current market value of a common share is $8.50 to $9.00.

SUD DORVAL LIMITED

Consolidated Income Statement
Year ended December 31, 19x3

	19x3	19x2
Revenue:		
Manufacturing and metal trading	$ 6,597,000	$ 6,233,000
Real estate operations	19,181,000	11,235,000
	25,778,000	17,468,000
Costs:		
Manufacturing and trading	5,401,000	5,317,000
Real estate operations	12,104,000	6,106,000
Interest expense less interest revenue	1,230,000	1,044,000
Overhead not included above	920,000	897,000
	19,655,000	13,364,000
Operating income before income taxes	6,123,000	4,104,000
Taxes on income	2,900,000	1,900,000
Net income	$ 3,223,000	$ 2,204,000

SUD DORVAL LIMITED

Consolidated Statement of Retained Earnings
Year ended December 31, 19x3

	19x3	19x2
Balance, January 1	$ 7,502,000	$6,711,000
Add net income	3,223,000	2,204,000
	10,725,000	8,915,000
Deduct dividends	2,826,000	1,413,000
Balance, December 31	$ 7,899,000	$7,502,000

SUD DORVAL LIMITED

Consolidated Balance Sheet
December 31, 19x3

	19x3	19x2
Assets		
Current:		
Cash	$ 18,000	$ 4,000
Receivables	535,000	606,000
Inventories, at lower of cost or net realizable value	2,688,000	3,028,000
Prepaid expenses	59,000	81,000
	3,300,000	3,719,000

	19x3	19x2
Noncurrent, at cost:		
Land held for resale	3,500,000	5,920,000
Land	2,100,000	2,100,000
Buildings	22,950,000	20,901,000
Construction in process	6,180,000	4,410,000
	34,730,000	33,331,000
Accumulated depreciation	8,945,000	8,260,000
	25,785,000	25,071,000
Other assets:		
Mortgages receivable	266,000	298,000
Goodwill, at cost	500,000	500,000
Investments in other companies, at cost	234,000	202,000
Deferred opening costs*	210,000	235,000
Unamortized discount on debt	95,000	105,000
	1,305,000	1,340,000
	$30,390,000	$30,130,000

	19x3	19x2

Liabilities and Owners' Equity

	19x3	19x2
Current liabilities:		
Bank loan	$ 1,700,000	$ 3,500,000
Accounts payable	1,769,000	1,905,000
Accrued liabilities	217,000	186,000
Construction holdbacks	712,000	604,000
Income taxes payable	400,000	318,000
Other liabilities	92,000	87,000
	4,890,000	6,600,000
Deferred income tax	121,000	152,000
Long term debt, secured, due 19x5 to 19x17, at 12% to 15% interest per annum	16,480,000	14,876,000
Owners' equity:		
Common shares, 100,000 issued	300,000	300,000
Contributed surplus	700,000	700,000
Retained earnings	7,899,000	7,502,000
	8,899,000	8,502,000
	$30,390,000	$30,130,000

* These are amortized over ten years from the date the project is declared open.

CHAPTER NINE

Unsolved Comprehensive Case III

INTRODUCTION

The final unsolved case is in the field of public accounting and deals in varying degrees of depth with financial and managerial accounting, income taxation, audit issues and related topics. Some may find it less directive than the previous case, whereas others may feel that they know precisely what is involved and what should be done. As with the previous unsolved cases allow yourself four hours and the usual present value tables and calculator.

Before you commence writing the required report try to design a flow or decision chart that indicates where you are headed and why. Naturally we would hope that you are now "sizing-up" the case, budgeting and instinctively performing the other recommendations that have been made in this book.

DARLENE'S SPECIALTY SHOPPES LTD.

Darlene's Specialty Shoppes Ltd. (DSSL) was incorporated on January 31, 19x3 under federal legislation. It was formed to bring together on that date three firms that were in related lines of business: Darlene's Dresses (DD), a proprietorship owned by Darlene Brown prior to its "acquisition" by DSSL; Blanche's Leathergoods Ltd. (BLL); and Grant Distributors (GD), a partnership owned equally by Elizabeth Grant and Darlene Brown.

DD operates four exclusive women's clothing and shoe stores in one Canadian city. It purchases goods from various manufacturers and distributors, including BLL and GD, and sells to the public. Although DD accepts the usual credit cards at its stores it also has its own charge accounts for credit-worthy customers. DD tends to have better than average quality goods in the stores.

BLL manufactures shoes, handbags, and related items in one manufacturing plant located in the same province as DD. BLL was incorporated 15 years ago by Blanche White. Prior to its "acquisition" by DSSL, BLL was owned by a trust created for Mrs. White and her children. During her life, Mrs. White would have voting control of BLL, but on her death the children would receive votes in proportion to the shares that they inherited. The trust is being rewritten to cover the 30 percent of the common shares of DSSL that Mrs. White and her children received when the administrator of the trust turned the shares of BLL over to DSSL.

DG was formed about 10 years ago by the two partners. They recognized that womens' clothing stores in smaller towns wanted to stock some top quality items but did not have the ability and funds to travel to European and other centres to acquire current fashions. Elizabeth Grant became business manager and sales manager of GD and Darlene Brown became the purchasing manager. Ms. Brown had previously been able to make an arrangement with Ms. Grant so that some high fashion goods could be bought directly for DD whereas other goods that are saleable to stores in smaller towns had to be channelled through GD. BLL's shoes can be bought directly from them by DD.

Ms. Brown and Ms. Grant each received 15 percent of the voting common shares of DSSL. Since Ms. Brown also received 40 percent of DSSL's voting shares in exchange for ownership of DD this gave her 55 percent of the common shares of DSSL outstanding at January 31, 19x3.

It is now April 19x3 and the owners of DSSL are recognizing that they need some financial and accounting advice. They have approached you, a public accountant, to analyze their financial operations and make suggestions for improving major or potentially serious problem areas. You have accepted the engagement and have assembled the information on the following schedules.

REQUIRED:
Assume the role of the public accountant and prepare a report that covers financial matters that should be of concern to the owners of DSSL.

SCHEDULE 1
Darlene's Dresses Division

1. As of January 31, 19x3 DD's balance sheet showed:

Current assets:			
Cash			$ 11,535
Accounts receivable			107,615
Inventories, at cost			256,850
Prepaid expenses			9,000
			385,000
Long-lived assets, at cost:			
Land		$100,000	
Building and equipment	$530,000		
Accumulated depreciation	110,000	420,000	
Leasehold improvements	125,000		
Amortization to date	109,000	16,000	536,000
Organization costs			4,900
			$925,900
Current liabilities:			
Accounts payable and accrued charges			$245,600
Bank loan, prime plus 2½%, secured			128,000
			373,600
Mortgage payable, 15%, due 19x4			220,000
Due to owner, 10%			40,000
Owner's capital			292,300
			$925,900

2. DD never had an audit by a public accountant during its existence, and was not audited by income tax assessors as far as can be determined.

3. Inventories and receivables vary widely throughout the year because sales tend to peak when new fashions arrive, which is generally twice per year. As of April 1, 19x3 in the DD division inventories were $298,700 and receivables were $139,770. No allowance for bad debts had been provided at January 31, 19x3; a figure of $4,500 probably would have been appropriate.

The receivables fit into two classes: those bearing interest; and those that are interest free. At April 1, 19x3 about $30,000 probably would be interest free because it would be paid by the 25th of April. The remainder would be paid over about a one year period because customers are allowed to pay as little as 10 percent per month of their outstanding balance. Interest rates are currently eighteen percent per year.

The average gross profit on sales revenue is about one-third. In the year ended January 31, 19x3 sales were approximately $1,300,000 and income before income tax was about $8,000. Ms. Brown drew a salary of $60,000, which was included as an expense in arriving at income before income tax.

4. The DD division's land was acquired several years ago along with

the building for Store #1. Some improvements were made to the building in August 19x2 and it was re-mortgaged on an interim basis. Monthly mortgage payments are $10,000 per month of principal, plus interest at 15 percent per annum.

DD has used income tax rates in the past to depreciate the building (five percent rate) and equipment (either 20 percent or 30 percent). As of January 31, 19x3 the undepreciated cost figures were:

Building (5%)	$298,000
Equipment (20%)	103,800
Equipment (30%)	18,200
	$420,000

The land and building can probably be sold for $600,000.

5. Leasehold improvements have been amortized over the period of the leases on Stores #2, #3 and #4. All three leases were for 10 year periods, and all expire in early 19x4. It is expected that all three leases can be renewed for five years, but at an increase of about $1,500 per month.
6. Organization costs were incurred years ago and it is not clear from DD's books and records what they represent.
7. Accounts payable at January 31, 19x3 includes a variety of items:

Salary due to Ms. Brown	$ 25,000
Miscellaneous accruals and deferred interest	14,600
Sales tax payable	7,840
Due to suppliers, including BLL ($12,500)	
and GD ($7,500)	198,160
	$245,600

8. As of January 31, 19x3 the interest rate on the bank loan was 16 percent per annum. The loan is secured by accounts receivable, with additional collateral being a second mortgage on the building and Ms. Brown's pledge of her personal assets.
9. The sum due to the owner, Ms. Brown, at January 31, 19x3 is not due on a particular date. Interest is accrued and paid quarterly.
10. In the year ended January 31, 19x4 Ms. Brown expects the DD division's sales to increase 10 percent over the previous year. Gross profits may decline to 30 percent if economic conditions are not favourable and inflation continues at the current 10-12 percent rate.
11. Suppliers tend to allow DD 60 days to pay invoices. After about 75 days from the invoice date interest is charged at 18 percent.

12. DD division employs the retail method of inventory control in its stores, supported by cash register computer analyses of different classes of inventory items. Inventory is counted once per year, usually in early July, and shortages are charged to cost of goods sold. Recently shortages have been around five to six percent of the cost of goods sold.

    If old merchandise is not sold after two price reductions in the retail locations, it is sold in bulk to discount houses. Generally, selling prices to discount houses are 20 to 25 percent of cost.

13. DD does not record interest revenue on those customer charge accounts that bear interest until such time as the customer has paid all of the principal balance outstanding, or has made regular payments for at least 10 months. Once the customer has made regular payments for 10 months, deferred interest is debited to accounts payable (which was previously credited) and credited to interest revenue.

SCHEDULE 2

Blanche's Leathergoods Division

1. Mrs. White has informed you that she is well aware of rising costs of producing footware and handbags, especially those having leather components. She believes that she has a special place in the market because several of her goods are handmade, especially many of the slippers. She feels that over the years BLL has built up a good following of repeat customers for expensive winter boots and slippers. She has no intention of competing with large manufacturers who operate many assembly lines and produce medium and low priced items.

    Mrs. White believes that the continuity of BLL is assured now that she has joined with DD and GD to form DSSL. One of her daughters and one son are now working daily in BLL and are quickly learning the production and marketing functions of the business. Design is very important to the success of BLL and Mrs. White believes that her daughter has "the natural instincts to stay ahead of competition."

    The main reason why Mrs. White joined DSSL is that she believes that DSSL will be a public company some day. Then, her children will be able to sell some of their shares and diversify as they please. She had "grave concerns" about a trust set up for "a small company like BLL." The second reason for joining DSSL is that she was given a salary of $60,000 a year, which is 50 percent higher than what she took out of BLL.

2. BLL is required to file quarterly financial statements with the

company's banker. Since BLL is now a subsidiary of DSSL Mrs. White is not sure which financial statements, BLL's or DSSL's, have to be filed. The bank loan is not guaranteed by DSSL.

3. BLL's balance sheet at January 31, 19x3 showed:

Current assets:		
Cash		$ 5,010
Accounts receivable		151,315
Inventories, at cost		239,770
Prepaid expenses		1,865
		397,960
Long-lived assets, at cost:		
Land	$ 52,000	
Building and equipment	616,800	
	668,800	
Accumulated depreciation	226,740	442,060
Development cost, less		
amortization $3,170		14,210
Incorporation cost		1,225
		$855,455
Current liabilities:		
Accounts payable and accrued		$228,110
Bank loan payable, 15%		110,000
Income tax payable		5,200
Other liabilities		17,680
		360,990
Loan payable, due February 15, 19x4,		
14%		125,000
Mortgage payable, 12½%, due 19x5		210,000
Owner's equity:		
Common shares, no par value	$ 10,000	
Retained earnings	149,465	159,465
		$855,455

4. BLL's accounts receivable at January 31, 19x3 includes $12,500 due from DD and $21,000 due from GD. The balance is reasonably current and is due from a number of customers. Present policy is to not charge interest on overdue accounts.

5. Most of the company's inventory at January 31 is finished goods ($127,500) awaiting orders for Spring delivery. The balance is raw materials that are bought in bulk and, depending upon the nature of the item, tend to be used over a period of a few months or up to one year.

BLL's operations are highly seasonal. Most of its sales are in

August and September (for retail sale in October to Christmas) with a second, lesser peak in March (for Spring retail sales). In the year ended January 31, 19x3 sales were $982,000, the gross profit was $267,300 and net income was $51,000. Approximately $140,000 of the sales were to DD, and $200,000 were to GD.

6. The company's land and building (cost at January 31, 19x3 is $360,000) were acquired five years ago. Current replacement cost in its present condition is about $500,000. Accounting and income tax figures for the long-lived assets are:

	Cost at January 31, 19x3	Accounting depreciation to date	Capital cost allowance (CCA) claimed to date	CCA rate
Land	$ 52,000	$ —	$ —	
Building	360,000	43,200	84,390	5%
Equipment	230,000	176,140	192,110	20%
Other	26,800	7,400	10,770	30%
	$668,800	$226,740	$287,270	

BLL is depreciating its assets for accounting purposes as follows: Building: straight-line over 40 years; Equipment: straight-line over 10 years; Other: straight-line over five years.

7. The development cost represents outlays for designs of new winter boots and slippers. The cost is being amortized at $3,475 per year.

8. Incorporation cost is the fee paid to the lawyer who incorporated BLL.

9. Accounts payable includes a variety of liabilities:

Due to suppliers	$120,890
Bonuses due to senior employees	10,500
Year end accruals, including interest	32,695
Accrued wages and commissions	25,960
Various taxes (other than income tax) payable	14,375
Miscellaneous	23,690
	$228,110

Suppliers allow, on average, about 60 days after the invoice date for payment, and charge 18 percent interest per annum thereafter. At January 31, 19x3 BLL was paying interest on about $40,000 of trade payables, most of which was leather specialty items to be used in manufacturing over the next several months.

10. BLL's bank loan is secured by accounts receivable of BLL, and

Mrs. White's home has been pledged as secondary collateral.

11. The loan payable is secured by inventories of BLL plus a second mortgage on the land and buildings.

12. No dividends have been paid since incorporation of BLL. The loan payable contains a restrictive covenant that does not allow dividends to be declared unless retained earnings exceed $125,000 after payment of the dividend.

13. Mrs. White expects sales revenue to increase about 12 percent in the year ended January 31, 19x4 and maybe 15 percent in the year ended January 31, 19x5. Cash operating costs likely will rise about 10 to 12 percent.

14. BLL does not have a cost or management accounting system. Cost figures for the 30-35 different finished products are based on estimates.

SCHEDULE 3

Grant Distributors Division

1. GD's balance sheet at January 31, 19x3 showed:

Current assets:		
Cash		$ 15,690
Accounts receivable		137,445
Inventories, at cost		276,850
Prepaid expenses		13,170
		443,155
Long-lived assets, at cost:		
Equipment and automobiles	$163,800	
Leasehold improvements	26,500	
	190,300	
Accumulated depreciation and		
amortization	77,235	113,065
		$556,220
Current liabilities:		
Accounts payable		$201,720
Accrued liabilities		68,195
Bank loan payable, 15%		110,000
Other		27,715
		407,630
Due to Blanche's Leathergoods Ltd.		21,000
Partners' capital		127,590
		$556,220

2. In the year ended January 31, 19x3 GD's sales were approxi-

mately $1,425,000 of which $235,000 were to DD. Gross profit on sales was about 28 percent and income before income tax was $141,000. Included in expenses were a $30,000 salary and bonus to Ms. Brown and $50,000 to Ms. Grant.

3. GD's experience has been that it has to encourage some smaller stores in northern towns to buy new lines of merchandise by allowing them to stock on a consignment basis. Very few goods have been returned in recent years, and full payment usually is received. Thus GD tends to recognize revenue when consignment goods are shipped to these small, northern stores. In the year ended January 31, 19x3 $185,000 goods at retail were shipped on consignment. As of January 31, 19x3 accounts receivable included $11,500 at selling price of goods shipped on consignment. The balance of the receivables, including $7,500 due from DD, seemed collectible with the possible exception of $4,900 for a store that is in receivership.

4. Inventories at January 31, 19x3 were saleable at amounts in excess of cost except for one line of dresses that cost $17,600. The supplier, in Europe, had used a new material on part of each dress and the material was not compatible with the thread that was used, eventually causing a ripple effect. GD is trying to settle with the supplier before selling the dresses to a discount house for $3,500. The supplier claims that a humidity problem during shipment must have caused the problem and has denied liability. Ms. Grant and the transportation company regard the supplier's explanation as "beyond belief."

5. GD's office and warehouse are in leased premises in a condominium row project. GD has an option to purchase the portion of the building that they now occupy any time before October 31, 19x3 for $150,000. The current market value would be around $185,000. GD would have to assume a mortgage of about $45,000 and pay $105,000 cash to the owner. If GD does not purchase the building it will probably have to re-locate because the owner will want to sell the asset.

6. Ms. Grant expects sales revenue to increase only five percent in the year ended January 31, 19x4. Unemployment in some northern sales territories is cutting into sales of retail stores, and some may be forced to close, or buy less expensive merchandise. Costs are expected to increase about 10 percent.

7. GD depreciates its equipment, automobiles and leasehold improvements at maximum rates allowable for income tax purposes. An exception occurred in 19x1 when GD, which self insures except for automobile coverage, had a fire that caused $70,000 damage to merchandise in the warehouse.

8. Accounts payable primarily represents trade payables for recent purchases of merchandise. Approximately $100,000 at January 31, 19x3 is payable in foreign currencies, and when due might cost as much as $110,000 in Canadian funds to pay off.
9. Accrued liabilities include $10,000 payable to Ms. Brown and $22,000 payable to Ms. Grant for wages and bonuses earned in the year ended January 31, 19x3.
10. The bank loan is secured by accounts receivable of GD, with additional collateral being personal guarantees of the partners.
11. Income tax auditors have never checked GD's records since it has been in existence.

SCHEDULE 4

Miscellaneous Matters

1. Ms. Brown has informed you that an owner of some retail stores that buy from GD has expressed interest in acquiring up to 25 percent of DSSL, either by buying unissued shares of DSSL or by purchasing outstanding shares from one or more of the shareholders. Ms. Brown stated that the prospective shareholder's stores are in a different region to DD's, and therefore that there would be no competition from them. She also mentioned that the prospective shareholder was quite knowledgeable, had a pleasant personality, and had told Ms. Brown that she would not interfere in the operations of DSSL if she were allowed to buy shares. The prospective buyer apparently is willing to pay between $350,000 and $400,000 for a 25 percent interest in the present capital of DSSL. She would be willing to pay proportionately more if she could buy enough unissued shares to acquire a 25 percent interest. Ms. Brown wants to know what you think of the offer and what financial factors should be kept in mind in making a decision. The prospective buyer would want to review DSSL's operations before making a definite offer and setting a specific price for the shares.
2. The latest (April 19x3) reports from Europe indicate that women's fashions are expected to change radically over the next two years.
3. Mrs. White mentioned to you that she was told by a government official that if BLL moved its manufacturing facilities to one of two regions that it would be eligible for a relocation grant of $150,000. It would also be given a $400,000 loan that would be forgivable in equal amounts over 10 years as long as she employed 15 people from the local region on a fulltime basis. She has asked your opinion of the idea of a possible move.
4. Both Ms. Grant and Mrs. White have asked you how they might lower operating costs and improve profitability.

Appendix

PRESENT VALUE TABLES

TABLE 1   PRESENT VALUE FACTORS

Periods Hence	1%	2%	3%	4%	5%	6%	7%	8%	9%	10%
1	.9901	.9804	.9709	.9615	.9524	.9434	.9346	.9259	.9174	.9091
2	.9803	.9612	.9426	.9246	.9070	.8900	.8734	.8573	.8417	.8264
3	.9706	.9423	.9151	.8890	.8638	.8396	.8163	.7938	.7722	.7513
4	.9610	.9238	.8885	.8548	.8227	.7921	.7629	.7350	.7084	.6830
5	.9515	.9057	.8626	.8219	.7835	.7473	.7130	.6806	.6499	.6209
6	.9420	.8880	.8375	.7903	.7462	.7050	.6663	.6302	.5963	.5645
7	.9327	.8706	.8131	.7599	.7107	.6651	.6227	.5835	.5470	.5132
8	.9235	.8535	.7894	.7307	.6768	.6274	.5820	.5403	.5019	.4665
9	.9143	.8368	.7664	.7026	.6446	.5919	.5439	.5002	.4604	.4241
10	.9053	.8203	.7441	.6756	.6139	.5584	.5083	.4632	.4224	.3855
11	.8963	.8043	.7224	.6496	.5847	.5268	.4751	.4289	.3875	.3505
12	.8874	.7885	.7014	.6246	.5568	.4970	.4440	.3971	.3555	.3186
13	.8787	.7730	.6810	.6006	.5303	.4688	.4150	.3677	.3262	.2897
14	.8700	.7579	.6611	.5775	.5051	.4423	.3878	.3405	.2992	.2633
15	.8613	.7430	.6419	.5553	.4810	.4173	.3624	.3152	.2745	.2394
16	.8528	.7284	.6232	.5339	.4581	.3936	.3387	.2919	.2519	.2176
17	.8444	.7142	.6050	.5134	.4363	.3714	.3166	.2703	.2311	.1978
18	.8360	.7002	.5874	.4936	.4155	.3503	.2959	.2502	.2120	.1799
19	.8277	.6864	.5703	.4746	.3957	.3305	.2765	.2317	.1945	.1635
20	.8195	.6730	.5537	.4564	.3769	.3118	.2584	.2145	.1784	.1486
21	.8114	.6598	.5375	.4388	.3589	.2942	.2415	.1987	.1637	.1351
22	.8034	.6468	.5219	.4220	.3418	.2775	.2257	.1839	.1502	.1228
23	.7954	.6342	.5067	.4057	.3256	.2618	.2109	.1703	.1378	.1117
24	.7876	.6217	.4919	.3901	.3101	.2470	.1971	.1577	.1264	.1015
25	.7798	.6095	.4776	.3751	.2953	.2330	.1842	.1460	.1160	.0923
26	.7720	.5976	.4637	.3607	.2812	.2198	.1722	.1352	.1064	.0839
27	.7644	.5859	.4502	.3468	.2678	.2074	.1609	.1252	.0976	.0763
28	.7568	.5744	.4371	.3335	.2551	.1956	.1504	.1159	.0895	.0693
29	.7493	.5631	.4243	.3207	.2429	.1846	.1406	.1073	.0822	.0630
30	.7419	.5521	.4120	.3083	.2314	.1741	.1314	.0994	.0754	.0573
31	.7346	.5412	.4000	.2965	.2204	.1643	.1228	.0920	.0691	.0521
32	.7273	.5306	.3883	.2851	.2099	.1550	.1147	.0852	.0634	.0474
33	.7201	.5202	.3770	.2741	.1999	.1462	.1072	.0789	.0582	.0431
34	.7130	.5100	.3660	.2636	.1904	.1379	.1002	.0730	.0534	.0391
35	.7059	.5000	.3554	.2534	.1813	.1301	.0937	.0676	.0490	.0356
36	.6989	.4902	.3450	.2437	.1727	.1227	.0875	.0626	.0449	.0323
37	.6920	.4806	.3350	.2343	.1644	.1158	.0818	.0580	.0412	.0294
38	.6852	.4712	.3252	.2253	.1566	.1092	.0765	.0537	.0378	.0267
39	.6784	.4619	.3158	.2166	.1491	.1031	.0715	.0497	.0347	.0243
40	.6717	.4529	.3066	.2083	.1420	.0972	.0668	.0460	.0318	.0221
41	.6650	.4440	.2976	.2003	.1353	.0917	.0624	.0426	.0292	.0201
42	.6584	.4353	.2890	.1926	.1288	.0865	.0583	.0395	.0268	.0183
43	.6519	.4268	.2805	.1852	.1227	.0816	.0545	.0365	.0246	.0166
44	.6454	.4184	.2724	.1780	.1169	.0770	.0509	.0338	.0226	.0151
45	.6391	.4102	.2644	.1712	.1113	.0727	.0476	.0313	.0207	.0137
46	.6327	.4022	.2567	.1646	.1060	.0685	.0445	.0290	.0190	.0125
47	.6265	.3943	.2493	.1583	.1009	.0647	.0416	.0269	.0174	.0113
48	.6203	.3865	.2420	.1522	.0961	.0610	.0389	.0249	.0160	.0103
49	.6141	.3790	.2350	.1463	.0916	.0575	.0363	.0230	.0147	.0094
50	.6080	.3715	.2281	.1407	.0872	.0543	.0339	.0213	.0134	.0085

TABLE 1 PRESENT VALUE FACTORS

Periods Hence	11%	12%	13%	14%	15%	16%	17%	18%	19%	20%
1	.9009	.8929	.8850	.8772	.8696	.8621	.8547	.8475	.8403	.8333
2	.8116	.7972	.7831	.7695	.7561	.7432	.7305	.7182	.7062	.6944
3	.7312	.7118	.6931	.6750	.6575	.6407	.6244	.6086	.5934	.5787
4	.6587	.6355	.6133	.5921	.5718	.5523	.5337	.5158	.4987	.4823
5	.5935	.5674	.5428	.5194	.4972	.4761	.4561	.4371	.4190	.4019
6	.5346	.5066	.4803	.4556	.4323	.4104	.3898	.3704	.3521	.3349
7	.4817	.4523	.4251	.3996	.3759	.3538	.3332	.3139	.2959	.2791
8	.4339	.4039	.3762	.3506	.3269	.3050	.2848	.2660	.2487	.2326
9	.3909	.3606	.3329	.3075	.2843	.2630	.2434	.2255	.2090	.1938
10	.3522	.3220	.2946	.2697	.2472	.2267	.2080	.1911	.1756	.1615
11	.3173	.2875	.2607	.2366	.2149	.1954	.1778	.1619	.1476	.1346
12	.2858	.2567	.2307	.2076	.1869	.1685	.1520	.1372	.1240	.1122
13	.2575	.2292	.2042	.1821	.1625	.1452	.1299	.1163	.1042	.0935
14	.2320	.2046	.1807	.1597	.1413	.1252	.1110	.0985	.0876	.0779
15	.2090	.1827	.1599	.1401	.1229	.1079	.0949	.0835	.0736	.0649
16	.1883	.1631	.1415	.1229	.1069	.0930	.0818	.0708	.0618	.0541
17	.1696	.1456	.1252	.1078	.0929	.0802	.0693	.0600	.0520	.0451
18	.1528	.1300	.1108	.0946	.0808	.0691	.0592	.0508	.0437	.0376
19	.1377	.1161	.0981	.0829	.0703	.0596	.0506	.0431	.0367	.0313
20	.1240	.1037	.0868	.0728	.0611	.0514	.0433	.0365	.0303	.0261
21	.1117	.0926	.0768	.0638	.0531	.0443	.0370	.0309	.0259	.0217
22	.1007	.0826	.0680	.0560	.0462	.0382	.0316	.0262	.0218	.0181
23	.0907	.0738	.0601	.0491	.0402	.0329	.0270	.0222	.0183	.0151
24	.0817	.0659	.0532	.0431	.0349	.0284	.0231	.0188	.0154	.0126
25	.0736	.0588	.0471	.0378	.0304	.0245	.0197	.0160	.0129	.0105
26	.0663	.0525	.0417	.0331	.0264	.0211	.0169	.0135	.0109	.0087
27	.0597	.0469	.0369	.0291	.0230	.0182	.0144	.0115	.0091	.0073
28	.0538	.0419	.0326	.0255	.0200	.0157	.0123	.0097	.0077	.0061
29	.0485	.0374	.0289	.0224	.0174	.0135	.0105	.0082	.0064	.0051
30	.0437	.0334	.0256	.0196	.0151	.0116	.0090	.0070	.0054	.0042
31	.0394	.0298	.0226	.0172	.0131	.0100	.0077	.0059	.0046	.0035
32	.0355	.0266	.0200	.0151	.0114	.0087	.0066	.0050	.0038	.0029
33	.0319	.0238	.0177	.0132	.0099	.0075	.0056	.0042	.0032	.0024
34	.0288	.0212	.0157	.0116	.0086	.0064	.0048	.0036	.0027	.0020
35	.0259	.0189	.0139	.0102	.0075	.0055	.0041	.0030	.0023	.0017
36	.0234	.0169	.0123	.0089	.0065	.0048	.0035	.0026	.0019	.0014
37	.0210	.0151	.0109	.0078	.0057	.0041	.0030	.0022	.0016	.0012
38	.0190	.0135	.0096	.0069	.0049	.0036	.0026	.0019	.0013	.0010
39	.0171	.0120	.0085	.0060	.0043	.0031	.0022	.0016	.0011	.0008
40	.0154	.0107	.0075	.0053	.0037	.0026	.0019	.0013	.0010	.0007
41	.0139	.0096	.0067	.0046	.0032	.0023	.0016	.0011	.0008	.0006
42	.0125	.0086	.0059	.0041	.0028	.0020	.0014	.0010	.0007	.0005
43	.0112	.0076	.0052	.0036	.0025	.0017	.0012	.0008	.0006	.0004
44	.0101	.0068	.0046	.0031	.0021	.0015	.0010	.0007	.0005	.0003
45	.0091	.0061	.0041	.0027	.0019	.0013	.0009	.0006	.0004	.0003
46	.0082	.0054	.0036	.0024	.0016	.0011	.0007	.0005	.0003	.0002
47	.0074	.0049	.0032	.0021	.0014	.0009	.0006	.0004	.0003	.0002
48	.0067	.0043	.0028	.0019	.0012	.0008	.0005	.0004	.0002	.0002
49	.0060	.0039	.0025	.0016	.0011	.0007	.0005	.0003	.0002	.0001
50	.0054	.0035	.0022	.0014	.0009	.0006	.0004	.0003	.0002	.0001

TABLE 1   PRESENT VALUE FACTORS

Periods Hence	21%	22%	23%	24%	25%	26%	27%	28%	29%	30%
1	.8264	.8197	.8130	.8065	.8000	.7937	.7874	.7813	.7752	.7692
2	.6830	.6719	.6610	.6504	.6400	.6299	.6200	.6104	.6009	.5917
3	.5645	.5507	.5374	.5245	.5120	.4999	.4882	.4768	.4658	.4552
4	.4665	.4514	.4369	.4230	.4096	.3968	.3844	.3725	.3611	.3501
5	.3855	.3700	.3552	.3411	.3277	.3149	.3027	.2910	.2799	.2693
6	.3186	.3033	.2888	.2751	.2621	.2499	.2383	.2274	.2170	.2072
7	.2633	.2486	.2348	.2218	.2096	.1983	.1877	.1776	.1682	.1594
8	.2176	.2038	.1909	.1789	.1678	.1574	.1478	.1388	.1304	.1226
9	.1799	.1670	.1552	.1443	.1342	.1249	.1164	.1084	.1011	.0943
10	.1486	.1369	.1262	.1164	.1074	.0992	.0916	.0847	.0784	.0725
11	.1228	.1122	.1026	.0938	.0859	.0787	.0721	.0662	.0607	.0558
12	.1015	.0920	.0834	.0757	.0687	.0625	.0568	.0517	.0471	.0429
13	.0839	.0754	.0678	.0610	.0550	.0496	.0447	.0404	.0365	.0330
14	.0693	.0618	.0551	.0492	.0440	.0393	.0352	.0316	.0283	.0254
15	.0573	.0507	.0448	.0397	.0352	.0312	.0277	.0247	.0219	.0195
16	.0474	.0415	.0364	.0320	.0281	.0248	.0218	.0193	.0170	.0150
17	.0391	.0340	.0296	.0258	.0225	.0197	.0172	.0150	.0132	.0116
18	.0323	.0279	.0241	.0208	.0180	.0156	.0135	.0118	.0102	.0089
19	.0267	.0229	.0196	.0168	.0144	.0124	.0107	.0092	.0079	.0068
20	.0221	.0187	.0159	.0135	.0115	.0098	.0084	.0072	.0061	.0053
21	.0183	.0154	.0129	.0109	.0092	.0078	.0066	.0056	.0048	.0040
22	.0151	.0126	.0105	.0088	.0074	.0062	.0052	.0044	.0037	.0031
23	.0125	.0103	.0086	.0071	.0059	.0049	.0041	.0034	.0029	.0024
24	.0103	.0085	.0070	.0057	.0047	.0039	.0032	.0027	.0022	.0018
25	.0085	.0069	.0057	.0046	.0038	.0031	.0025	.0021	.0017	.0014
26	.0070	.0057	.0046	.0037	.0030	.0025	.0020	.0016	.0013	.0011
27	.0058	.0047	.0037	.0030	.0024	.0019	.0016	.0013	.0010	.0008
28	.0048	.0038	.0030	.0024	.0019	.0015	.0012	.0010	.0008	.0006
29	.0040	.0031	.0025	.0020	.0015	.0012	.0010	.0008	.0006	.0005
30	.0033	.0026	.0020	.0016	.0012	.0010	.0008	.0006	.0005	.0004
31	.0027	.0021	.0016	.0013	.0010	.0008	.0006	.0005	.0004	.0003
32	.0022	.0017	.0013	.0010	.0008	.0006	.0005	.0004	.0003	.0002
33	.0019	.0014	.0011	.0008	.0006	.0005	.0004	.0003	.0002	.0002
34	.0015	.0012	.0009	.0007	.0005	.0004	.0003	.0002	.0002	.0001
35	.0013	.0009	.0007	.0005	.0004	.0003	.0002	.0002	.0001	.0001
36	.0010	.0008	.0006	.0004	.0003	.0002	.0002	.0001	.0001	.0001
37	.0009	.0006	.0005	.0003	.0003	.0002	.0001	.0001	.0001	.0001
38	.0007	.0005	.0004	.0003	.0002	.0002	.0001	.0001	.0001	.0000
39	.0006	.0004	.0003	.0002	.0002	.0001	.0001	.0001	.0000	
40	.0005	.0004	.0003	.0002	.0001	.0001	.0001	.0001		
41	.0004	.0003	.0002	.0001	.0001	.0001	.0001	.0000		
42	.0003	.0002	.0002	.0001	.0001	.0001	.0000			
43	.0003	.0002	.0001	.0001	.0001	.0000				
44	.0002	.0002	.0001	.0001	.0001					
45	.0002	.0001	.0001	.0001	.0000					
46	.0002	.0001	.0001	.0001						
47	.0001	.0001	.0001	.0000						
48	.0001	.0001	.0000							
49	.0001	.0001								
50	.0001	.0000								

TABLE 1 PRESENT VALUE FACTORS

Periods Hence	31%	32%	33%	34%	35%	36%	37%	38%	39%	40%
1	.7634	.7576	.7519	.7463	.7407	.7353	.7299	.7246	.7194	.7143
2	.5827	.5739	.5653	.5569	.5487	.5407	.5328	.5251	.5176	.5102
3	.4448	.4348	.4251	.4156	.4064	.3975	.3889	.3805	.3724	.3644
4	.3396	.3294	.3196	.3102	.3011	.2923	.2839	.2757	.2679	.2603
5	.2592	.2495	.2403	.2315	.2230	.2149	.2072	.1998	.1927	.1859
6	.1979	.1890	.1807	.1727	.1652	.1580	.1512	.1448	.1386	.1328
7	.1510	.1432	.1358	.1289	.1224	.1162	.1104	.1049	.0997	.0949
8	.1153	.1085	.1021	.0962	.0906	.0854	.0806	.0760	.0718	.0678
9	.0880	.0822	.0768	.0718	.0671	.0628	.0588	.0551	.0516	.0484
10	.0672	.0623	.0577	.0536	.0497	.0462	.0429	.0399	.0371	.0346
11	.0513	.0472	.0434	.0400	.0368	.0340	.0313	.0289	.0267	.0247
12	.0392	.0357	.0326	.0298	.0273	.0250	.0229	.0210	.0192	.0176
13	.0299	.0271	.0245	.0223	.0202	.0184	.0167	.0152	.0138	.0126
14	.0228	.0205	.0185	.0166	.0150	.0135	.0122	.0110	.0099	.0090
15	.0174	.0155	.0139	.0124	.0111	.0099	.0089	.0080	.0072	.0064
16	.0133	.0118	.0104	.0093	.0082	.0073	.0065	.0058	.0051	.0046
17	.0101	.0089	.0078	.0069	.0061	.0054	.0047	.0042	.0037	.0033
18	.0077	.0068	.0059	.0052	.0045	.0039	.0035	.0030	.0027	.0023
19	.0059	.0051	.0044	.0038	.0033	.0029	.0025	.0022	.0019	.0017
20	.0045	.0039	.0033	.0029	.0025	.0021	.0018	.0016	.0014	.0012
21	.0034	.0029	.0025	.0021	.0018	.0016	.0013	.0012	.0010	.0009
22	.0026	.0022	.0019	.0016	.0014	.0012	.0010	.0008	.0007	.0006
23	.0020	.0017	.0014	.0012	.0010	.0008	.0007	.0006	.0005	.0004
24	.0015	.0013	.0011	.0009	.0007	.0006	.0005	.0004	.0004	.0003
25	.0012	.0010	.0008	.0007	.0006	.0005	.0004	.0003	.0003	.0002
26	.0009	.0007	.0006	.0005	.0004	.0003	.0003	.0002	.0002	.0002
27	.0007	.0006	.0005	.0004	.0003	.0002	.0002	.0002	.0001	.0001
28	.0005	.0004	.0003	.0003	.0002	.0002	.0001	.0001	.0001	.0001
29	.0004	.0003	.0003	.0002	.0002	.0001	.0001	.0001	.0001	.0001
30	.0003	.0002	.0002	.0002	.0001	.0001	.0001	.0001	.0001	.0000
31	.0002	.0002	.0001	.0001	.0001	.0001	.0001	.0000	.0000	
32	.0002	.0001	.0001	.0001	.0001	.0001	.0000			
33	.0001	.0001	.0001	.0001	.0001	.0000				
34	.0001	.0001	.0001	.0000	.0000					
35	.0001	.0001	.0000							
36	.0001	.0000	.0000							
37	.0000									

TABLE 1 PRESENT VALUE FACTORS

Periods Hence	41%	42%	43%	44%	45%	46%	47%	48%	49%	50%
1	.7092	.7042	.6993	.6944	.6897	.6849	.6803	.6757	.6711	.6667
2	.5030	.4959	.4890	.4823	.4756	.4691	.4628	.4565	.4504	.4444
3	.3567	.3492	.3420	.3349	.3280	.3213	.3148	.3085	.3023	.2963
4	.2530	.2459	.2391	.2326	.2262	.2201	.2142	.2084	.2029	.1975
5	.1794	.1732	.1672	.1615	.1560	.1507	.1457	.1408	.1362	.1317
6	.1273	.1220	.1169	.1122	.1076	.1032	.0991	.0952	.0914	.0878
7	.0903	.0859	.0818	.0779	.0742	.0707	.0674	.0643	.0613	.0585
8	.0640	.0605	.0572	.0541	.0512	.0484	.0459	.0434	.0412	.0390
9	.0454	.0426	.0400	.0376	.0353	.0332	.0312	.0294	.0276	.0260
10	.0322	.0300	.0280	.0261	.0243	.0227	.0212	.0198	.0185	.0173
11	.0228	.0211	.0196	.0181	.0168	.0156	.0144	.0134	.0125	.0116
12	.0162	.0149	.0137	.0126	.0116	.0107	.0098	.0091	.0084	.0077
13	.0115	.0105	.0096	.0087	.0080	.0073	.0067	.0061	.0056	.0051
14	.0081	.0074	.0067	.0061	.0055	.0050	.0045	.0041	.0038	.0034
15	.0058	.0052	.0047	.0042	.0038	.0034	.0031	.0028	.0025	.0023
16	.0041	.0037	.0033	.0029	.0026	.0023	.0021	.0019	.0017	.0015
17	.0029	.0026	.0023	.0020	.0018	.0016	.0014	.0013	.0011	.0010
18	.0021	.0018	.0016	.0014	.0012	.0011	.0010	.0009	.0008	.0007
19	.0015	.0013	.0011	.0010	.0009	.0008	.0007	.0006	.0005	.0005
20	.0010	.0009	.0008	.0007	.0006	.0005	.0005	.0004	.0003	.0003
21	.0007	.0006	.0005	.0005	.0004	.0004	.0003	.0003	.0002	.0002
22	.0005	.0004	.0004	.0003	.0003	.0002	.0002	.0002	.0002	.0001
23	.0004	.0003	.0003	.0002	.0002	.0002	.0001	.0001	.0001	.0001
24	.0003	.0002	.0002	.0002	.0001	.0001	.0001	.0001	.0001	.0001
25	.0002	.0002	.0001	.0001	.0001	.0001	.0001	.0001	.0000	.0000
26	.0001	.0001	.0001	.0001	.0001	.0001	.0000	.0000		
27	.0001	.0001	.0001	.0001	.0000	.0000				
28	.0001	.0001	.0000	.0000						
29	.0000	.0000								

TABLE 2 CUMULATIVE PRESENT VALUE FACTORS

Periods 0 to:	1%	2%	3%	4%	5%	6%	7%	8%	9%	10%
1	.990	.980	.971	.962	.952	.943	.935	.926	.917	.909
2	1.970	1.942	1.913	1.886	1.859	1.833	1.808	1.783	1.759	1.736
3	2.941	2.884	2.829	2.775	2.723	2.673	2.624	2.577	2.531	2.487
4	3.902	3.808	3.717	3.630	3.546	3.465	3.387	3.312	3.240	3.170
5	4.853	4.713	4.580	4.452	4.329	4.212	4.100	3.993	3.890	3.791
6	5.795	5.601	5.417	5.242	5.076	4.917	4.767	4.623	4.486	4.355
7	6.728	6.472	6.230	6.002	5.786	5.582	5.389	5.206	5.033	4.868
8	7.652	7.325	7.020	6.733	6.463	6.210	5.971	5.747	5.535	5.335
9	8.566	8.162	7.786	7.435	7.108	6.802	6.515	6.247	5.995	5.759
10	9.471	8.983	8.530	8.111	7.722	7.360	7.024	6.710	6.418	6.145
11	10.378	9.787	9.253	8.760	8.306	7.887	7.499	7.139	6.805	6.495
12	11.255	10.575	9.954	9.385	8.863	8.384	7.943	7.536	7.161	6.814
13	12.134	11.348	10.635	9.986	9.394	8.853	8.358	7.904	7.487	7.103
14	13.004	12.106	11.296	10.563	9.899	9.295	8.745	8.244	7.786	7.367
15	13.865	12.849	11.938	11.118	10.380	9.712	9.108	8.559	8.061	7.606
16	14.718	13.578	12.561	11.652	10.838	10.106	9.447	8.851	8.313	7.824
17	15.562	14.292	13.166	12.166	11.274	10.477	9.763	9.122	8.544	8.022
18	16.398	14.992	13.754	12.659	11.690	10.828	10.059	9.372	8.756	8.201
19	17.226	15.678	14.324	13.134	12.085	11.158	10.336	9.604	8.950	8.365
20	18.046	16.351	14.877	13.590	12.462	11.470	10.594	9.818	9.129	8.514
21	18.857	17.011	15.415	14.029	12.821	11.764	10.836	10.017	9.292	8.649
22	19.660	17.658	15.937	14.451	13.163	12.042	11.061	10.201	9.442	8.772
23	20.456	18.292	16.444	14.857	13.489	12.303	11.272	10.371	9.580	8.883
24	21.243	18.914	16.936	15.247	13.799	12.550	11.469	10.529	9.707	8.985
25	22.023	19.523	17.413	15.622	14.094	12.783	11.654	10.675	9.823	9.077
26	22.795	20.121	17.877	15.983	14.375	13.003	11.826	10.810	9.929	9.161
27	23.560	20.707	18.327	16.330	14.643	13.211	11.987	10.935	10.027	9.237
28	24.316	21.281	18.764	16.663	14.898	13.406	12.137	11.051	10.116	9.307
29	25.066	21.844	19.188	16.984	15.141	13.591	12.278	11.158	10.198	9.370
30	25.808	22.396	19.600	17.292	15.372	13.765	12.409	11.258	10.274	9.427
31	26.542	22.938	20.000	17.588	15.593	13.929	12.532	11.350	10.343	9.479
32	27.270	23.468	20.389	17.874	15.803	14.084	12.647	11.435	10.406	9.526
33	27.990	23.989	20.766	18.148	16.003	14.230	12.754	11.514	10.464	9.569
34	28.703	24.499	21.132	18.411	16.193	14.368	12.854	11.587	10.518	9.609
35	29.409	24.999	21.487	18.665	16.374	14.498	12.948	11.655	10.567	9.644
36	30.108	25.489	21.832	18.908	16.547	14.621	13.035	11.717	10.612	9.677
37	30.780	25.969	22.167	19.143	16.711	14.737	13.117	11.775	10.653	9.706
38	31.485	26.441	22.492	19.368	16.868	14.846	13.193	11.829	10.691	9.733
39	32.163	26.903	22.808	19.584	17.017	14.949	13.265	11.879	10.726	9.757
40	32.835	27.355	23.115	19.793	17.159	15.046	13.332	11.925	10.757	9.779

TABLE 2   CUMULATIVE PRESENT VALUE FACTORS

Periods 0 to:	11%	12%	13%	14%	15%	16%	17%	18%	19%	20%
1	.901	.893	.885	.877	.870	.862	.855	.848	.840	.833
2	1.712	1.690	1.668	1.647	1.626	1.605	1.585	1.566	1.546	1.528
3	2.444	2.402	2.361	2.322	2.283	2.246	2.210	2.174	2.140	2.106
4	3.102	3.307	2.974	2.914	2.855	2.798	2.743	2.690	2.639	2.589
5	3.696	3.605	3.517	3.433	3.352	3.274	3.199	3.127	3.058	2.991
6	4.230	4.111	3.998	3.889	3.784	3.685	3.589	3.498	3.410	3.326
7	4.712	4.564	4.423	4.288	4.160	4.039	3.922	3.812	3.706	3.605
8	5.146	4.968	4.799	4.639	4.487	4.344	4.207	4.078	3.954	3.837
9	5.537	5.328	5.132	4.946	4.772	4.607	4.451	4.303	4.163	4.031
10	5.889	5.650	5.426	5.216	5.019	4.833	4.659	4.494	4.339	4.192
11	6.206	5.938	5.687	5.453	5.234	5.029	4.836	4.656	4.486	4.327
12	6.492	6.194	5.918	5.660	5.420	5.197	4.988	4.793	4.610	4.439
13	6.750	6.424	6.122	5.842	5.583	5.342	5.118	4.910	4.715	4.533
14	6.982	6.628	6.303	6.002	5.724	5.468	5.229	5.008	4.802	4.611
15	7.191	6.811	6.463	6.142	5.847	5.576	5.324	5.092	4.876	4.676
16	7.379	6.974	6.604	6.265	5.954	5.668	5.405	5.162	4.938	4.730
17	7.549	7.120	6.729	6.373	6.047	5.749	5.475	5.222	4.990	4.775
18	7.702	7.250	6.840	6.468	6.128	5.818	5.534	5.273	5.033	4.812
19	7.839	7.366	6.938	6.550	6.198	5.877	5.584	5.316	5.070	4.844
20	7.963	7.469	7.025	6.623	6.259	5.929	5.628	5.353	5.101	4.870
21	8.075	7.562	7.102	6.687	6.312	5.973	5.665	5.384	5.127	4.892
22	8.176	7.645	7.170	6.743	6.358	6.011	5.696	5.410	5.149	4.910
23	8.266	7.718	7.230	6.792	6.399	6.044	5.723	5.432	5.167	4.925
24	8.348	7.784	7.283	6.835	6.434	6.073	5.746	5.451	5.182	4.937
25	8.422	7.843	7.330	6.873	6.464	6.097	5.766	5.467	5.195	4.948
26	8.488	7.896	7.372	6.906	6.490	6.118	5.783	5.480	5.206	4.956
27	8.548	7.942	7.409	6.935	6.513	6.136	5.797	5.492	5.215	4.964
28	8.601	7.984	7.441	6.961	6.533	6.152	5.810	5.502	5.223	4.970
29	8.650	8.022	7.470	6.983	6.551	6.166	5.820	5.510	5.229	4.975
30	8.694	8.055	7.496	7.003	6.566	6.177	5.829	5.517	5.235	4.979
31	8.733	8.085	7.518	7.020	6.579	6.187	5.837	5.523	5.239	4.983
32	8.768	8.112	7.538	7.035	6.590	6.196	5.844	5.528	5.243	4.986
33	8.800	8.135	7.556	7.048	6.600	6.203	5.849	5.532	5.246	4.988
34	8.829	8.157	7.572	7.060	6.609	6.210	5.854	5.535	5.249	4.990
35	8.855	8.176	7.586	7.070	6.616	6.215	5.858	5.538	5.251	4.992
36	8.878	8.192	7.598	7.079	6.623	6.220	5.862	5.541	5.253	4.993
37	8.900	8.208	7.609	7.087	6.629	6.224	5.864	5.543	5.255	4.994
38	8.918	8.221	7.619	7.094	6.634	6.228	5.867	5.545	5.256	4.995
39	8.936	8.233	7.627	7.100	6.638	6.231	5.869	5.547	5.257	4.996
40	8.951	8.244	7.635	7.105	6.642	6.234	5.871	5.548	5.258	4.997

TABLE 2   CUMULATIVE PRESENT VALUE FACTORS

Periods 0 to:	21%	22%	23%	24%	25%	26%	27%	28%	29%	30%
1	.826	.820	.813	.806	.800	.794	.787	.781	.775	.769
2	1.509	1.492	1.474	1.457	1.440	1.424	1.407	1.392	1.376	1.361
3	2.074	2.042	2.011	1.981	1.952	1.924	1.896	1.868	1.842	1.816
4	2.540	2.494	2.448	2.404	2.362	2.320	2.280	2.241	2.203	2.166
5	2.926	2.864	2.804	2.746	2.689	2.635	2.583	2.532	2.483	2.436
6	3.244	3.167	3.092	3.021	2.951	2.885	2.821	2.759	2.670	2.643
7	3.508	3.416	3.327	3.242	3.161	3.083	3.009	2.937	2.868	2.802
8	3.725	3.619	3.518	3.421	3.329	3.241	3.156	3.076	2.998	2.925
9	3.905	3.786	3.673	3.566	3.463	3.366	3.273	3.184	3.100	3.019
10	4.054	3.923	3.799	3.682	3.570	3.465	3.364	3.269	3.178	3.092
11	4.177	4.036	3.902	3.776	3.656	3.544	3.437	3.335	3.239	3.147
12	4.278	4.128	3.985	3.852	3.725	3.606	3.493	3.387	3.286	3.190
13	4.362	4.203	4.053	3.912	3.780	3.656	3.538	3.427	3.322	3.223
14	4.431	4.265	4.108	3.962	3.824	3.695	3.573	3.459	3.351	3.249
15	4.489	4.315	4.153	4.001	3.859	3.726	3.601	3.483	3.372	3.268
16	4.536	4.357	4.190	4.033	3.887	3.751	3.623	3.503	3.390	3.283
17	4.575	4.391	4.219	4.059	3.910	3.771	3.640	3.518	3.403	3.295
18	4.608	4.419	4.243	4.080	3.928	3.786	3.654	3.530	3.413	3.304
19	4.634	4.442	4.263	4.097	3.942	3.799	3.664	3.539	3.421	3.310
20	4.656	4.460	4.279	4.110	3.954	3.808	3.673	3.546	3.427	3.316
21	4.675	4.476	4.292	4.121	3.963	3.816	3.679	3.552	3.432	3.320
22	4.690	4.488	4.302	4.130	3.970	3.822	3.684	3.556	3.435	3.323
23	4.702	4.499	4.311	4.137	3.976	3.827	3.688	3.559	3.438	3.325
24	4.712	4.507	4.318	4.143	3.981	3.831	3.692	3.562	3.440	3.327
25	4.721	4.514	4.323	4.147	3.985	3.834	3.694	3.564	3.442	3.328
26	4.728	4.520	4.328	4.151	3.988	3.837	3.696	3.566	3.443	3.329
27	4.734	4.524	4.332	4.154	3.990	3.839	3.698	3.567	3.444	3.330
28	4.739	4.528	4.335	4.156	3.992	3.840	3.699	3.568	3.445	3.331
29	4.743	4.531	4.337	4.158	3.994	3.841	3.700	3.569	3.446	3.331
30	4.746	4.534	4.339	4.160	3.995	3.842	3.701	3.570	3.446	3.332
31	4.749	4.536	4.341	4.161	3.996	3.843	3.701	3.570	3.447	3.332
32	4.751	4.538	4.342	4.162	3.997	3.844	3.702	3.571	3.447	3.332
33	4.753	4.539	4.343	4.163	3.997	3.844	3.702	3.571	3.447	3.332
34	4.754	4.540	4.344	4.164	3.998	3.845	3.703	3.571	3.448	3.333
35	4.756	4.541	4.345	4.164	3.998	3.845	3.703	3.571	3.448	3.333
36	4.756	4.542	4.345	4.165	3.998	3.845	3.703	3.571	3.448	3.333
37	4.757	4.543	4.346	4.165	3.999	3.846	3.703	3.571	3.448	3.333
38	4.758	4.543	4.346	4.165	3.999	3.846	3.703	3.571	3.448	3.333
39	4.759	4.544	4.347	4.166	3.999	3.846	3.703	3.571	3.448	3.333
40	4.759	4.544	4.347	4.166	3.999	3.846	3.703	3.572	3.448	3.333

TABLE 2   CUMULATIVE PRESENT VALUE FACTORS

Periods 0 to:	31%	32%	33%	34%	35%	36%	37%	38%	39%	40%
1	.763	.758	.752	.746	.741	.735	.730	.725	.719	.714
2	1.346	1.332	1.317	1.303	1.289	1.276	1.263	1.250	1.237	1.224
3	1.791	1.766	1.742	1.719	1.696	1.674	1.652	1.630	1.609	1.589
4	2.130	2.096	2.062	2.029	1.997	1.966	1.936	1.906	1.877	1.849
5	2.390	2.345	2.302	2.260	2.220	2.181	2.143	2.106	2.070	2.035
6	2.588	2.534	2.483	2.433	2.385	2.339	2.294	2.250	2.209	2.168
7	2.739	2.677	2.619	2.562	2.508	2.455	2.404	2.355	2.308	2.263
8	2.845	2.786	2.721	2.658	2.598	2.540	2.485	2.431	2.380	2.331
9	2.942	2.868	2.798	2.730	2.665	2.603	2.544	2.486	2.432	2.379
10	3.009	2.930	2.855	2.784	2.715	2.649	2.587	2.526	2.469	2.414
11	3.060	2.978	2.899	2.824	2.752	2.683	2.618	2.555	2.496	2.438
12	3.100	3.013	2.931	2.854	2.779	2.708	2.641	2.576	2.515	2.456
13	3.130	3.040	2.956	2.876	2.799	2.727	2.658	2.592	2.528	2.468
14	3.152	3.061	2.974	2.892	2.814	2.740	2.670	2.602	2.538	2.478
15	3.170	3.076	2.988	2.905	2.825	2.750	2.679	2.610	2.546	2.484
16	3.183	3.088	2.999	2.914	2.834	2.757	2.685	2.616	2.551	2.488
17	3.193	3.097	3.006	2.921	2.840	2.763	2.690	2.620	2.554	2.492
18	3.201	3.104	3.012	2.926	2.844	2.767	2.693	2.624	2.557	2.494
19	3.207	3.109	3.017	2.930	2.847	2.770	2.696	2.626	2.559	2.496
20	3.211	3.113	3.020	2.933	2.850	2.772	2.698	2.627	2.560	2.497
21	3.215	3.116	3.022	2.935	2.852	2.773	2.699	2.628	2.561	2.498
22	3.217	3.118	3.024	2.937	2.853	2.774	2.700	2.629	2.562	2.498
23	3.219	3.120	3.026	2.938	2.854	2.775	2.701	2.630	2.563	2.499
24	3.221	3.121	3.027	2.939	2.855	2.776	2.701	2.630	2.563	2.499
25	3.222	3.122	3.028	2.939	2.855	2.776	2.702	2.631	2.563	2.499
26	3.223	3.123	3.028	2.940	2.856	2.777	2.702	2.631	2.564	2.500
27	3.224	3.123	3.029	2.940	2.856	2.777	2.702			
28	3.224	3.124	3.029	2.941	2.856	2.777	2.702			
29	3.224	3.124	3.029	2.941	2.856	2.777	2.702			
30	3.225	3.124	3.030	2.941	2.857	2.777	2.702	2.631	2.564	2.500
31	3.225	3.124	3.030	2.941	2.857	2.778	2.703			
32	3.225	3.124								
33	3.225	3.125								
34	3.225	3.125								
35	3.225	3.125	3.030	2.941	2.857	2.778	2.703			
36	3.226	3.125								
37	3.226									
38	3.226									
39	3.226									
40	3.226	3.125								

TABLE 2   CUMULATIVE PRESENT VALUE FACTORS

Periods 0 to:	41%	42%	43%	44%	45%	46%	47%	48%	49%	50%
1	.709	.704	.699	.694	.690	.685	.680	.676	.671	.667
2	1.212	1.200	1.188	1.177	1.165	1.154	1.143	1.132	1.122	1.111
3	1.569	1.549	1.530	1.512	1.493	1.475	1.458	1.441	1.424	1.407
4	1.822	1.795	1.769	1.744	1.720	1.695	1.672	1.649	1.627	1.605
5	2.001	1.968	1.937	1.906	1.876	1.846	1.818	1.790	1.763	1.737
6	2.129	2.090	2.054	2.018	1.983	1.949	1.917	1.885	1.854	1.824
7	2.219	2.176	2.135	2.096	2.057	2.020	1.984	1.949	1.916	1.883
8	2.283	2.237	2.192	2.150	2.108	2.068	2.030	1.993	1.957	1.922
9	2.328	2.279	2.232	2.188	2.144	2.102	2.061	2.022	1.984	1.948
10	2.360	2.309	2.260	2.214	2.168	2.124	2.083	2.042	2.003	1.965
11	2.383	2.330	2.280	2.232	2.185	2.140	2.097	2.055	2.015	1.977
12	2.400	2.345	2.294	2.244	2.196	2.151	2.107	2.064	2.024	1.984
13	2.411	2.356	2.303	2.253	2.204	2.158	2.114	2.071	2.029	1.990
14	2.419	2.363	2.310	2.259	2.210	2.163	2.118	2.075	2.033	1.993
15	2.425	2.368	2.315	2.263	2.214	2.166	2.121	2.078	2.036	1.995
16	2.429	2.372	2.318	2.266	2.216	2.169	2.123	2.079	2.037	1.996
17	2.432	2.375	2.320	2.268	2.218	2.170	2.125	2.081	2.038	1.998
18	2.434	2.377	2.322	2.270	2.219	2.171	2.126	2.082	2.039	1.998
19	2.436	2.378	2.323	2.271	2.220	2.172	2.126	2.082	2.040	1.999
20	2.437	2.379	2.324	2.271	2.221	2.173	2.127	2.083	2.040	1.999
21	2.437	2.379	2.324	2.272	2.221	2.173	2.127	2.083	2.040	2.000
22	2.438	2.380	2.325	2.272	2.222	2.173	2.127			
23	2.438	2.380	2.325	2.272	2.222	2.173	1.127			
24	2.438	2.380	2.325	2.273	2.222	2.174	2.128			
25	2.439	2.380	2.325	2.273	2.222	2.174	2.128	2.083	2.040	2.000
26	2.439	2.381	2.326	2.273	2.222	2.174	2.128			
27										
28										
29										
30	2.439	2.381	2.326	2.273	2.222	2.174	2.128			